100 GREATEST MODERN WORLD COINS

Charles Morgan and Hubert Walker

Foreword by Donald Scarinci

Whitman Publishing, LLC
PUBLISHING SINCE 1934
Whitman.com

100 Greatest Modern World Coins

© 2020 Whitman Publishing, LLC
1974 Chandalar Drive • Suite D • Pelham, AL 35124

100 GREATEST is a registered trademark of Whitman Publishing, LLC.

Correspondence concerning this book may be directed to the publisher,
Attn: 100 Greatest Modern World Coins, at the address above.

ISBN: 0794846335
Printed in China

If you enjoy the fascinating history and color images of the *100 Greatest Modern World Coins,* you will also enjoy the other books in this collection, including *100 Greatest U.S. Coins, 100 Greatest Ancient Coins, 100 Greatest American Currency Notes, 100 Greatest American Medals and Tokens, 100 Greatest U.S. Modern Coins, 100 Greatest U.S. Error Coins, 100 Greatest Women on Coins, 100 Greatest American Stamps,* and *100 Greatest Comic Books.*

For a complete catalog of numismatic reference books, supplies, and storage products,
visit Whitman Publishing online at www.Whitman.com.

CONTENTS

When you pick up a book about "modern" coins, you might expect to see pictures of everyday pocket change. To numismatists, the modern period in coins generally does not include the ones in your pocket, nor does it include the commercially made commemorative and "collector" coins and bullion sold today. Rather, the term modern describes the period of numismatic history that starts from the widespread use of the Janvier reducing machine in the mid- to late 1800s and continues to about the dawn of the space age or the era of computers.

Those 100 or so years were a time of great transition in just about every aspect of life. In numismatics, they were a bridge between the classic designs of the great eighteenth- and nineteenth-century engravers, like Pierre-Simon-Benjamin Duvivier and William Wyon, and the contemporary masterpieces of sculptors such as Herbert Wähner and Donald N. Everhart Jr.

STRONG DEMAND FOR COINS AND THE TECHNOLOGICAL CHANGES TO MEET THAT DEMAND

Historically, demand for coins and advances in technology may be the two most significant variables that influenced coin design. As demand for coins in commerce increased in the ancient world, their methods of production improved and the number of mints increased.

Demand continued to increase from the seventeenth century forward. Manufacturing methods improved and the demand was met on a widespread scale. Instead of each coin being individually hammered by hand, mechanically operated devices increased the speed and efficiency of production.

As the speed of production increased, the need for artists to design the coins expanded. New technology assisted the designers just as it increased the production of coins. A medieval hammered coin looks very different from a coin produced on a screw press or a steam press. All coins made after the invention and widespread use of the Janvier reducing machine look very different from the coins made before.

In the nineteenth century the Janvier allowed sculptors to participate in what had theretofore been the province of engravers. The sculptors brought a new eye to coin design and saw coins as three-dimensional objects, like bas relief and sculpture. They could sculpt a 12-inch bas relief, put it on the Janvier, and reduce the sculpture to a 40 mm stackable coin.

In the modern era, before credit and debit cards, more people than ever before in the history of the world used coins and paper currency to transact business. Their coins needed to be functional for everyday use. It is no surprise, therefore, that the design trends in the decorative arts—art nouveau, beaux arts, art deco—and not trends such as expressionism, cubism, surrealism, modernism, or post-modernism came to dominate coin and medal design before the 1960s.

It can be argued whether the involvement of sculptors in coin design made coins more aesthetically competitive or whether the marketplace demanded more pleasing coin designs and mints responded to the demand. It is certain, however, that while *function* has driven the weight, size, and shape of the coins of the modern era, *sculptors* have driven the excellence of coin designs.

FOR MODERN COINS, THE ART IS AS IMPORTANT AS THE HISTORICAL CONTEXT

Collectors who discover these "bridge" coins that we have labeled "modern" have a unique opportunity to understand the world nation-by-nation. The 1907-S peso from the Philippines makes a statement about that country and its relationship with America, just as the 1938 pattern penny of Ireland teaches something about the sentiment of the Irish people when they changed the inscription from *Saorstát Éireann* (Irish Free State) to *Eire*.

When we study the coinage of the modern era, we begin to appreciate the importance of the art as much as the subject matter it conveys and the importance of a coin in its historical context. Increasingly, modern coins are studied and appreciated almost more for their art than for their history. With modern coins, numismatists strive to understand the life and work of artists such as Georges Guiraud, who designed the 1950 50 franc, and Giuseppe Romagnoli, who designed the impressive 1928 20 lire.

The trend is toward understanding the art of coins and the work of the artists who make them. Beginning in 1982, coin designs and artists were singled out with recognitions like the Krause Coin of the Year Award. At many world mints, the designs on coins are reviewed and approved by committees rather than by individuals, thereby creating a written numismatic record.

The advent of computer modeling in the twenty-first century allows artists to translate two-dimensional drawings into three-dimensional coins. Today, graphic artists are replacing sculptors in the same way that sculptors replaced engravers in the 1800s when the Janvier reducing machine was introduced. Fortunately, sculptors are still required in the translation process, but this too will likely change.

ASSEMBLING YOUR OWN GREAT COIN COLLECTION

While this book debunks the notion that coins of the modern era are too common to warrant much of a premium for collecting purposes, the emphasis on rarity in this 100 Greatest list should not deter collectors who are interested in the coins of this important period.

Coins of the late nineteenth and early twentieth centuries were manufactured in the millions. Accordingly, they are often available quite inexpensively. The challenge with collecting modern coins is not so much the scarcity of the coins, but the scarcity of the condition.

The best uncertified modern coins often sell for just a slight premium over their less-pristine siblings. If you can grade properly and develop an interesting collecting plan, your efforts will be rewarded economically as well as by the knowledge you gain from the collecting experience.

Authors Charles Morgan and Hubert Walker have created a wonderful study of modern world coinage. They cover the period of 1900 to date (extending the "modern" era to include in their rankings a half dozen significant and well-deserving coins from more recent decades), setting each coin in context and bringing each to life. *100 Greatest Modern World Coins* will inspire, inform, and entertain you. Enjoy the journey and let it spark ideas for building your own significant collection.

Donald Scarinci

Donald Scarinci is the senior partner in one of the largest law firms in New Jersey. He has collected coins since high school. Scarinci is considered an international authority in the field of contemporary coins and medals, having assembled one of the largest privately held collections of modern and contemporary art medals in the United States. He is a life member of the American Numismatic Association and a fellow of the American Numismatic Society, where he serves as chairman of the J. Sanford Saltus Award Committee for excellence in medallic art. He is also the ranking member (serving since 2005) of the U.S. Treasury Department's Citizens Coinage Advisory Committee. He has written four books, including *Coin of the Year*, published in English and Chinese by Krause Publications, where he continues to lend his expertise as one of the ten prime Coin of the Year nominators.

A CENTURY LIKE NO OTHER: UNDERSTANDING WORLD COINS
OF THE TWENTIETH CENTURY AND WHY WE COLLECT THEM

When we look at the coins we spend on a day-to-day basis, even the less numismatically inclined among us might ask: *How did we end up with coins like this?* The effigies, the inscriptions, the use of dates, the different sizes and shapes—all of these details have held remarkably consistent over the years. Until recently (in the United States, anyway), our paper money seemed to change more often than our coins.

But if we can see past our own experience with coins and look back just a few generations, the striking and radical changes to coinage that have taken place over the last century or so come into sharper focus.

THE CHANGING SIGNIFICANCE OF COINS

A great shift has taken place in attitudes about coins and their role in commerce. The situation, obviously, is not the same everywhere, but major economic factors such as inflation, a change from precious metals to base metals, consumer preference for paper money, and the rapid growth of electronic payment systems have had a dramatic effect on the utility of coins as a circulating medium. Bimetallism and the "gold standard" have been replaced by base-metalism.

International trade, which in previous centuries was heavily reliant upon special trade coinage, has matured to the point where debits and credits of astronomical amounts can be moved around digitally. Even paper cash, the physical-money replacement of coinage, has become increasingly irrelevant and its authenticity and use sometimes suspect.

This monetary evolution may seem sudden and surprising, but the reality is that this is a shift born of both necessity and expedience. Simply put, we are presently bearing witness to the end of one era of money, dominated by physical coins and paper currency, and the transition into another, dominated by electronic credits and debits.

This new era is filled with possibilities and conveniences (the ability to shop and pay bills online, for example, or to use a debit card to buy a cup of coffee), but it can also be dangerous due to the publicly understated risks of theft and other types of crime. In spite of risks and weaknesses, the computers and other devices we use in our daily lives grow more and more sophisticated, and we interact with them to ever greater degrees. Resist it as we may, the need for digital payment technologies is not going away. Coins and other physical forms of money may not become extinct within our lifetime, but they will certainly undergo many changes as they become less and less important to commerce.

If history is any guide, we will continue to develop the forms of and the ideas behind "money" well into this and any subsequent era.

So, when we think of coins, it's important to appreciate the broader context in order to understand the dramatic developments in money that many of us have experienced personally. Looking back at the modern period of the world's coinage—essentially the twentieth century—what one sees is nothing less than a major revision of the meaning of the word "coin."

Of course, the mints of the world still produce coinage for circulation and new coins of each denomination are struck every year, which we receive and spend freely. But the production of circulating coinage is just part of the workloads that the mints now undertake.

The twentieth century saw the proliferation of coinage **not intended for circulation** (i.e., not meant to be used as money); chief among these the modern bullion coin and the mass-produced collector coin, which have become two of the industry's main sources of revenue and the principal drivers behind many of the new technologies being employed.

This, we are convinced, justifies the categorical separation of this new type of coinage from those that precede it because it is coinage *in name only* and is not struck with any bearing on a respective country's monetary system. For the most part, we have not included such *postmodern* coinage in this book, as we feel the topic deserves serious study in its own right. Where we have included such bullion or collector-specific pieces, it is as much for their value to the narrative of the modern age of world coins as it is for their worth or beauty.

WHAT CAUSED THIS MODERN CHANGE IN COINAGE?

If we accept that almost all the new products a collector might buy directly from world mints today are something other than modern (some have called them *ultra*modern), then what, exactly, is a "modern" coin?

For us, the era of modern coinage overlaps with the changes wrought by the rapid industrialization that many countries experienced in the first eighty years of the twentieth century. We don't believe this is too controversial a concept, though as American coin collectors born in the second half of that century, we are familiar with the way terms like "classic" and "modern" are applied to U.S. coinage. Current usage in the American hobby is (mostly) a reaction to the transition to copper-nickel–clad coinage in 1965, but the terms meant something different in 1915, and they certainly meant something different in 1865.

It just so happens these changes were accelerated around the close of the nineteenth century as industry spread from its beginnings in Western Europe to Europe's colonies and the rest of the world. Many reformers, revolutionaries, and opportunists in Asia and Latin America saw the desperate need for modernization, as it was the only real means of repelling the imperialist West and asserting their independence. Sometimes these modernizing forces encountered stiff resistance from entrenched power, as in China; sometimes these forces emanated from the seat of power, as in Japan. In both instances, new coinage was required to meet the needs of a different socioeconomic structure than the one that came before.

Besides enabling the steamships and armaments that allowed Europe to conquer much of the world, industrialization effected other changes in its home continent. Foremost among these was a new sense of political identity transcending the petty fiefdoms of an older age. Nationalism began to mold the borders of Europe into those we know today, creating powerful new nation-states like the larger German kingdoms and a consolidated Italy, which produced their own coinage to reflect their newfound national pride and economic power.

The railroads of the nineteenth century started to shrink the world, but the invention of aviation and electronic communications finished the job. While what happened in one part of the world had always had an impact on events in another, that fact was now laid bare, and the effects were more immediate. A global economic nervous system came into place, forcing those in a position to see the big picture to rethink what they thought they knew about money. For example, many of the coins in this book were struck according to the standards and rules of the Latin Monetary Union, an early attempt at a multinational currency and a precursor to such super-states as the European Union.

Beyond the perceived benefits of a single currency for a unitary international market, perhaps the most penetrating aspect of this rethink was the permanent debasement of most of the world's coinage in the twentieth century. Even as some parts of the world (such as Tibet) were only just beginning to create a gold coinage, other parts began to abandon the gold standard as too inflexible for the new age. As nationalism and technology combined to fight for the scraps of imperialism in the World Wars, it became evident that even the continued use of silver was unsustainable for modern economies. In turn, nations around the world began to adopt base-metal coinage for commerce, made legal tender by government fiat.

These are but a few of the fascinating changes to world coins that have taken place in the modern moment. The essays within this book demonstrate the effects of others.

WHY ARE MODERN WORLD COINS GREAT?

Coins are interesting and important objects no matter what era they come from. Excitement and discovery are possible in any field of numismatic endeavor.

But when it comes to the field of world coins, we believe no era has produced as wide a range of fascinating material as the modern era. This seems only fitting for a time when disparate parts of the world began to learn more about each other precisely at a moment of intense and unprecedented social and technological change. Even when a nation's own identity was in flux, what better way to transmit something of its essence to the rest of the world (and to posterity) than with a coin?

Because the record of events of the twentieth century came fast and furious, the study of numismatic objects leads to a more profound understanding of events contemporaneous with each coin.

Plus, the hobby itself is evolving, and each new coin produced—and each new coin one studies—adds to the story in often surprising ways. By studying the coins of the modern era (and, by extension, its greatest coins), one can watch as mints adopt best practices from one country to the next, or trace a notable innovation back to its source. One can see historical trends in metal use, design, and bullion programs—to name just a few—that become invaluable to an understanding of numismatics in general.

Along with many in the hobby community, we share a conviction that world coins comprise a field of collecting that is bound to experience immense growth in the United States over the next several years. It is our hope that, in addition to stimulating many conversations and arguments about the subject, this book serves to give the curious collector a more sophisticated appreciation of the topic.

100 GREATEST MODERN WORLD COINS: DEFINING GREATNESS

When it comes to coins, how does one define greatness? This is a daunting question and one that has been posed to generations of collectors and numismatic researchers. As it pertains to Whitman Publishing's library of "100 Greatest" books, we see a number of criteria. Taking from the very first numismatic book in the line, *100 Greatest U.S. Coins*, authors Jeff Garrett and Ron Guth outline six factors: rarity, value, quality, popularity, beauty, and history. Given that Garrett and Guth were writing about a finite set of homogeneous U.S. coin issues, the over-emphasis of any one of these factors (save perhaps beauty) might lead to a rather uninteresting book.

Fortunately for all of us, in the first (and each subsequent) edition, this pair of top-tier numismatic researchers found a successful mix that works great for the U.S. coin series. Their books have spawned many lively discussions among the hobby faithful.

When it came to developing our own criteria for this book, we had to consider that the sweep of twentieth-century world-coin production was far more complex than an expert survey of the 100 greatest U.S. coin issues, nearly all of which have years of documented price performance and reasonably familiar back stories. Many rare world coins struck in the past 120 years are not well known outside of their issuing countries. Exploring historic auction data for the sale of these coins often requires specialist knowledge and years of market participation. Furthermore, as a collector steeped in American culture, one must be careful not to overemphasize Western aesthetics concerning art produced by other cultures. It's a delicate dance, to be sure, but one we took a tremendous amount of care to execute as fairly as possible.

To us, compiling a list of 100 coins was more a matter of informed compromise.

When we set out to make our selections, we started by looking at the coinage output of every country around the globe spanning the past 120 years. We started with the year 1901, not because a valid case couldn't be made that "modern coinage" started decades, or even a century or more, before, but because we felt the twentieth century was such a consequential period for numismatics that the coins of this century deserved to be considered among their peers. From a numismatic perspective, we consider this period to be an essential area of study to understand the present and future role of coins in society. Over the course of 100 coins, we will embark on an effort to tell that story.

To choose the coins on our list, we opted to take into consideration the following criteria.

Rarity. Generally speaking, coins are struck to be instruments of commerce that trade freely in exchange for goods and services, and, in order to achieve this goal, should not be rare. But there are instances where coins are struck in very limited numbers.

Among our selections, you will find coins struck for kings and queens; coins struck in limited numbers as presentation pieces for important members of government; pattern coins accidentally released into circulation; Proof issues struck in lower numbers than their circulation-strike counterparts; and coins that, for whatever reason, have had most of their mintages lost to time.

Rarity is an important factor that affects a coin's numismatic value, but it is not the sole indicator of it.

Innovation. Over the course of the twentieth century, mints around the world introduced a number of important innovations that changed the global landscape of coins. Some of these creations were technical and involved processes and alloys used to strike coins. Some were artistic and introduced bold new aesthetics for coin design that paved the way for a global reimagining of the art form. Other innovations were driven by necessity or the needs of the market, such as long overdue coinage reforms or the introduction of bullion coins as investment instruments.

The twentieth century introduced enormous challenges to the continued utility of coins as a circulating medium. Every step of the way, the world's coin producers, both big and small, rose to the challenge and secured a viable place for coinage.

Coin Sets. Some of the greatest coins of the century need to be viewed in a broader context. Not every entry in our 100 Greatest Modern World Coins is an individual coin. In certain instances, coin sets are included. These sets may include one or more coins that, if considered individually, are sufficiently important to be included on our list. Other entries are known to collectors primarily as sets and it would be inconceivable to talk about one coin without discussing the others. Our goal was to valorize as many of the highlights of twentieth-century world coinage as possible, and in doing this we've included a fair number of sets.

Oddities and Emergency Issues. Human beings are amazing and resilient, and some of the most fascinating numismatic stories to unfold in the twentieth century center around coins that are a little off the beaten path. Some are limited-run vanity issues projecting the power and prestige of failed kings and despots, issued on the cusp of their overthrow, while others are crudely made pieces of emergency money issued by revolutionaries or by desperate people whose "revolutionary" idea was to survive no matter the cost. If holding a coin is like holding history in your hands, then coins struck in these ironic, unusual, and desperate circumstances tell us something about human nature and have an intrinsic greatness that is hard to ignore.

Auction Data and Market Values. In taking on this project, we were presented an interesting challenge: How does one weigh an entire range of factors relating to modern world-coin issues and organize the coins so that the broadest survey of issues is possible and auction data, certified-coin populations, and collector popularity aren't overemphasized? We made every effort to review a variety of auction sources, historical records, and market-maker insights about the coins presented in this book. But as we complete this edition, we know that not every auction for every world coin included in (or excluded from) this book has been taken into consideration.

We provide certain auction data and market values for general interest, but we do not want readers to get the mistaken impression that every modern world coin that has ever sold for a significant sum of money was automatically included in our selection. Conversely, some of the coins on our list are readily available to collectors and hardly considered rare at all. If you are using this book to make purchasing decisions about rare and valuable coins, know that our ranking system is an opinion and should not outweigh your due diligence and appreciation of a piece. Lists are conversation starters and not the final word. The beauty of this is that the numismatic hobby is forever evolving and there is no shortage of stories to tell.

WHY GREAT COINS MATTER

Many coins described in this book fall outside the financial means of most collectors, and some pieces are so rare that the only known examples are held in museums or institutional collections. Others are so seldom encountered that it may take generations for an example to come to market. That's okay. More important than *owning* one of the world's greatest coins is the enrichment that comes from knowing its story and relating this information to the pursuit of other coins of the type, of the period, or of the country.

The rarest of the rare coins that we consider the greatest are truly landmarks on the numismatic skyline.

Other great coins might be expensive but approachable, or not very expensive at all. A few of the coins on our list may be available for a small premium over current market value or even a small premium over face value. Regardless of cost or even the public's general perception of them, these greatest world coins have an important story to tell . . . but then, so do *great* coins, so do *good* coins, and so do *average* coins. No matter the scope or scale of your collection, the coins you select have stories. Every coin ever struck plays some role in making coin collecting a dynamic hobby. It is our hope that in reading this book you find yourself inspired to discover these stories and propel forward our hobby community's appreciation for coins both great and ordinary.

And if you disagree with the selections that we've made or the order of our list, that's okay too. We understood when writing this book that, ultimately, it is the reader and not the author who gets the last word as to which coins are truly the greatest. In that spirit, we considered our narratives to be the first salvo in a lengthy conversation about this remarkable period of numismatic history. We invite you to share with us your thoughts on which modern world coins would make *your* list, and why.

COIN COLLECTING DIFFICULTY CRITERIA:

Easy: Under $2,500
Moderate: $2,500 to $5,000
Moderately Difficult: $5,001 to $10,000
Difficult: $10,001 dollars to $20,000
Extremely Difficult: $20,000+ and seldom seen
Virtually Impossible: 5 or fewer known
Impossible: No known examples in the market

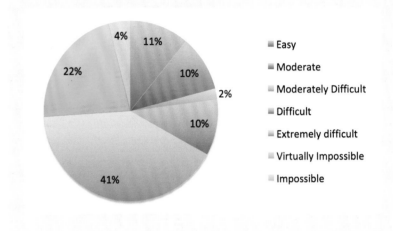

- Easy
- Moderate
- Moderately Difficult
- Difficult
- Extremely difficult
- Virtually Impossible
- Impossible

Numismatic study is a collaborative effort and we, like most authors, do appreciate all the help, encouragement, and support that we can get. If you'd like to contact us, you can do so by sending us an email at morganwalker@whitman.com or writing to Whitman Publishing, Attn: 100 Greatest Modern World Coins, 1974 Chandalar Drive, Suite D, Pelham AL 35124.

Also, please, if you have not done so already, expand your collecting horizons by adding these important Whitman Publishing "100 Greatest" books to your numismatic library:

- *100 Greatest U.S. Coins* by Jeff Garrett with Ron Guth
- *100 Greatest U.S. Modern Coins* by Scott Schechter and Jeff Garrett
- *100 Greatest American Currency Notes*
  by Q. David Bowers and David M. Sundman
- *100 Greatest U.S. Error Coins*
  by Nicholas Brown, David Camire, and Fred Weinberg
- *100 Greatest American Medals and Tokens*
  by Katherine Jaeger and Q. David Bowers
- *100 Greatest Ancient Coins* by Harlan J. Berk
- *100 Greatest Women on Coins* by Ron Guth

The following abbreviations can be found throughout this book.

REFERENCES

Bitkin	Bitkin, Vladimir (*Composite Catalogue of Russian Coins, 1700-1917*)
BW	Bailey, Don/Bailey, Lois (*Whitman Encyclopedia of Mexican Money*)
DC	Drake, M. (*Charlton Coin Guide*)
Dav	Davenport, John S. (*European Crowns and Talers, Since 1800, 2nd Edition*)
Divo	Divo, Jean-Paul (*Modern Greek Coins: 1828–1968*)
Eliz	Elizondo, Carlos A. (*Eight Reales and Pesos of the New World*)
Fr	Friedberg, Arthur/Friedberg, Ira (*Gold Coins of the World: From Ancient Times to the Present*)
GB	Guthrie, Hugh S. (*Mexican Revolutionary Coinage: 1913–1917: Based on the Bothamley Collection*)
Gill	Gill, Dennis (*The Coinage of Ethiopia, Eritrea and Italian Somalia*)
Hede	Hede, Holger (*Danmarks og Norges Mønter 1541–1814–1977*)
Herinek	Herinek, Ludwig (*Österreichische Münzprägungen von 1740–1969*)
Hern	Hern, Brian (*Hern's Handbook of South African Coins*)
HMZ	Richter, Juerg, and Ruedi Kunzmann (*Der neue HMZ-Katalog, Band 2: Die Münzen der Schweiz und Liechtensteins 15//16. Jahrhundert bis Gegenwart*)
HW	Wood, Howland (*The Coinage of the Mexican Revolutionists 1913–1917*)
J	Jaeger, Kurt (*Die deutschen Münzen seit 1871: Bewertungen mit aktuellen Marktpreisen, Die Münzprägungen der deutschen Staaten vom Ausgang de alten Reiches*)
J&V	Jacobs, Norman/Vermeule, Cornelius (*Japanese Coinage: A Monetary History of Japan*)
JNDA	JNDA (*The Catalog of Japanese Coins and Bank Notes*)
K	Kann, Eduard (*Illustrated Catalog of Chinese Coins: Gold, Silver, Nickel, and Aluminum*)
KM	Krause-Mishler (*Standard Catalog of World Coins*)
L&M	Lin Gwo Ming/Ma Tak Wo (*Illustrated Catalog of Chinese Gold & Silver Coins*)
Marsh	Marsh, Michael (*The Gold Sovereign*)
McD	McDonald, Greg (*Australian Coins and Banknotes*)
Par	Parchimowicz, Janusz (*Katalog Monet Polskich*)
Russo	Russo, Arnaldo (*Catalogo de Moedas do Brasil*)
Schön	Schön, Gunter (*Welt-Munzkatalog*)
Schou	Schou, H.H. (*Beskrivelse af Danske og Norske Mønter, 1815–1923*)
Sev	Severin, H.M. (*Gold and Platinum Coinage of Imperial Russia*)
Spink	Howard, Emma/Kitchen, Geoff (*Coins of England and the United Kingdom: Pre-Decimal Issues*)
Uzd	Uzdenikov, V.V. (*Russian Coins 1700-1917*)
Vogt & Bruce	Vogt, George/Bruce, Colin (*Standard Catalog of Mexican Coins, Paper Money, Stocks, Bonds and Medals*)
WS	Wright, Richard N. J. (*The Modern Coinage of China 1866–1949: The Evidence in Western Archives*)
Y	Yeoman (*Catalog of Modern World Coins, 1850–1964; Catalog of Current World Coins*)

GRADING FIRMS

NGC: Numismatic Guaranty Corporation. NGC has certified more than 35 million U.S., international, and ancient coins, tokens, and medals. The company, founded in 1987, provides grading, authentication, attribution, and encapsulation, as well as online research tools and a census report of the coins it has graded. NGC is the official grading service of the American Numismatic Association and the Professional Numismatists Guild.

PCGS: Professional Coin Grading Services. Founded in 1985, PCGS offers grading, authentication, attribution, and encapsulation for U.S. and foreign coins. The service has graded more than 38 million coins. PCGS also keeps a census of the coins it has graded, including quality details, to provide population reports for particular denominations, as well as other informational resources for coin collectors.

A NOTE ABOUT TRANSCRIPTIONS OF ASIAN PROPER NOUNS AND NAMES

When referring to Chinese names and places in this book, we use Pinyin instead of the traditionally used Wade-Giles style for Chinese transliteration. This style change, much like BC and AD being BCE and CE in academic history circles for the past 40 years, is long overdue. Our decision to do this was to facilitate further research on the part of the reader. In addition, we use revised romanization for Korean. For Japanese, we use Hepburn romanization. This is an older system, but it is in common usage around the world and whatever flaws it may have in reproducing Japanese grammar they do not outweigh its familiarity to most readers. The over-reliance on Wade-Giles in the numismatic hobby is, at this late point, an unnecessary detriment to the future study and enjoyment of Chinese numismatics in the United States.

The Dominion of Canada was the last of three major countries in North America to open a mint for domestic coin production. With the permission of the home government in London, England, Canada established the Canadian Mint in Ottawa as a branch of the Royal Mint, opening for business on January 2, 1908.

Before the establishment of the nation's own branch mint, Canadian coinage developed from trade tokens to provincial issues to national coins struck at the privately owned Heaton Mint in Birmingham, England. These circulated alongside a great number of coins from the United States that had migrated north (partially explaining why the Canadians modelled their monetary system after that of the United States).

The system worked, but it was hardly efficient.

While the establishment of the Ottawa Mint was meant to facilitate the flow of new coinage into commercial channels, the Currency Act of 1910 was seen as a necessary reform. The law adjusted the weight of Canada's subsidiary coinage to ease rounding, authorized the issue of gold coins produced domestically from gold discovered in the Yukon, and called for production of a much-needed Canadian silver dollar. It was an ambitious mandate.

The Mint opened to great fanfare. Albert Grey, governor general of Canada and the fourth Earl Grey, struck the Mint's first coin, a 1908 50-cent piece. Grey's wife, Countess Alice Holford, then struck the nation's first domestically produced 1-cent coin[1]. Plasters and dies for the silver dollar would not come into play for another two years, but in the interim a number of events both at home and abroad set about a turbulent time for Mint Deputy Master Dr. James Bonar and the government in Ottawa.

A collapse in demand for new coinage, brought about by the Panic of 1907, meant most of the coins being struck at the facility wound up in government stockpiles. A trickle of worn silver coins arrived at the Mint for re-coining, but banks were reluctant to bear the costs of redemption. The absence of a *refinery* on Mint grounds left it without the means to assay its own gold, which made it difficult to strike gold coins. These issues led many in the government to question the worth of having a domestic mint in the first place. The staff was threatened with layoffs, but they soldiered on anyway.

The death of King Edward VII on May 6, 1910, only compounded the Mint's problems.

British tradition holds that upon the death of a monarch, the Crown mints are authorized to continue to produce coinage bearing the likeness of the late king or queen through the year's end. This is meant to give the mints time to create new designs without a sudden disruption in production.

The process of creating new designs for 1911 overwhelmed the Royal Mint in London, which delayed the delivery of dies to the Ottawa Mint until almost halfway through 1911. Such was the rush to produce new dies that one glaring omission was made. The inscription DEI GRA, a truncation of *Dei Gratia* ("By the Grace of God")—which had been standard since the time of King Richard III—was omitted from the coinage produced for the new king, George V (who would rule from 1910 to 1936). After drawing attention to the issue, the Royal Mint promised to revise the dies the following year. In the interim, the Canadians would have to make do with the "godless" designs.

Given the cascading issues facing the new mint, work continued on the development of a Canadian dollar coin.

In *Striking Impressions: The Royal Canadian Mint and Canadian Coinage* (1983), numismatic researcher and author Dr. James A. Haxby shows a master hub of a 1910-dated reverse design and notes that a wax impression of the design was produced and shipped to Canada for review[2]. In 1911, "godless" obverse designs were made up, but no known examples

CANADA 1911 SILVER DOLLAR PATTERN

"Emperor of Canadian Coinage" and the "Most Valuable Coin in the World" (once).

Obverse: An enlarged left-facing portrait of King George V. Inscription GEORGIVS V DEI GRA REX ET IND IMP (abbreviated Latin for GEORGIUS V DEI GRATIA REX ET INDIAE IMPERATOR ["George V, King by the Grace of God and Emperor of India"]). Designer's initials B.M. in bust truncation.
Reverse: Inscription ONE DOLLAR CANADA. Date 1911 below a dividing bar. A wreath (of maple) cradles the inscription starting at the bottom. There is a small rendition of the imperial state crown atop the central design.

Composition	Weight	Diameter	Alignment	Edge
.925 silver (sterling)	23.25 grams	36 mm	Medal	Reeded

Mintage	Mint	Collecting Difficulty	References
2	Royal Canadian Mint (Ottawa)	Virtually impossible	DC-6; KM-Pn15

Albert Grey, governor general of Canada, struck the Ottawa Mint's first coin in 1908.

King George V in 1911.

exist of this type. Instead, at least two pieces with the corrected legend were struck up in silver by the London Mint and held as patterns. When Canada received the dies and punches, it struck its own trial piece in lead and sent it to the finance minister in Ottawa for review. (The existence of the lead trial was forgotten until it was rediscovered in 1977, still in the same brown paper bag it was mailed in 65 years earlier.)

Despite calling for the production of a dollar coin in legislation a year earlier, the new Conservative majority shelved the program, informing the Mint in writing not to proceed. As a result, the Ottawa Mint would not strike a dollar coin until 1935.

The 1911 pattern silver dollars, only one of which made its way into private hands, would become the ultimate rarity in the Canadian series.

In fact, the existence of the 1911 silver dollars was little more than a rumor for almost 50 years, before London-based coin dealer B. A. Seaby made knowledge of his purchase of one of the patterns public in 1960. Ultimately, it was revealed that the coin was sourced from the family of former Mint Master Sir William Grey Ellison-MacCartney, though the Royal Mint does not believe that he leaked the coin into the numismatic wild.

Dubbed the "Emperor of Canadian Coinage," the sole privately held example has been actively sought after by an elite class of collector for the better part of a century. It has served as the cornerstone of the famed John L. McKay-Clements and Sid and Alicia Belzberg Collections. In 1976, stateside coin dealer Gene L. Henry of Rare Coin Galleries of Seattle, purchased the piece for US$135,000. At the time of the sale, Henry noted that the coin was underpriced[3].

Noted U.S. collector Jay Parrino bought the Belzberg specimen in 1988.

In March 1990, the coin became the first Canadian coin ever certified by Professional Coin Grading Service (PCGS), from whom it earned the

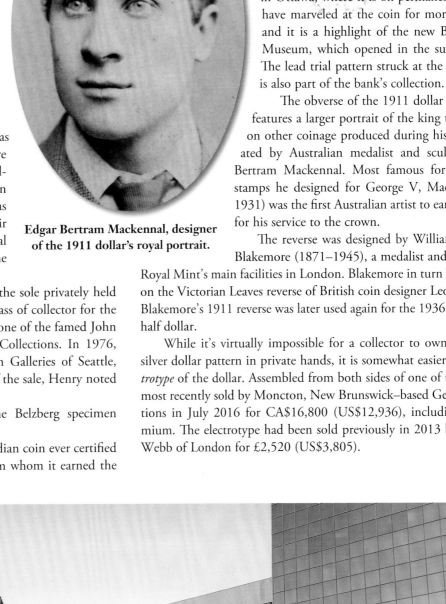

Edgar Bertram Mackennal, designer of the 1911 dollar's royal portrait.

grade SP-65[4]. The last time the coin publicly traded was in 2003, when Heritage Auctions sold it for $690,000[5]. At one time, it was listed as the most valuable coin in the world by the *Guinness Book of World Records*.

As for the second known example, Seaby's investigations revealed that it resided at the Royal Mint Museum in London. It was eventually transferred to the Bank of Canada National Currency Collection in Ottawa, where it is on permanent loan. Visitors have marveled at the coin for more than 30 years and it is a highlight of the new Bank of Canada Museum, which opened in the summer of 2017. The lead trial pattern struck at the Canadian Mint is also part of the bank's collection.

The obverse of the 1911 dollar patterns, which features a larger portrait of the king than that found on other coinage produced during his reign, was created by Australian medalist and sculptor Sir Edgar Bertram Mackennal. Most famous for the coins and stamps he designed for George V, Mackennal (1863–1931) was the first Australian artist to earn a knighthood for his service to the crown.

The reverse was designed by William Henry James Blakemore (1871–1945), a medalist and engraver at the Royal Mint's main facilities in London. Blakemore in turn based his design on the Victorian Leaves reverse of British coin designer Leonard C. Wyon. Blakemore's 1911 reverse was later used again for the 1936 Canadian silver half dollar.

While it's virtually impossible for a collector to own the only 1911 silver dollar pattern in private hands, it is somewhat easier to own an *electrotype* of the dollar. Assembled from both sides of one of the coins, it was most recently sold by Moncton, New Brunswick–based Geoffrey Bell Auctions in July 2016 for CA$16,800 (US$12,936), including buyer's premium. The electrotype had been sold previously in 2013 by Dix Noonan Webb of London for £2,520 (US$3,805).

The Bank of Canada Museum's National Currency Collection in Ottawa houses one of the two known 1911 dollars.

CHINA 1903 SILVER FENGTIEN TAEL PATTERN

Unique among the Chinese tael patterns.

Obverse. In the center, a Chinese dragon curled around a flaming pearl. English legend FEN-TIEN-PROVINCE at top, and ONE TAEL at bottom. Two rosettes, one on either side of the dragon, with each rosette separating the top and bottom inscriptions. A ring of denticles surrounds along the rim.

Reverse. Four large Chinese characters in the center: 光緒元寶 (Guāngxù Yuánbǎo ["Guangxu Ingot"]). A closed circle of very small dots or beads surrounds. Inscription along the top half of the coin (reading right to left): 奉天省造 (Fèngtiān Shěng Zào ["Made in Fengtien Province"]). Chinese characters for "Gui" and "Mao" (癸卯, Guǐ Mǎo; representing the date 1903) on the right and left, respectively. Along the bottom (right to left): 庫平銀一兩 (Kùpíng Yín Yī Liǎng ["Treasury Standard Silver One Tael"]). A ring of small denticles surrounds the design along a relatively wide rim.

Composition	Weight	Diameter	Alignment	Edge
Silver	37.5 grams	40 mm	Coin	Reeded

Mintage	Mint	Collecting Difficulty	References
1	Fengtien Machinery Bureau/ Shenyang Mint	Virtually impossible	K-931i; KM-PnA15; L&M-486

Imperial portrait of the Emperor Guangxu of China.

The tael—pronounced more like the English word *tile* than the word *tail*—is a unit in the traditional Chinese system of weights, though it is also used in other East Asian cultures. It is derived (via Portuguese traders) from the Malay word *tahil,* which means "weight." Different standards were applied using the same word, but a range of 35 to 40 grams is about right (though the People's Republic of China reduced it to as low as 31.25 grams in 1959). Coins were issued in these weights instead of in monetary denominations, though China had two systems to denominate coins: the cash and the dollar. About 1,000 cash equaled one tael, and 100 cash equaled one cent, 100 of which equaled a dollar.

The characters 元寶 *(Yuánbǎo)* inscribed on the coin refer to Chinese ingots of gold or silver, also known as sycee. These unminted, privately struck units of weight—famous for the various shapes they were made into—became an especially important form of currency in China during the late Ming dynasty (1368–1644 AD), as silver from Spanish mines in the Americas made its way into Asian markets. Sycee, or yuanbao, continued to play an important role in Chinese commerce until the very end of the Qing dynasty in the early twentieth century.

The 1903 Fengtien tael silver pattern coin is unique. It was certified by PCGS at the April 2012 Hong Kong International Coin Convention, having been submitted by a Taiwanese coin dealer on behalf of a collector who wishes to remain private. In 2013 it was insured for US$5 million.

Lin Gwo Ming's *Illustrated Catalog of Chinese Gold & Silver* states the coin is unique ("so far"). It is pedigreed to such owners as Eduard Kann (1880–1962), whom the *New York Times* said owned the "finest collection of Chinese coins" and who published what is considered one of the authoritative texts on the subject of Chinese coins beginning in 1953, after he left China during the Maoist takeover in 1949. He had lived there for 47 years, working as a banker and adviser to the Chinese monetary authorities. Other owners of this coin over the years have included collectors Irving Goodman and Chou Chien-Fu.

The province of Fengtien (奉天, *Fèngtiān;* renamed Liaoning in 1929) was established in its modern form in 1907. It is the southern part of Manchuria, sharing a border with what is now North Korea. As such, it was an area where different nations and cultures interacted, whether in trade or at war. Fengtien was an early seat of power for the Manchus, who conquered China in the seventeenth century, but by the mid- to late nineteenth century the Han Chinese became the dominant ethnic group in the

THE GUANGXU EMPEROR

In Chinese tradition, rulers choose or receive a propitious "era name" by which their reign is known and by which histories and calendars refer to the time period. The Qing ruler whose personal name was Zaitian (載湉, Zǎitián) became known as the Guangxu (Kuang Hsu) Emperor (光緒帝, Guāngxù Dì), with his era name meaning "Glorious Succession." Guangxu lived from 1871 to 1908, and he inherited the throne around the age of four, in 1875, with the Empress Dowager Cixi (慈禧太后, Cíxǐ Tàihòu) serving as regent.

Confronted by China's failure to keep pace with the modernization of rival nations such as Japan, Guangxu set about to reform the Chinese system. This effort is widely known as the Hundred Days' Reform. Unfortunately, these modernization initiatives put him on a collision course with the very powerful forces of tradition within Chinese culture, and the Empress Dowager overthrew the young emperor in an 1898 coup. Guangxu was imprisoned within his own household until his death in 1908, which means the 1903 Fengtien silver tael was actually issued under Cixi's auspices.

area. When Russia and Japan went to war in 1904, several battles took place within the province, including the historic Battle of Mukden (the Manchurian name for the capital of Shenyang).

This coin was made at the Fengtien Machinery Bureau, which is now the Shenyang Mint. It features an iconic Chinese dragon on the obverse, which differs from a Western or European dragon in its serpentine body form and long whiskers, antlers, and claws. The dragon makes frequent appearances on Chinese coins as a symbol of wisdom and imperial power. Especially powerful is the five-toed variety, since it is capable of grasping a mystical pearl called a *ruyizhu* (如意珠, *Rúyìzhū*) that can materialize whatever is desired by the one who wields it. In Buddhist legend the pearl fell from the sky. This is likely the reason for the flames coming from the pearl as shown on the coin, while the dragon appears to attempt to catch the pearl as it falls.

The date, given by the characters 癸卯 *(Guǐ Mǎo)*, is represented using the Chinese "stem-branch" calendar, an ancient system that dates back to approximately 3000 BCE. "Gui" (癸) is one of the 10 heavenly stems and "Mao" (卯) represents one of the 12 earthly branches. When combined,

these stems and branches are capable of uniquely identifying every year in a 60-year cycle. "Mao" also corresponds to the Year of the Rabbit in the Chinese zodiac. The 2014 *Standard Catalog of World Coins* briefly mentions that the sole known specimen of this pattern (K931-i) sold at the March 1991 Superior Goodman auction for US$187,000; this is considered by many to be a turning point for the rising reputation of Chinese coins in the global market. The seventh edition of Lin Gwo Ming's *Illustrated Catalog of Chinese Gold & Silver Coins* (2012) states that the tael pattern is worth $3 million in Uncirculated condition.

A circa 1900 map of China, produced by Fort Dearborn Publishing Co.

LIANG VS. TAEL

Liǎng (兩, or 两 in simplified Chinese) is the abstract Chinese "ounce," while tael is specifically an ounce of silver. The Chinese used both terms, depending on the context. Europeans, however, insisted on using the word tael. The denomination "seven mace two candareens" (7.2 mace), encountered frequently in Chinese numismatics, corresponds to one tael. A Kùpíng or "treasury standard" tael weighs 37.5 grams, while other standards used for commerce and shipping may weigh less.

A Chinese New Year festival in Melbourne, Australia, in 2014 includes a dragon puppet.

CHINA 1910 YUNNAN SPRING SILVER DOLLAR

First Chinese coin to sell for more than US$1 million.

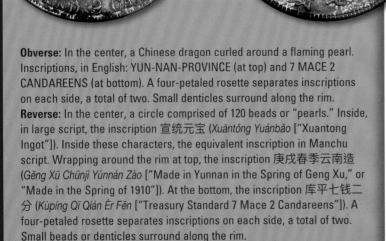

Obverse: In the center, a Chinese dragon curled around a flaming pearl. Inscriptions, in English: YUN-NAN-PROVINCE (at top) and 7 MACE 2 CANDAREENS (at bottom). A four-petaled rosette separates inscriptions on each side, a total of two. Small denticles surround along the rim.

Reverse: In the center, a circle comprised of 120 beads or "pearls." Inside, in large script, the inscription 宣统元宝 (*Xuāntǒng Yuánbǎo* ["Xuantong Ingot"]). Inside these characters, the equivalent inscription in Manchu script. Wrapping around the rim at top, the inscription 庚戌春季云南造 (*Gēng Xū Chūnjì Yúnnán Zào* ["Made in Yunnan in the Spring of Geng Xu," or "Made in the Spring of 1910"]). At the bottom, the inscription 库平七钱二分 (*Kùpíng Qī Qián Èr Fēn* ["Treasury Standard 7 Mace 2 Candareens"]). A four-petaled rosette separates inscriptions on each side, a total of two. Small beads or denticles surround along the rim.

Composition	Weight	Diameter	Alignment	Edge
Silver	37.5 grams	40 mm	Medal	Reeded

Mintage	Mint	Collecting Difficulty	References
2 known	Yunnan	Virtually impossible	Y-260.1

Pu Yi, the "Last Emperor" (of the Qing dynasty).

Collectors who are not well-versed in Chinese history may yet have some historical perspective on the time of this coin's striking and the volatile politics of China at the start of the twentieth century, as the era is the subject of Italian filmmaker Bernardo Bertolucci's 1987 Academy Award–winning epic biopic, *The Last Emperor*.

Minted during the tumultuous years of the reign of Pu Yi (溥儀, *Pǔyí*)—otherwise known as the Xuantong Emperor (宣统帝, *Xuāntǒng Dì* [an era name meaning "declaration of unity" or "herald of unity"])—and the last member of the Qing dynasty—the Yunnan Spring dollar is as enigmatic as it is rare.

Yunnan (云南, *Yúnnán*) is a southern Chinese province that borders Myanmar, Laos, and Vietnam to the south, the Chinese province of Sichuan (四川, *Sìchuān*) to the north, and the provinces of Guizhou (贵州, *Guìzhōu*) and Guangxi (广西, *Guǎngxī*) to the east. At the start of the twentieth century, this rugged and rustic area was relatively isolated, but after the overthrow of the Qing in 1912, the events of the Warlord Era (1916–1928) and the Second Sino-Japanese War (1937–1945) would make Yunnan of great strategic importance.

In 1910, the province's isolation possibly led to the creation of the Spring dollar.

On April 15 of that year, the Qing government issued monetary reforms that sought to standardize silver coinage. All production of silver coins would be centralized at the Tientsin Mint, except for those provinces that were too isolated for this restriction to be enforced. Yunnan was one such province, and its mint was now considered a branch of Tientsin. These secondary mints were not permitted to strike silver until they were able to strike coins according to the central standard weight, size, fineness, and design.

For some reason, Yunnan knowingly disobeyed this order. To circumvent the new reforms, the province specified a date of "Spring" (understood to mean the first three months of the year) directly on the coins themselves.

Quite possibly the only Chinese coin to include the season within which it was struck (春季, *Chūnjì* ["Spring"]), the Yunnan Spring dollar also features another form of traditional Chinese dating, seen on more than one coin on our list (see number 2 and number 11). The date, given by the characters 庚戌 (*Gēng Xū*), is represented using the Chinese "stem-branch" calendar. "Geng" (庚) is one of the 10 heavenly stems and "Xu" (戌) represents one of the 12 earthly branches. When combined, these stem-branch combinations are capable of uniquely identifying every year in a 60-year cycle. "Xu" also corresponds to the Year of the Dog in the Chinese zodiac.

The denomination "seven mace two candareens" (7.2 mace) is often seen in Chinese numismatics and corresponds to one tael. A *Kùpíng* or "treasury standard" tael weighs 37.5 grams, while standards used for commerce and shipping may weigh less.

The characters 元宝 (*Yuánbǎo*) inscribed on the coin refer to Chinese ingots of gold or silver also known as sycee. These privately struck units of weight were made in various shapes and were an especially important form of currency in China during the late Ming dynasty (1368–1644), often made with silver from Spanish mines in the Americas. Sycee, or yuanbao, were used in Chinese commerce until the very end of the Qing dynasty in the early-twentieth century.

A Chinese dragon, a symbol of wisdom and imperial power, is featured on the obverse. Its five toes mean it is a particularly powerful and venerable dragon, capable of grasping a mystical, wish-granting pearl (如意珠, *Rúyìzhū*) that makes the holder omnipotent. The flames on the pearl likely refer to its falling from the sky in Buddhist legend.

Only two genuine examples of the Spring dollar are known. The finer of the two was one of many captivating treasures from the collection of numismatic author and Far East specialist Norman Jacobs. The Jacobs

Collection was offered for sale in September 2011 by Heritage Auctions and brought US$546,250.

Asian coin specialist Michael Chou notes that the Yunnan Spring Dollar was the first Chinese coin to reach 1 million renminbi (approximately US$140,000 in early 2019) when one was offered at a 2001 Beijing auction. Since then, the market for rare Asian coins has heated up dramatically and in 2010, the Yunnan Spring Dollar became the first Chinese coin to surpass US$1 million.

INSIGHTS FROM ASIAN COIN SPECIALIST MICHAEL CHOU

"The China Yunnan Spring 1910 dollar has a wonderful story. The coin was discovered in Yunnan by a former Kuomintang official's family member and then purchased by a Taiwanese dealer before it was consigned to a 2001 auction in Beijing, where it sold and became the first Chinese coin to reach 1 million renminbi. The coin was purchased by a collector from Hong Kong, who consigned it five years later to auction, where it sold for a record 3.68 million renminbi. The coin was consigned to my company, Champion Auction, in 2010 and when we sold it, it became the first Chinese coin to sell for over $1 million."

Dragons on a dish from the Qing dynasty.

A mountain scene in China's remote Yunnan Province.

AUSTRALIA 1920 SYDNEY GOLD SOVEREIGN

Rarest of all sovereign issues.

Obverse. A portrait of King George V, facing left and sharply truncated at the neck. Initials B.M. in the truncation. Inscription GEORGIVS V D. G. BRITT: OMN: REX F. D. IND: IMP: (abbreviated Latin for *GEORGIUS V DEI GRATIA BRITANNIARUM OMNIUM REX FIDEI DEFENSOR INDIAE IMPERATOR* ["George V, by the Grace of God, King of all the Britons, Defender of the Faith, Emperor of India"]), clockwise around the top. Denticles surround along the rim.

Reverse. A rendering of lightly clad St. George in a crested Roman helmet, soldier's cloak, and leather boots, atop a steed, which rears up to trample a European-style dragon. St. George pulls back the reins with his left hand and brandishes a short Roman sword *(gladius)* in the right. His left foot is barely visible under the horse. the point of his spear is broken off in the dragon's side; the spear shaft is on the ground behind his horse. The date 1920 is beneath this tableau. Mintmark S is above the date, in the ground. Above and to the right of the date are the initials, B.P. An incuse denticle design surrounds along the rim.

Composition	Weight	Diameter	Alignment	Edge
.9167 gold	7.9881 grams	21 mm	Medal	Reeded

Mintage	Mint	Collecting Difficulty	References
360,000 (reported by Krause; estimated 4–9 actually struck)	Royal Mint (Sydney)†	Virtually impossible	Fr-38; KM-29; Marsh-280; McD-264; S-4003

† Mintmark: S

As one of the twentieth century's greatest rarities, the 1920-S sovereigns flew under the radar for at least 60 years after their emission—perhaps because no one was looking (the reported mintage was 360,000 pieces), or perhaps because so few ever turned up at auction that it was impossible to get a true grasp of just how rare they were in reality.

The coin was struck in Sydney, then one of three Australian branch mints operating under the Royal Mint in London. Gold had become too expensive to coin in the immediate years after World War I, and so the Royal Mint suspended production of the sovereign. But apparently, Sydney had already minted a handful before word arrived of this suspension. According to Australian numismatic researcher Barrie Winsor, a local politician named Jacob Garrard was responsible for the mega-rarity when he placed a personal order with the mint for gold sovereigns to present to himself, his wife, and their seven children on the occasion of the Garrards' 50th anniversary.

One of the four known surviving 1920-S sovereigns is part of the Royal Australian Mint Collection in Canberra. Only three are known to be in private hands.

The sovereign's reverse is iconic. It utilizes Italian medalist and engraver Benedetto Pistrucci's *St. George and the Dragon* design. The long-serving design first appeared in 1817 and was struck to honor St. George, the patron saint of England. Unfortunately, most known examples of the coin feature a somewhat rough surface on the reverse due to corrosion on the dies, which was caused by the extensive journey by sea from London to Sydney.

In medieval legend, George, a Christian Roman soldier, was riding by a lake in Libya that was being poisoned by a dragon. The nearby townspeople, fearful of the dragon, were forced to feed it with sheep; when they ran out of sheep, the town's children were supplied according to the drawing of lots. On the day George rode by, the king's daughter had been selected. He decided to put an end to this barbaric sacrifice and met the dragon in battle, where he wounded it with his lance. He then took the princess's girdle and leashed it to the dragon. He and the princess led the dragon back to town, whereby George offered to kill it if the townspeople converted to Christianity. They did, and thus the beast was slain.

The obverse features a portrait of King George V (1865–1936; reigned 1910–1936) created by Australian medalist and sculptor Sir Edgar Bertram Mackennal, an artist most famous for the coins and stamps he designed for King George. He was the first Australian artist to earn a knighthood, as Knight Commander of the Royal Victorian Order, for his personal service to the monarch.

Krause Publications for some reason reports a mintage of 360,000 in its *Standard Catalog of World Coins*. Clearly aware of the issue's rarity, however, the publication's editors give estimated values of US$75,000 in VF-20, $150,000 in XF-40, and $275,000 in MS-60.

Numismatist Neil S. Berman tracked published prices and sales records of the 1920-S sovereign, which, when it was offered, brought as little as AU$4,250 in 1979 (approximately US$4,720). Thirteen years later, Spink Auctions sold a Good Extremely Fine example for the equivalent of US$195,200. An example from the Bentley Collection of milled gold sovereigns sold in a 2006 auction in Australia for AU$582,500 (about $426,796 in contemporaneous U.S. dollars). It was offered again at a 2011 A.H. Baldwin and Sons auction and sold for £780,000 (about US$998,400), setting a record for an Australian coin—as well as for British imperial gold sovereigns.

A replica of a circa 1420 painting depicting St. George slaying the dragon.

Struck in the waning years of the short-lived Great Korean Empire (1897–1910), the 5-, 10-, and 20-won denominations were made in Osaka, Japan (after local Korean coin production was shut down), from 1906 to 1909.

The 5-won coin debuted in 1908, the second year of the reign of Emperor Yunghui. In total, 10,000 of the coins were struck. Almost all were held as a reserve currency until Japan annexed Korea on August 29, 1910, at which point the majority were melted down. The very few that escaped the smelter's pot were spirited away to private collections and museums.

The 10-won and 20-won coins debuted in 1906 and were struck with modest mintages of 5,012 and 2,506 pieces, respectively. As was the case with the 1908 5 won, all but a very few of the 10- and 20-won coins are now lost, making the offering of any existent piece a major news event in international numismatic circles.

It is because of their absolute rarity and their ties to a tumultuous and important point in Korean history that these early-twentieth-century Korean gold coins have become among the most desirable objects for builders of the finest world-coin cabinets. Famed American collectors Henry Christensen and Louis Eliasberg Sr. took turns owning a single specimen of the 20-won gold coin of 1906. That coin was last offered at a 2012 Bonham's sale (lot 1064). It has, to the best of our knowledge, been off the market since then.

The 1909 coins are unlike the debut issues in this three-denomination gold series (coins that were struck in some quantity

KOREA 1909 YUNGHUI THREE-COIN GOLD SET

A golden celebration of the Confucian virtues.

Common Obverse: In the center, a curled Korean dragon clutching a Yeouiju. 76 beads encircle the dragon. Clockwise around the beads, reading right to left: 大韓 (Dae Han ["Great Korea"]) * (small five-petaled plum flower) 隆熙三年 (Hyeon-hui Sam Nyeon ["Yunghui Three Years"]) * (plum flower) (denomination) * (plum flower). The denominations are 원십이 (I-Sip Won ["20 Won"]), 십원 (Sip Won ["10 Won"]), and 오원 (O Won ["5 Won"]). Denticles surround the design.
Common Reverse: In the center, top to bottom, is the denomination in Japanese: 二十圓 (I-Sip Won — "20 Won"), 十圓 (Sip Won ["10 Won"]), and 五圓 (O Won ["5 Won"]). Large five-petaled Korean plum flower, top. Surrounding the denomination, a rose-and-plum-leaf wreath tied with a ribbon at the bottom. Denticles surround the design.

5 Won				
Composition	Weight	Diameter	Alignment	Edge
Gold	4.1225 grams		Coin	Reeded
Mintage	Mint		Collecting Difficulty	References
2 (known)	Japan Mint (Osaka)		Virtually impossible	J&V-AD8; KM-1142

10 Won				
Composition	Weight	Diameter	Alignment	Edge
Gold	8.245 grams		Coin	Reeded
Mintage	Mint		Collecting Difficulty	References
2 (known)	Japan Mint (Osaka)		Virtually impossible	J&V-AD6; KM-A1130

20 Won				
Composition	Weight	Diameter	Alignment	Edge
Gold	16.49 grams	28.8 mm	Coin	Reeded
Mintage	Mint		Collecting Difficulty	References
2 (known)	Japan Mint (Osaka)		Virtually impossible	J&V-AD3; KM-1144

but all but lost to time). The emissions of 1909 were made in very small numbers, presumably as presentation pieces. Only two examples of each denomination are known today. One three-coin set is impounded in the permanent collection of the Bank of Japan at the Bank of Japan Currency Museum in Tokyo. The other set was held for many years in the collection of Dr. Norman Jacobs (1924–2004), a Harvard-educated author, professor, and pioneer in the field of Asian numismatics.

It was Dr. Jacobs's 1953 collaboration with numismatist and art historian Dr. Cornelius C. Vermeule, entitled *Japanese Coinage: A Monetary History,* that served as the first real English-language roadmap to the collecting of Asian coins.

The Jacobs set was broken up and its coins sold individually in 2011 by Heritage Auctions at their September Long Beach Signature Auction. This was the first (and so far, only) time these coins were ever publicly offered. The set realized a combined total of US$1,391,500 (the 20-won coin brought $632,500). According to Asian coin expert and auctioneer Michael Chou, the Jacobs set has been reconstituted and repatriated to its Korean homeland, where it now resides in the cabinet of a prominent collector.

It may be many years before the coins resurface, if they are ever offered for sale again.

The obverse of all three coins is based on the design of the Meiji-era Japanese yen, which was originally created in 1869 by nineteenth-century artist Kano Natsuo (1828–1898)—arguably the greatest designer of Japanese sword fittings in history. It features an excellent example of an Asian dragon (용, *yong*), replete with antlers, whiskers, spines, and skin like fish scales. In Korean folklore, an immature dragon could not enter into its full power and majesty until it had caught something known as a *yeouiju* (여의주)—a jewel or pearl that falls from the sky and has the ability to make thoughts and desires real. The yeouiju grants omnipotence to the one who wields it, and only dragons with "thumbs" (four claws or toes instead of three) are capable of using this powerful pearl. It has its origins in Hindu and Buddhist legend.

The prominent plum-flower blossom on the reverse serves as an imperial seal and a symbol of the Korean nation. It represents perseverance, hope, and the Confucian virtues of loyalty, honesty, charity, integrity, and correct behavior in all aspects of life.

Yunghui, the second and last emperor of Korea.

The mint in Osaka, 1909.

King Edward VIII (1894–1972; reigned January 20–December 11, 1936) ascended to the British throne following the death of King George V, his father.

In one of the great aristocratic traditions, Prince Edward showed great scorn for aristocratic tradition. His freewheeling lifestyle and numerous affairs were cause for concern to his father before, but early in the 1930s his contrarian nature threatened to upend British social order.

The future king met American socialite Wallis Simpson in 1931 and she became his mistress by 1934—even though she was married to her second husband. Edward and Mrs. Simpson's very public affair gave consternation to the king and the royal family. Upon King George's death and Edward's succession, Mrs. Simpson divorced her husband in order that she might marry the newly crowned Edward VIII. Beyond the social embarrassment their marriage would have caused—not to mention the potential crisis of having Americans in line for the throne—the king, who was traditionally the supreme governor of the Church of England, was simply not allowed, on religious grounds, to wed a divorcée.

So, on December 11, 1936, King Edward announced his abdication over BBC airwaves after a mere 326 days in power, before there had even been an official coronation ceremony. His younger brother was made king on December 12, becoming King George VI.

Edward and the former Mrs. Simpson married on June 3, 1937, being granted the titles of Duke and Duchess of Windsor.

Due to the brevity of his reign, coins of Edward VIII never entered circulation (production would have started on New Year's Day, 1937). According to legend, and keeping in character, the new king insisted the coins feature what he considered his best side—his left—despite the almost 400-year numismatic tradition that the new monarch's portrait face the direction opposite to their predecessor's (the portrait of George V faced left). This tradition dates back to King Charles II (reigned 1660–1685), who requested that his portrait look in the opposite direction of the dictator Oliver Cromwell (ruled 1653–1658).

The Royal Mint came up with a compromise: to model Edward's portrait on his left side and reverse it for the coin, so that it faced right. For whatever reason, this plan was rejected by the new king.

English medalist Thomas Humphrey Paget, OBE (1893–1974), was chosen by the Mint to design the new coinage, based on the strength of his design for an earlier medal honoring Prince Edward.

Only a few sets of 1937 Edward VIII coinage were ever struck, and the former king himself asked the Royal Mint for one. This request was passed up to his brother, the new king, who refused to allow it.

The Mint struck six Edward VIII gold sovereigns dated 1937 but, in order to spare the royal family any awkward feelings, hid the coins away until 1970, when a cardboard box was pulled from the safe of retiring Deputy Master of the Royal Mint (1957–1970) Sir Jack James (though according to A.H. Baldwin and Sons, the Mint had taken an inventory of the contents of the box back in 1950). The box held the six gold sovereigns and 43 other Edward VIII coins and patterns. The Royal Mint Museum has added to this collection of Edward VIII coinage since 1974.

The British Museum in London currently holds four of the six sovereigns, while another specimen is part of a complete set of English sovereigns. The sixth coin is in private hands and has been sold a few times over the last three decades or so. Spink sold it for £40,000 in 1984 as part of the Professor R.E. Gibson Collection, having been sold privately by the firm in 1981. The company offered it again in 2007 but it was not sold. Then, after it was purchased at a 2008 auction in Tokyo, the coin garnered £516,000 (US$874,258 at the time of sale) at the Baldwin and Sons auction of the Hemisphere Collection of gold sovereigns on May 8, 2014, where it became the most valuable British coin ever put up for auction.

GREAT BRITAIN 1937 KING EDWARD VIII GOLD SOVEREIGN

The most expensive British coin ever sold.

Obverse. A left-facing portrait of clean-shaven King Edward VIII. Clockwise from left: inscription EDWARDUS VIII D: G: BR: OMN: REX F: D: IND: IMP. (abbreviated Latin for EDWARDUS VIII DEI GRATIA BRITANNIARUM OMNIUM REX FIDEI DEFENSOR INDIAE IMPERATOR ["Edward VIII, by the Grace of God, King of All Britain, Defender of the Faith, Emperor of India"]). Designer's initials H.P. under the truncation of the neck. An enclosed ring of denticles encircles the entire design.

Reverse. A muscular rendering of St. George, clad in a crested Roman helmet, soldier's cloak, and leather boots, atop a steed, which rears up to trample a European-style dragon. St. George pulls back the reins with his left hand and brandishes a short Roman sword *(gladius)* in his right. His left foot is barely visible under the horse. The point of his spear is broken off in the dragon's side; the spear shaft is on the ground behind the horse. The date 1937 is beneath this tableau. Above and to right of the date are the initials B.P.

Composition	Weight	Diameter	Alignment	Edge
.9167 gold	7.98 grams	22.05 mm	Medal	Reeded
Mintage	**Mint**		**Collecting Difficulty**	**References**
6 (per Krause)	Royal Mint (London)		Extremely difficult	KM-Pn132

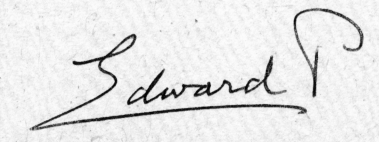

Edward's autograph as Prince of Wales.

AUSTRALIA 1930 MELBOURNE PENNY, PROOF

The "King of Australian Coins."

Obverse. A left-facing effigy of King George V, crowned and wearing a robe. Inscription GEORGIVS V D. G. BRITT: OMN: REX F.D. IND: IMP: (abbreviated Latin for *GEORGIUS V DEI GRATIA BRITANNIARUM OMNIUM REX FIDEI DEFENSOR INDIAE IMPERATOR* ["George V, by the Grace of God, King of all the Britons, Defender of the Faith, Emperor of India"]) wraps around the rim clockwise from lower left; a large dot divides the two ends of the inscription at the bottom, below the bust. The designer's initials B.M. are in the bust truncation. Denticles surround the design along the rim.

Reverse. The denomination ONE PENNY in large letters in the center. Two filigree ornaments, one above and one below the denomination. A beaded ring surrounds. the legend COMMONWEALTH OF AUSTRALIA encircles a beaded ring clockwise from the lower left. Beneath the beaded ring, at bottom, is the date 1930. A single dot on each side separates the legend from the date. Denticles wrap around the rim.

Composition	Weight	Diameter	Alignment	Edge
Bronze (.955 copper, .030 tin, .015 zinc)	9.4 grams	30.8 mm	Medal	Smooth

Mintage	Mint	Collecting Difficulty	References
6	Royal Mint (Melbourne)	Extremely difficult	KM-23

1933 portrait of King George V by Arthur Stockdale Cope.

The 1930 Australian penny is as popular with Australian collectors as the 1909-S VDB Lincoln cent is with U.S. collectors, yet it is much scarcer and many times more valuable. As with the 1909-S VDB cent, the 1930 Australian penny is avidly sought by everyday collectors who wanted to fill their penny albums.

What Australian hobbyists of the mid-twentieth century soon realized while searching their pocket change was that the 1930 penny, bearing an obverse portrait of King George V, was extremely hard to find. It was certainly much more challenging to locate a 1930 penny than other scarce Australian pennies, including semi-key issues like the 1919, 1920, 1925, 1933, and 1946 pennies. Each of those coins has decidedly low mintages of between 240,000 and nine million pieces each; the 1930 penny, however, saw a *very* limited mintage. Most sources, including the *Standard Catalog of World Coins* by Krause Publications, estimate that 3,000 business strikes and a tiny run of just six Proofs were all that were ever made.

This was because of the Great Depression, which began in October 1929 with the stock market crash in New York City and quickly spread around the world. Since Australia's economic outlook was so bleak, there was little need to strike new coinage in 1930.

Silver coins could only be struck after an order was received and silver stocks were allocated for the ordered run, while bronze could be stockpiled regardless of the order status for copper-based coins. So Mint officials were free to change dies to reflect the 1930 date in anticipation of incoming orders, and they decided to test the dies by producing bronze coins.

The Mint had a substantial number of 1929 pennies on hand, and thus only a small number of 1930 pennies were struck as trials. The output was not officially recorded, and these coins were interspersed with the Mint's stockpiled 1929 issues. Both the 1929 and 1930 pennies were released into circulation together, and the next official order for new bronze coins would not arrive at the Mint until 1931.

The background behind the Proof 1930 pennies is relatively well recorded. Six were made during the calendar year (presumably for completionist reasons), and soon delivered to the nation's two major public coin collections at the National Gallery of Victoria and the Art Gallery of South Australia.

The obverse design was created by Australian medalist and sculptor Sir Edgar Bertram Mackennal (1863–1931), who had designed coins and stamps for King George V, as well as his official coronation medal in 1910. The reverse was designed by William Henry James Blakemore (1871–1945), a medalist and engraver at the Royal Mint's main facilities in London.

One of two privately held specimens of the "King of Australian Coins" (as the 1930 Proof penny is known) sold for AU$16,000 in 1974. The same coin sold for US$100,000 in 1982—equivalent to almost $534,000 as of late 2019.

A different coin, removed from the British Museum's collections, sold in 2005 for almost US$620,000 (about $803,000 in 2019) and again in 2009 for $800,000 (about $938,000 today).

In 2011, one specimen sold for $1.05 million, becoming the first Australian coin to join the "million-dollar coin" club.

Like several other coins in this list, the sheer difficulty of trying to collect a coin with only one or two examples in private hands makes the acquisition of a copy, circulation strike, or base metal version relatively more reasonable. Since the 3,000 or so circulation-strike versions of the 1930 penny were released during the nadir of the Great Depression, even specimens with a fair amount of wear can be valuable. Heritage Auctions sold a PCGS EF Details coin for US$9,987.50 in 2013 and an NGC VF-25 example for $14,100. International Auction Gallery sold an NGC EF-45 Brown specimen for a whopping $31,684.80 in 2015.

If the 1936 "Dot" issues are the ultimate rarities in Canadian numismatics (and there is quite the competition for that title), then the unique "Dot" specimen set, which houses special strikes of all three coins, is the ultimate presentation of these ultimate rarities.

King George V died on January 20, 1936, and tradition dictated that the Royal Mint soon would have to prepare dies and strike new coins bearing the portrait of his successor, King Edward VIII. The process was complicated enough, and during the Great Depression there wasn't as much demand for coinage as during more prosperous times, so the coinage the Mint produced for a new king might not even circulate much. Still, the Mint and its branches around the world had managed the situation before, so there was no reason to believe this time would be different. But on December 11 of the same year, the rebellious new king abdicated the throne to marry an American divorcée, making his younger brother Albert king.

This historic turn of events compounded the work the Mint had to do, meaning its branch facilities around the world would have to wait that much longer to receive new dies for the coinage of King George VI (as Albert came to be known). Therefore, the Royal Mint decided that Canada would have to use the George V 1936 dies until George VI dies could be made. To denote that they were actually made in 1937, these coins were to have a small dot below the year 1936.

Three "Dot" cents are currently known; four "Dot" 10 cents are also known, with two of those impounded in the Bank of Canada's coin collection. It is believed that only four "Dot" quarters were produced in Specimen—and like the 10 cents, two are in the Bank of Canada collection—but the exact number is unknown. All other "Dot" issues are believed to have been melted.

The common obverse design was created by Sir Edgar Bertram Mackennal (1863–1931), an Australian medalist and sculptor most famous for the coins and stamps he designed for King George V. Mackennal also created the memorial tomb of King Edward VII in St. George's Chapel and sculpted statues of Edward for the Australian cities of Melbourne and Adelaide; Calcutta, in India; and London. When his bronze equestrian statue of King Edward was unveiled in London in 1921, King George made him a Knight Commander of the Royal Victorian Order.

CANADA 1936 SIX-COIN SPECIMEN SET (WITH "DOT" ISSUES)

The ultimate presentation of Canada's "ultimate rarity."

Common Obverse: A left-facing portrait of King George V. Clockwise from left, the inscription GEORGIVS V DEI GRA: REX & IND IMP (abbreviated Latin for GEORGIUS V DEI GRATIA REX ET INDIAE IMPERATOR ["George V King by the Grace of God and Emperor of India"]). The designer's initials B.M. are on the right side of the bust truncation. Denticles border the rim.

Cent Reverse: The inscription CANADA wraps around the rim at the top. In the center, justified, is the denomination ONE CENT, bordered above and below by an arrow-dot-arrow ornament. The date 1936 is below. Maple leaves bookend the left and right of the denomination. A tiny dot is beneath the left edge of the 3.

5 Cents Reverse: The inscription CANADA clockwise along the rim at the top. A large numeral 5 (with a small curlicue at its inside tip) is slightly above the center of the coin; the words FIVE and CENTS are to the left and right, respectively. Two detailed, mirror-image maple leaves are below, leaning left and right. The year 1936 runs clockwise at the bottom.

10 Cents Reverse: The inscription 10 CENTS CANADA in the center, justified. A bar is beneath the text. The year 1936 is beneath the bar. Two sprigs of maple arc around the rim on left and right (its leaves are a different shape than those of other coins of the set), bound with ribbon at the bottom of the coin. A royal crown is between the top leaves of both sprigs. Denticles surround the entire design. A tiny dot is below the left edge of the 3.

25 Cents Reverse: The inscription 25 CENTS CANADA in the center, justified. A bar is beneath the text. The year 1936 is beneath the bar. Two sprigs of maple arc around the rim on the left and right, bound with ribbon at the bottom. The royal crown is between the top leaves of both sprigs. Denticles surround the entire design. A tiny dot is below the left edge of the 3.

50 Cents Reverse: The inscription 50 CENTS CANADA in the center, justified, with a bar beneath the text. The year 1936 is beneath the bar. Two sprigs of maple arc around the rim at left and right, bound with a ribbon at the bottom. A royal crown is between the top leaves of both sprigs. Denticles surround the entire design.

Dollar Reverse: Facing right, a voyageur (a French-Canadian fur trader) and an Inuit guide paddle a canoe. Two trees and Northern Lights (aurora borealis) are in the background. CANADA and DOLLAR wrap around the rim at the top and bottom, respectively. The date 1936 is centered and justified above DOLLAR. Below the keel on the left are the designer's initials, E.H. Denticles border the rim.

Cent (Dot)				
Composition	Weight	Diameter	Alignment	Edge
Bronze (.955 copper, .030 tin, .015 zinc)	3.24 grams	19.05 mm	Medal	Smooth
Mint	Mintage	Collecting Difficulty	References	
Royal Canadian Mint (Ottawa)	3 known	Extremely difficult	KM-28	

5 Cents				
Composition	Weight	Diameter	Alignment	Edge
.999 nickel	4.54 grams	21.21 mm	Medal	Smooth
Mint	Mintage	Collecting Difficulty	References	
Royal Canadian Mint (Ottawa)		Extremely difficult	KM-29	

10 Cents (Dot)				
Composition	Weight	Diameter	Alignment	Edge
.800 silver, .200 copper	2.32 grams	18.034 mm	Medal	Reeded
Mint	Mintage	Collecting Difficulty	References	
Royal Canadian Mint (Ottawa)	4 known	Extremely difficult	KM-23a	

25 Cents (Dot)				
Composition	Weight	Diameter	Alignment	Edge
.800 silver, .200 copper	5.83 grams	23.62 mm	Medal	Reeded
Mint	Mintage	Collecting Difficulty	References	
Royal Canadian Mint (Ottawa)	4 (estimated)	Extremely difficult	KM-24a	

50 Cents				
Composition	Weight	Diameter	Alignment	Edge
.800 silver, .200 copper	11.62 grams	29.72 mm	Medal	Reeded
Mint	Mintage	Collecting Difficulty	References	
Royal Canadian Mint (Ottawa)		Extremely difficult	KM-25a	

Dollar				
Composition	Weight	Diameter	Alignment	Edge
.800 silver, .200 copper	23.3276 grams	36.06 mm	Medal	Reeded
Mint	Mintage	Collecting Difficulty	References	
Royal Canadian Mint (Ottawa)		Extremely difficult	KM-31	

A military parade during the 1937 coronation of King George VI.

His portrait graces more than 10 percent of the coins on this list, so it is only fitting that we say a little something about him. King George V was a complex and important monarch during a transformative period of history. Reigning from 1910 to the beginning of 1936, George saw firsthand the rise in Europe of revolutionary political movements such as fascism and communism—with the latter even taking the life of his cousin and doppelganger, Czar Nicholas II (see coins number 12 and number 22 among the 100 Greatest). The domains of the British Empire, upon which the sun proverbially never set, began to clamor for independence. And, of course, George was king during the thoroughly modern "Great War" (1914–1918) and the build-up to its totalizing sequel. Besides perhaps his granddaughter Queen Elizabeth II, no other person better embodies the modern age of coinage in their numismatic portraiture than King George V.

King George V.

The reverse of the dollar coin was created by German-Canadian sculptor Emanuel Hahn (1881–1957). The Voyageur design, beloved by collectors, appeared on the dollar from 1935 through 1986 and has made appearances on commemorative coins since. Hahn was also responsible for the later reverse designs of the Schooner dime and the Caribou quarter.

The reverses of the 25-, 10-, and 5-cent coins were created by the British medalist and engraver William Henry James Blakemore (1871–1945) at the Tower Mint in London. Blakemore also adapted his reverse for the 1911 Canadian silver dollar pattern (see number 1 in the 100 Greatest) for use on the 50-cent coin, the 1911 design itself was based on the Victorian Leaves reverse of British coin designer Leonard C. Wyon.

The reverse of the cent was designed in 1920 by Royal Mint artist Fred Lewis, with Blakemore serving as engraver.

One "Dot" specimen set is known, and it was broken up in 2003 when Heritage Auctions offered it piecemeal as part of the historic Sid and Alicia Belzberg Collection of Canadian coinage. Five of the six coins in the set sold (the 25-cent did not) and they brought a combined total of US$334,075. The reassembly of this set would rate as a great accomplishment for any serious collector of the Canadian series.

The pedigree of the set has been traced back to Royal Canadian Mint employee T. Roberts, whose widow sold it to American collector John Jay Pittman after her husband's death in 1954. Pittman, the savvy collector that he was, accomplished the impressive feat of acquiring all three known "Dot" cents, among many other notable world and U.S. coin rarities and "under-appreciated" issues.

According to research carried out by Heritage in preparation for the Belzberg sale, Pittman is said to have offered Roberts's widow the paltry sum of $250 for the six-coin set; the two apparently agreed to a price of a little more than double that amount[1].

Pittman bought a second complete set from another RCM employee, Maurice La Fortune, for $400. This set was stolen from Pittman's house in 1964, but the "Dot" cent and dime were, confoundingly but thankfully, returned in an unmarked envelope.

Etching of oil painting *Canoes in a Fog, Lake Superior* by Frances Anne (Beechey) Hopkins, published in 1873.

GREAT BRITAIN 1953 QUEEN ELIZABETH II FOUR-COIN GOLD PROOF SET

The first depiction of a new queen.

As of the writing of this book, Her Majesty Queen Elizabeth II is the current monarch of the United Kingdom and 16 other countries, including numismatic heavyweights Canada, Australia, and New Zealand. She is both the longest-reigning monarch in British history—having celebrated 65 years of her reign with the Sapphire Jubilee in 2017 (the only British monarch to do so)—and the longest-lived. During her reign, billions upon billions of coins, of all different types and from all around the world, have borne her portrait. It is a singular numismatic record, one that we often find ourselves marveling at when we think of where numismatics has been and where it is going.

All of this began in 1953.

Elizabeth ascended to the throne of the United Kingdom and the other nations of the Commonwealth on February 6, 1952, upon the death of her father, King George VI. In an age of social, political, and technological upheaval, with the world still recovering from the trauma of World War II, the new queen inspired hope for the future while simultaneously harking back to England's golden age. In order to prepare for what would be the first such televised ceremony in human history, the official coronation in Westminster Abbey was held more than a year later, on June 2, 1953.

The previous year, the Royal Mint held a contest to design what would become the first of five official coin effigies. The model for the designs was the first official state photograph of the queen, taken by Dorothy Wilding, and eventually the Mint selected English sculptor Mary Gaskell Gillick, OBE (1881–1965), to create this historic effigy.

Queen Elizabeth II and Prince Philip visiting Bermuda in 1953.

As is tradition (not always obeyed; see number 6 among the 100 Greatest Modern World Coins, the 1937 Edward VIII sovereign), the new ruler's portrait faced in the opposite direction of the preceding monarch. As George had faced the left, Elizabeth would face right.

Another significant design change (besides a new monarch and subsequent inscription) was Gillick's decision to include some of the queen's shoulders in the bust. This was an unusual choice for coinage at the time, when most effigies featured a sharp neck truncation.

The first coins to utilize this portrait were dated 1953. To commemorate the coronation, the Royal Mint struck three sets of pattern coins, each with Proof versions of a 5-pound coin, a 2-pound coin, a

Common Obverse. A laureate portrait of Queen Elizabeth II, facing right. From above the queen's head, the clockwise inscription ELIZABETH II DEI GRA: BRITT: OMN: REGINA F: D: + (abbreviated Latin for *ELIZABETH II DEI GRATIA BRITANNIARUM OMNIUM REGINA FIDEI DEFENSOR* ["Elizabeth II, By the Grace of God, Queen of All Britons, Defender of the Faith"]).

Common Reverse. A muscular rendering of St. George, clad in a crested Roman helmet, soldier's cloak, and leather boots, atop his steed, which rears up to trample a European-style dragon. St. George pulls back the reins with his left hand, brandishing a short Roman sword *(gladius)* in his right. His left foot is barely visible under the horse. the point of his spear is broken off in the dragon's side; the spear shaft is on the ground behind his horse. The date 1953 is beneath this tableau. Above and to the right of the date are the initials B.P.

Half Sovereign				
Composition	Weight	Diameter	Alignment	Edge
.9167 gold	3.994 grams	19.3 mm	Medal	Reeded
Mintage	Mint		Collecting Difficulty	References
3	Royal Mint (London)		Impossible	Fr-272; KM-Pn135; Spink-4123

Sovereign				
Composition	Weight	Diameter	Alignment	Edge
.9167 gold	7.98805 grams	22.05 mm	Coin	Reeded
Mintage	Mint		Collecting Difficulty	References
3	Royal Mint (London)		Impossible	Fr-270; KM-Pn136; Spink-4122

2 Pounds				
Composition	Weight	Diameter	Alignment	Edge
.9167 gold	15.9761 grams	28.4 mm	Medal	Reeded
Mintage	Mint		Collecting Difficulty	References
3	Royal Mint (London)		Impossible	Fr-269; KM-Pn137; Spink-4121

5 Pounds				
Composition	Weight	Diameter	Alignment	Edge
.9167 gold	39.9403 grams	36 mm	Medal	Reeded
Mintage	Mint		Collecting Difficulty	References
3	Royal Mint (London)		Impossible	Fr-268; KM-Pn138; Spink-4120

Plaster of Mary Gillick's definitive coin portrait of Her Majesty Queen Elizabeth II.

sovereign, and a half sovereign. The common reverse features the iconic *St. George and the Dragon* design by Italian medalist and de facto chief engraver Benedetto Pistrucci. First appearing in 1817, it honors the patron saint of England, a Christian military officer who served under the Roman emperor Diocletian (reigned 284–305 CE).

Unfortunately, these 12 coins are unavailable to the collector, as the Mint gave one set to the British Museum and one to the royal coin collection, keeping the third for the Royal Mint Museum.

Still, they are some of the most significant coins of the modern era, establishing a design that may well resonate for centuries to come.

Time magazine, Volume 61 Issue 1. Front cover is a drawing of the Queen Elizabeth II of the United Kingdom in the year of her coronation.

A portrait of Queen Elizabeth II.

GREAT BRITAIN 1933 PENNY

Elusive cornerstone of the British penny series.

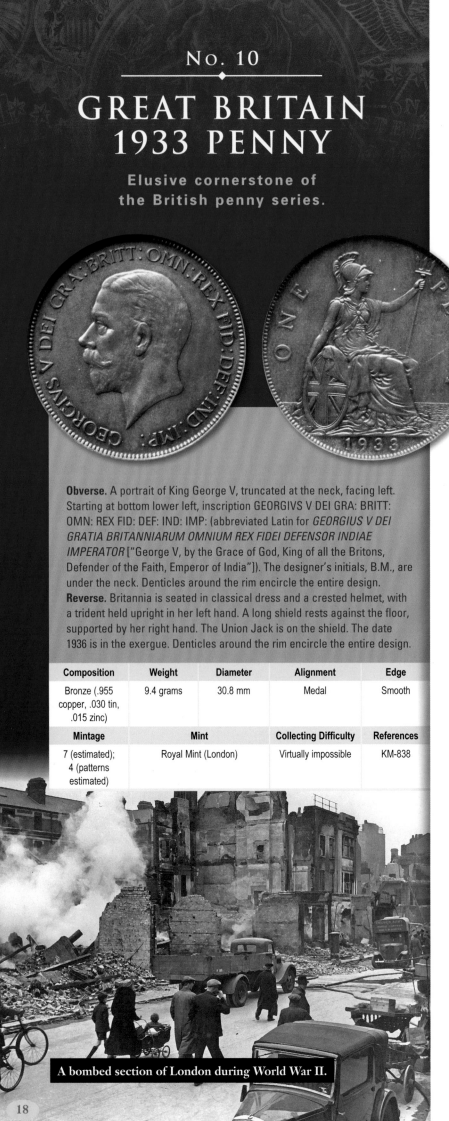

Obverse. A portrait of King George V, truncated at the neck, facing left. Starting at bottom lower left, inscription GEORGIVS V DEI GRA: BRITT: OMN: REX FID: DEF: IND: IMP: (abbreviated Latin for *GEORGIUS V DEI GRATIA BRITANNIARUM OMNIUM REX FIDEI DEFENSOR INDIAE IMPERATOR* ["George V, by the Grace of God, King of all the Britons, Defender of the Faith, Emperor of India"]). The designer's initials, B.M., are under the neck. Denticles around the rim encircle the entire design.
Reverse. Britannia is seated in classical dress and a crested helmet, with a trident held upright in her left hand. A long shield rests against the floor, supported by her right hand. The Union Jack is on the shield. The date 1936 is in the exergue. Denticles around the rim encircle the entire design.

Composition	Weight	Diameter	Alignment	Edge
Bronze (.955 copper, .030 tin, .015 zinc)	9.4 grams	30.8 mm	Medal	Smooth

Mintage	Mint	Collecting Difficulty	References
7 (estimated); 4 (patterns estimated)	Royal Mint (London)	Virtually impossible	KM-838

A bombed section of London during World War II.

With a surplus of relatively low-mintage 1932 pennies sitting in stockpiles, officials at the Royal Mint deemed it unnecessary to strike the denomination in 1933. The United Kingdom, along with the rest of the world, was in the midst of the Great Depression. Despite the production pause, the Mint did get requests for 1933 pennies, including three that were ordered by King George V so he could personally place them under the cornerstones of certain buildings that were being erected in England at the time[1]. Three Proofs and four circulation strikes are known to have been subsequently produced[2].

One Proof was buried under a cornerstone of the University of London Senate House in Bloomsbury, London. A second Proof was placed under a foundation stone of the Church of St. Cross in Middleton, Leeds. The third was buried under a foundation stone at St. Mary's Church in Kirkstall, Leeds. Meanwhile, the British Museum and the Royal Mint Museum each received a circulation strike, and two other circulation pieces went into private hands[3].

Interest in the 1933 penny reached a fever pitch following World War II. The German bombing campaign had razed many buildings in London and an urban legend developed that a number of these rare coins had entered into circulation. Generations of treasure hunters undoubtedly gave a second glance at their change before spending any old penny.

The historical record notes one high-profile situation of a 1933 penny being stolen from the foundation of the Church of St. Cross. This theft occurred in 1970, while the building was undergoing renovation. It was a year before the United Kingdom decimalized its coinage, and this may have contributed to the public's increased awareness of the value of the coin entombed at the construction site. The whereabouts of the stolen coin are unknown to this day.

To avoid another theft, the Bishop of Ripon of the diocese of Leeds ordered neighboring St. Mary's Church to dig up and sell its Proof 1933 penny, to avoid damage by possible theft. Sotheby's sold the coin on November 24, 1972.

One circulation-strike example owned by a private collector was sold in 1969 at a Glendining's auction. The Emory May Norweb specimen (graded NGC MS-63BN) sold at a Heritage auction on August 11, 2016, for US$193,875 (£149,364 at the time).

In addition to the seven 1933 pennies that were struck mostly for ceremonial purposes, four pennies bearing the 1933 date were minted as patterns to test design modifications. These coins are even rarer. The design enhancements were commissioned to help eliminate "ghosting," or progressive indirect design transfer, of the obverse King George V portrait upon the reverse of the coin. Many George V pennies produced throughout the run of the series, which began in 1911 and lasted until the king's passing in 1936, are notorious for this ghosting, due to the king's bust consuming such a large portion of the obverse (the design was also struck in a relatively high relief, thus displacing more metal). The result was a weaker reverse often bearing a "ghost-like" silhouette outline of King George V.

The king's head was modified in 1926 and, beginning with 1928-dated pennies, was made smaller—to no avail. In 1931 Deputy Master of the Royal Mint Sir Robert Johnson called for further modifications on the effigy and commissioned French artist André Lavrillier to produce a design that would eliminate once and for all the ghosting issue that had plagued the King George V–type penny for years.

Four Proof pennies were produced from revised dies bearing Lavrillier's modified George V head and reverse design. The results were not satisfactory, and that series of die experiments was discontinued[4].

One of these patterns realized £86,400 (US$126,495) at a May 4, 2016, auction in London.

The Tientsin Mint, located in the northern city of Tientsin (天津市, *Tiānjīn*) in the former province of Chihli (直隸, *Zhílì*), was founded in 1901 on the premise that it would strike the national coinage of China and that these coins would replace the output of China's provincial mints. This was a much-needed monetary reform for the country, but the effort was overshadowed by larger societal fissures that continued to erode and ultimately bring down the Qing dynasty.

As mentioned earlier (see coin number 2, the 1903 China Fengtien Tael Pattern), the phrase "Kuping" (or "treasury standard") tael denotes a weight and purity standard of 37.5 grams. Other standards used for commerce and shipping may weigh less. This coin, the 1906 Kuping tael, as well as the 1907 issue, was created as a pattern. Very few survive.

The date as given in the inscription 光緒丙午年造 ("Made in the Bing Wu year of [the] Guangxu [Emperor]", or "Made in 1906") is based on the incredibly ancient Chinese stem-branch 60-year calendar. "Bing" (丙) is one of the 10 heavenly stems and "Wu" (午) represents one of the 12 earthly branches. "Wu" also corresponds to the Year of the Horse in the Chinese zodiac.

The Chinese dragon again appears on this coin, reflecting its status as a cultural symbol of wisdom and imperial power. According to legend, its five toes mean it is a particularly powerful and venerable dragon since it is capable of grasping a mystical pearl called a *ruyizhu* (如意珠, *Rúyìzhū*), which can materialize anything at the desire of the one who wields it. Altogether, the coin motif is an action shot of the dragon mid-flight, attempting to seize the pearl as it falls from the sky.

A specimen from the Ultima Collection sold on August 8, 2014, at a Heritage Auctions sale for US$305,500, including the buyer's premium.

A Chinese dragon statue.

CHINA 1906 GOLD KUPING TAEL PATTERN

An attempt at monetary reform during a fading dynasty.

Obverse. A bearded and whiskered Chinese dragon, five claws or toes on each of its four feet, fills most of the side as it curls around to face the viewer head on. In the very center, a pearl, replete with fingers of flame, is on top. Swirling clouds surround the dragon, filling in much of the rest of the field. A relatively thin solid ring separates the design from a thick rim.
Reverse. In the center, top to bottom: 大清 (*Dà Qīng* ["Great Qing [Dynasty]]"); right to left: 金幣 (*Jīnbì* ["Gold Coin"]; *jīn* can refer to any precious metal but is often used to mean gold). A ring of small beads surrounds. Along the top of the coin (right to left): 光緒丙午年造 (*Guāngxù Bǐng Wǔ Nián Zào* ["Made in the Bing Wu year of [the] Guangxu [Emperor]," or "Made in 1906"]). Along the bottom (right to left): 庫平一兩 (*Kùpíng Yī Liǎng* ["Treasury Standard One Tael"]). On either side of the coin is a five-petaled rosette (made of larger beads). There is a relatively thick solid ring along the rim.

Composition	Weight	Diameter	Alignment	Edge
Gold	37.5 grams		Medal	Smooth
Mintage	**Mint**		**Collecting Difficulty**	**References**
Unknown	Tientsin Mint		Virtually impossible	K-1540; KM-Pn301; L&M-1023

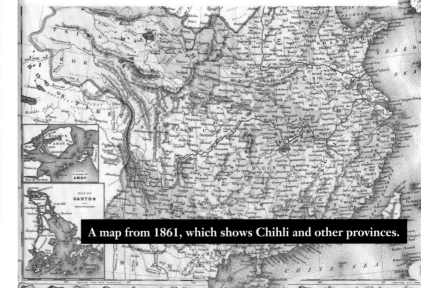

A map from 1861, which shows Chihli and other provinces.

RUSSIA 1908 GOLD 25 RUBLES, PROOF

A man called czar.

Obverse. A left-facing portrait of Czar Nicholas II. Inscription S. M. НИКОЛАЙ II ИМПЕРАТОРZ И САМОДЕРЖЕЦZ ВСЕ РОСС ("S. M. Nicholas II Emperor and Autocrat of all Russia"). Small, spade-shaped denticles surround entire design around rim.

Reverse. The Russian imperial eagle, crowned, displayed (spread out), and langued (tongue protruding), and the lesser coat of arms of the Russian Empire in a circle. Denominations denoted in two ways: At the top, 2 ½ ИМПЕРИАЛА (2-½ Imperials); at bottom, 25 РУБЛЕЙ ЗОЛОТОШЬ (25 gold rubles). 1908 Г (Year 1908).

Composition	Weight	Diameter	Alignment	Edge
.900 gold	32.25 grams	33.5 mm	Medal	Lettered†
Mintage	**Mint**		**Collecting Difficulty**	**References**
150 (including 25 struck in 1910 but dated 1908); 25 Proofs (estimated)	Paris Mint, Monnaie de Paris (* on edge)		Extremely difficult	Bitkin-314; Fr-153 (now Fr-171); RK-370a; Sev-587; Uzd-4213; Y-A65

† ЧИСТАГО ЗОЛОТА 6 ЗОЛОТНИКОВЪ 77,4 ДОЛИ * ("Pure Gold 6 Zolotniks 77.4 Dolyas")

Czar Nicholas II of Russia, 1912.

The 1908 Russian 25-ruble gold coin is one of the most coveted Russian coins of the twentieth century. Struck to mark the czar's 40th birthday, the coin was issued during a period of declining imperial power and political anxiety. Indeed, the large denomination was probably intended more as a store of wealth than as a coin to be spent in commerce.

While the reign of Nicholas II is marred by failure, obtuseness, military adventurism, national defeat, and (ultimately) collapse, accounts of the czar's personal life reveal a devoted family man, perhaps even someone who wanted a better outcome for his country but simply did not have the tools or judgment necessary to stem the tide of history.

The only Russian gold coin struck in 1908—and the last year of issue for the denomination—the 25-ruble gold coin of that year is very scarce. There were 150 examples actually struck that year, with an additional 25 pieces struck in 1910 that bear the date 1908. Proofs are rare, with a reported mintage of just 25 pieces.

The issue was struck in France at the Paris Mint (as denoted by the asterisk mintmark on the edge), in conformity with the standards of the treaty organization known as the Latin Monetary Union. Founded in 1865 by France, Italy, Switzerland, and Belgium, it was an early attempt to coordinate the monetary systems of Europe into a single currency.

At the time of publication, NGC has graded one Mint State example (MS-61); PCGS has graded none. Four total grading events of the Proof have been reported by PCGS (2) and NGC (2). One Proof specimen sold for £99,000 (approximately US$111,800 at the time) at a November 2009 auction by St. James Auctions of London—just within the presale estimate of £80,000 to £100,000.

The top population example (PCGS PR-65) is pedigreed to the Mortimer Hammel Collection of nineteenth- and twentieth-century foreign gold coins, which Stack's sold on September 15, 1982 (lot 601). Against a presale estimate of $100,000 to $125,000, the same coin brought a record $329,000 at the Stack's Bowers World Coins Auction on August 12, 2016, at the American Numismatic Association (ANA) World's Fair of Money (lot 21445). This notable example is fully brilliant and features a hint of frost on the devices. It is a truly remarkable example of one of the century's greatest coins.

THE IMPERIAL EAGLE AND THE LESSER COAT OF ARMS OF THE RUSSIAN EMPIRE

The reverse design of the 1908 Russian 25-ruble gold coin features the lesser coat of arms of the Russian Empire as it was designed in 1883, the chief element of which is a double-headed eagle. It is a well-known motif, with some variety of detail, from Russian imperial coinage.

The double eagle was originally an imperial symbol of the Byzantine Empire, but it became the seal of the Grand Duchy (or Principality) of Moscow in 1472 after Grand Prince Ivan III ("the Great") married Sophia (formerly Zoe) Palaiologina, a Byzantine princess and niece of Constantine XI, the last Byzantine emperor. After the Fall of Constantinople to the Ottoman Turks in 1453, many leaders in the Eastern Orthodox Church had removed themselves to Moscow and thought of the grand princes of the city as the successors to the Byzantine throne. Sophia embraced this conceit and encouraged Ivan to adopt the pomp and symbols of the fallen empire. Russians ever since have regarded their nation as the "Third Rome."

The escutcheon in the middle of the eagle's breast presents an image of St. George killing the famous dragon. This is the shield of St. George the Victor, which has been a symbol of Moscow since the 1400s. To the immediate left of the shield of St. George is the coat of arms of the United Principalities of Kiev,

Vladimir, and Novgorod. Right above the United Principalities shield is the Polish eagle from the coat of arms of Poland. Below the Polish eagle and to the left of the United Principalities is the black double-headed eagle of Taurida. Above the Polish eagle is the coat of arms of Kazan.

On the other side of the eagle are the coats of arms of (from top to bottom) Astrakhan, Siberia, Georgia, and Finland. Each coat of arms represents a territory under imperial control and signifies one of the czar's royal titles.

Surrounding the shield of St. George the Victor is the collar chain of the Order of St. Andrew—itself another double eagle, replete with three imperial crowns—which hangs below the shield. Atop the imperial eagle motif on the order is the X-shaped cross of St. Andrew, who was crucified on such an instrument. An early companion of Jesus, St. Andrew was said to have preached in the southern portion of Ukraine and is the patron saint of that country as well as Russia (St. Andrew's cross is also seen on the flag of the Russian Navy, among other places). The cross of St. Andrew recurs throughout the chain.

The crowned double eagle, emblem of czarist Russia, holds a globus cruciger (an orb with a cross on top of it) in its left talon and a scepter in its right. Both objects are traditional symbols of royal authority with roots in antiquity, and the cross-bearing orb has Christian religious connotations. Atop the scepter is a smaller version of the imperial coat of arms, which means the design is somewhat self-referential. Above and between the eagle's heads is the Imperial Crown of Russia, which features a cross at the pinnacle (as do the smaller Imperial Crowns that the eagle wears). Two ribbons extend from under each side of the imperial crown to the heads (and crowns) of the eagle.

The lesser coat of arms of the Russian Empire.

A Russian imperial family photo shows the Romanovs, including: seated, (left to right) Maria, Queen Alexandra, Czar Nicholas II, Anastasia, Alexei (front), and standing, (left to right) Olga and Tatiana. Circa 1919.

CHINA 1903 SILVER HU POO TAEL PATTERN

Ultra-rare pattern coin.

Obverse. Clockwise, top: English inscription 29TH YEAR OF KUANG HSU. Counterclockwise, bottom: HU POO. Single dots on each side separate the beginning and end of the inscriptions. A Chinese bearded dragon, facing viewer, curls around a flame atop a pearl, and its long whiskers reach down to the pearl. it has four legs and claws with five toes extended. Swirling, wispy clouds surround the dragon. A ring of denticles encircles the entire design along the rim.

Reverse. Chinese inscription in middle: 光緒元寶 (Guāngxù Yuánbǎo ["Guangxu Ingot"]); a ring of small dots surrounds this. Along the rim at the top: a Manchu script inscription of the same. Bottom inscription (right to left): 庫平一兩 (Kùpíng Yī Liǎng ["Treasury Standard One Tael"]. Chinese characters for "Hu" and "Poo" (戶部, Hùbù) on the right and left, respectively. Larger dots or lozenges separate the Chinese and Manchu inscriptions, one per side. Denticles encircle the entire design along the rim.

Composition	Weight	Diameter	Alignment	Edge
Silver	37.3 grams	43.5 mm	Medal	Smooth
Mintage	**Mint**		**Collecting Difficulty**	**References**
Unknown	Tientsin Mint		Virtually impossible	K-927; KM-Pn296; L&M-1019

Empress Dowager Cixi.

The 1903 China Hu Poo 1-tael silver pattern coin was issued by the imperial Ministry (or Board) of Revenue (戶部, Hùbù; literally "Household Ministry") in Beijing as part of an attempt at reforming Chinese currency and creating one unified system of silver coinage in 1 tael and 5-, 2-, 1- and half mace denominations. The Board was operating independent of any other government or provincial mint. Unfortunately, due to internal conflict and external pressure, the attempt failed.

One of the reasons the plan failed to take root was because the scheme called for the creation of a central mint. The provincial mints balked at ceding their authority—as well as their profits. Under the proposed system, silver coinage would have been denominated according to a gold standard.

The coin was struck at the Tientsin Mint in Chihli (直隸, Zhílì) province, but the dies were created at the Osaka Mint in Japan. The British diplomat Sir Robert Hart, who served as the inspector general of China's Imperial Maritime Customs Service from 1863 to 1911 and is credited with modernizing China's customs system, ordered the dies and supervised their production.

It was struck in the 29th year of the reign of the Guangxu Emperor (光緒帝, Guāngxù Dì), the de jure ruler of China who was in reality merely a figurehead once the Empress Dowager Cixi (慈禧太后, Cíxǐ Tàihòu) led a coup against him in 1898. Before that, he had ruled under her influence. Still, the coins bear his name.

The coin's design carries forward the popular Chinese dragon motif seen multiple times in this list. The dragon, the five-toed variety of which was the most powerful and a favorite motif of the Qing, symbolizes wealth and imperial power as it curls around a mystical pearl called a ruyizhu (如意珠, Rúyìzhū). According to Buddhist legend, the ruyizhu materializes whatever the one who wields it desires. The pearl is depicted in flames because it is believed to have fallen from the sky like other mystical objects.

The characters 元寶 (Yuánbǎo) inscribed on the coin refer to Chinese ingots of gold or silver also known as sycee. These privately-struck units of weight—were often minted in shapes such as squares, boats, flowers, and tortoises. These were an especially important form of currency during the late Ming dynasty (ruled 1368–1644) and continued to be part of Chinese commerce until the very end of the Qing dynasty in the early-twentieth century. Even today, sycee are seen as a symbol of wealth and prosperity in China and are often part of celebrations of the new year.

Since the Qing was a Manchu dynasty, coins struck under Qing rulers tend to feature Manchu script in addition to Chinese and sometimes English characters. In the case of the 1903 Hu Poo tael silver pattern coin, Manchu script is found at the top of the reverse, near the rim.

A PCGS SP-63 1-tael Hu Poo silver pattern was sold by Stack's Bowers in its August 2013 Hong Kong auction for US$227,050. Baldwin's sold an example in its April 5, 2012, Hong Kong auction for $206,500 (including an 18 percent buyer's fee). Baldwin's sold another in 2011 for $271,400, against a high estimate of $180,000. That particular coin was part of the Norman Jacobs Collection, which Baldwin's had sold previously in 2008. Beware the plentiful counterfeits of this particular coin.

Palace where Emperor Kuang Hsu (Guangxu) was imprisoned.

In 1928, the Mint of Rome (Zecca di Stato) celebrated the 10th anniversary of the end of WWI with a commemorative 20-lire silver coin, a gold medal, and a 20-lire gold coin—all of the same design (with the exception of the medal, which had no denomination)—by Italian medalists Giuseppe Romagnoli and Atilio Silvio Motti. Romagnoli served as the head of the Mint's medal school from 1909 through 1954.

The coin's design is unique and draped in fascist political imagery.

On the coin's obverse is the helmeted head of King Victor Emmanuel III (1869–1947; reigned 1900–1946). His effigy dominates the planchet. The helmet is tipped slightly upward, the king's facial features rigid and serious. The reverse is equally intense: the king's fierce facial expression is replaced by the allegorical lion, and the fasces, a stalwart motif of fascist coinage, dominates the left third of the coin.

The fasces is a bundle of wooden rods bound with leather straps, often surrounding an axe. It served as a prop representing the authority of government as derived from the unity of the people; each stick or rod by itself could be broken, but together they could not. On a literal level, the fasces represented the power of the state over the very lives of those under its control. For this reason, plus its roots in classical antiquity, Italian fascists adopted the fasces as a fundamental symbol (indeed, taking its name from the object).

As an organization, the National Fascist Party (*Partito Nazionale Fascista*, or PNF) was founded in 1921 by Benito Mussolini, but its roots are in the politics of nineteenth-century Italy and the nationalist reaction to World War I. The party came to power after the fascist March on Rome on October 28, 1922, which King Victor Emmanuel III allowed to happen without military opposition. The king made Mussolini prime minister the day after the march.

Excepting the economic and political tensions following the First World War, the king enjoyed popular support for more than half of his 46-year reign. Many from the working classes and the bourgeoisie looked to both fascism and the monarch as bulwarks against radical leftist forces, but even as the public began to sour on Mussolini, the king himself remained beloved. This affection began to fade only with the Ethiopian and Albanian conquests, which were condemned abroad and held in little esteem at home. Victor Emmanuel would depose and arrest Mussolini and renounce the foreign crowns in 1943, reaching an armistice with Allied forces. Despite this, many felt that as long as he was king, fascism remained. So, Victor Emmanuel abdicated in May 1946 to make way for his son Umberto II, but Italians voted to abolish the monarchy that June.

Most collectors of twentieth-century Italian coins are familiar with the silver 1928-R 20 lire, as it is a highly collected type. The gold version, however, is extremely rare—so rare, in fact, that it is almost entirely unknown. Krause does not list a mintage for the issue in this composition and the $40,000 price they publish in their *Standard Catalog* is inconceivably low for such an important issue. A Gem Proof example would likely exceed $100,000 if offered at public auction.

Benito Mussolini and other leaders during the March on Rome.

ITALY 1928-R GOLD 20 LIRE, PROOF

Fascists honor king who brought them to power—and ultimately toppled them.

Artist's depiction.

Obverse. The inscription VITT * EM * III * RE * ("Vittorio Emmanuel III King," with four-sided diamond shapes between each section) is written clockwise, starting at the bottom left. A left-facing portrait of a mustachioed King Victor Emmanuel III wearing an M16 Adrian helmet without chin straps. A star on each side of the collar. On the right side, starting at the edge of the helmet, the inscription G. ROMAGNOLI A. MOTTI, INC.

Reverse. A fasces with the year 1918 in Roman numerals (MCMXVIII) at the top and the year 1928 (MCMXXVIII) at bottom. Beneath the year 1928 is the inscription A.VI, which stands for the sixth year of fascist rule in Italy. To the left are the denomination L. 20 and the mintmark R for Rome. To the right of the fasces, at the top of the coin, is the inscription ITALIA. Below ITALIA is a lion-headed axe. A 1922 quote from Benito Mussolini is found on the cheek and toe of the blade: MEGLIO VIVERE UN GIORNO DA LEONE CHE CENTO ANNI DA PECORA ("Better to live one day as a lion than one hundred years as a sheep").

Composition	Weight	Diameter	Alignment	Edge
.900 gold	6.45 grams	21 mm	Coin	Reeded
Mintage	**Mint**		**Collecting Difficulty**	**References**
Unknown	Zecca di Stato†		Virtually impossible	KM-Pr53
	† Mintmark: R			

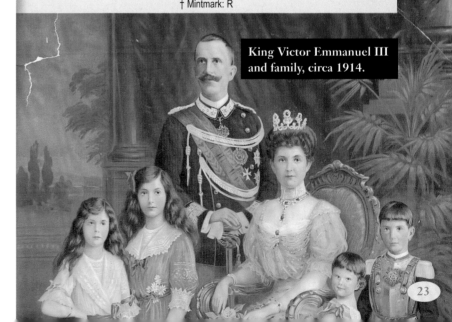

King Victor Emmanuel III and family, circa 1914.

CHINA 1949 KWEICHOW 50 CENTS

Made rare by war.

Obverse. The central inscription 半圓銀幣 (*Bàn Yuán Yín Bì* ["Half Yuan Silver Coin"]) within an inner circle of beads, surrounding a small dot at the very center. Above (right to left), the legend 中華民國卅八年 (*Zhōnghuá Mínguó Sàbā Nián* ["Republic of China, 38th Year"]). Along the bottom from right to left, the legend 贵州省造 (*Guìzhōu Shěng Zào* ["Made in Kweichow Province"]). Two four-petaled rosettes or rosaces, one on each side, separate the legends. A Greek meander or key pattern is engraved along the circumference near the rim. Solid rings are on top of and below the meander; the outer ring is thicker than the inner ring.

Reverse. A large Arabic numeral 50 is in the center, each numeral consisting of an outer border surrounding an inner crosshatch pattern. The numeral 5 has a serif at top and a curled lobe at the other end. A circle of beads or "pearls" is around the large 50; a circle of 32 smaller Arabic numeral 50s surrounds the beads. A Greek meander pattern encircles the entire design along the outer rim, between the thicker outer solid ring and the thinner inner solid ring.

Composition	Weight	Diameter	Alignment	Edge
Silver	12.46 grams		Coin	Reeded

Mintage	Mint	Collecting Difficulty	References
Unknown	Kweichow	Extremely difficult	K-758I; L&M-614; WS-1114; Y-432

The first half of the twentieth century was a time of immense change and terrible conflict, and few nations saw as much change and conflict in that time as China. Opening with the anti-colonial Boxer Rebellion of 1899–1901 and subsequent fall of the ultra-conservative Qing dynasty in 1912, the modernization of China gave way to the Warlord Era (1916–1928), civil war (1927–1937), the Second Sino-Japanese War (1937–1945), and the resumption of civil war (the Communist Revolution of 1945–1949).

During the 1940s, internal strife and the chaos of war had brought about inflation (as it often does) that greatly weakened the purchasing power of Chinese paper currency. This forced the provinces to come up with local solutions, and many chose to mint their own coins to fulfill the commercial needs of the people. Kweichow (州省造; *Guìzhōu*), a landlocked, mountainous province in the southern part of China—already famous for its Warlord Era "auto dollar"—did just that.

This silver half dollar is a fractional denomination associated with the Kweichow "Bamboo Dollar" minted under the authority of Kweichow governor Kuo Tseng Lun. There is also a 20-cent piece with a design much like that of the half dollar, with the Arabic numeral "20" replacing all instances of the 50 as found on the present coin.

The Republic mentioned in the coin's legend was founded in 1911 at the end of the Qing dynasty, making 1949 the 38th anniversary of its rule—however tenuous in parts it may have been. By 1949, however, the Communists under Mao Zedong (毛泽东) had taken control of the mainland, forcing General Chiang Kai-Shek (蔣介石) and the Nationalists to flee to Taiwan. Many coins issued under the auspices of the Nationalists (including those struck in Kweichow, and especially those struck in the waning years of the civil war) were confiscated and repurposed by the Communists. This is primarily why the 1949 Kweichow half dollar is so rare now, with some surviving examples being recovered from caches of coins buried or hidden by people at the time.

General Chiang Kai-shek.

A specimen of this coin, graded AU-58 NGC and pedigreed to the collections of Irving Goodman and Eduard Kann himself, garnered US$358,500 in the Stack's Bowers April 2014 Hong Kong Showcase Auction. The same coin previously sold at a Superior Stamp & Coin Company auction in June 1991 for $5,280—which clearly shows how the global market for Chinese coins has grown over the last few decades.

Krause's *Standard Catalog* (2014) states values of $5,500 in VF(20), $12,500 in XF(40), and $17,500 in UNC (MS-60). Lin Gwo Ming's *Illustrated Catalog of Chinese Gold & Silver Coins* (2012) says $80,000 in UNC and $450,000 in BU.

Mao Zedong, leader of China's Communists, addresses some of his followers, circa 1944.

It is hard to pin down a "true" market value for the 1934 Proof set.

For starters, the set is rare with just 100 issued (it was the first year of commercial Proofs for Melbourne), and a number of them are lost to time. Some measure of the set's scarcity can be seen by the number of possible complete sets that can be assembled with coins certified by PCGS and NGC. While it's true that the American grading services don't have the world coin grading market locked up like they have major U.S. rarities, market realities provide an excellent incentive for high-ticket coins to be in these holders.

That said, barring resubmissions and crossovers, approximately 10 percent of the total mintage has been certified, with PCGS having a distinct edge.

Heritage Auctions has recorded four sales of complete certified sets since 2005, with prices ranging from US$37,600 to a record price of $276,000 that was realized at a January 2010 Heritage Auctions Signature World Coin Auction.

The record-setting set was described as being "absolutely spectacular" by the cataloger and included Gem or better examples of every coin in the set, featuring coins tied for the finest known in the sixpence, shilling, and florin denominations.

Amazingly, based on what's been certified, one could assemble a set even finer, with notable improvements in the half penny, penny, and three-pence denominations. A superior set in today's market would likely bring a sum above six figures but would probably not match the 2010 record price.

With the exception of the half penny and penny, Australian coins struck in 1934 bear a common obverse featuring King George V and

AUSTRALIA 1934 SIX-COIN PROOF SET

Blending Australian wildlife with British heraldry.

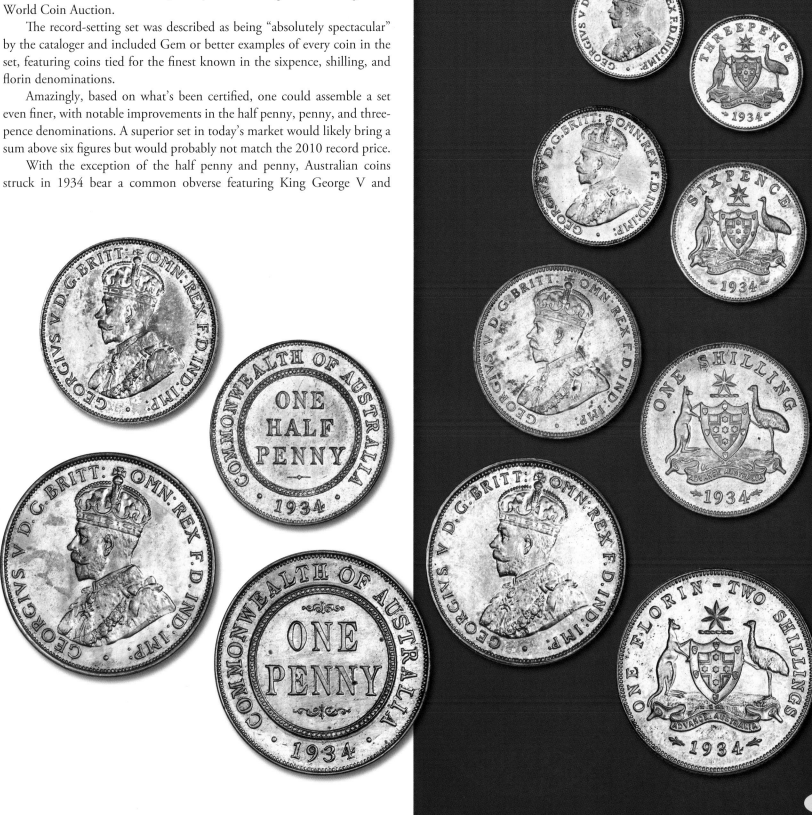

Common Obverse. A crowned bust of King George V, facing left. Initials B.M. in truncation. Clockwise around the rim, starting beneath the bust truncation, is the inscription GEORGIVS V D. G. BRITT: OMN: REX F. D. IND: IMP: (abbreviated Latin for *GEORGIUS V DEI GRATIA BRITANNIARUM OMNIUM REX FIDEI DEFENSOR INDIAE IMPERATOR* ["George V, by the Grace of God, King of all the Britons, Defender of the Faith, Emperor of India"]). A large dot or bead is beneath the bust, between the start and end of the inscription. Denticles surround along the rim.

Half Penny Reverse. Center: Denomination ONE HALF PENNY in large letters in three lines. Line and dart ornament beneath. A ring of beads or dots between the inner and outer solid rings encircles the denomination. Clockwise starting from left is the legend COMMONWEALTH OF AUSTRALIA. At the bottom is the date 1934. A large dot is on each side of the date. Denticles surround along the rim.

Penny Reverse. Center: Denomination ONE PENNY in large letters in two lines. Curlicue ornaments above and below. A ring of beads or dots between the inner and outer solid rings encircles the denomination. Clockwise starting from left is the legend COMMONWEALTH OF AUSTRALIA. At the bottom is the date 1934. A large dot is on each side of date. Denticles surround along the rim.

Threepence, Sixpence, Shilling, and Florin Reverse. Center: The Australian coat of arms; red kangaroo (left) and emu (right) supporting a heraldic shield (escutcheon). Six shields, or inescutcheons, represent each of Australia's six states. St. George's cross is in the center of the shield. A commonwealth star atop a torse of white and blue, and a scroll (ADVANCE AUSTRALIA) below a grassy field. The denomination—THREEPENCE, SIXPENCE, SHILLING, or ONE FLORIN — TWO SHILLINGS—arcs along the top. The date 1934 is at bottom, with a three-pronged ornament on either side. Denticles surround along the rim.

Half Penny				
Composition	Weight	Diameter	Alignment	Edge
Bronze (.970 copper, .025 zinc, .005 tin)	5.6 grams	25.5 mm	Medal	Smooth
Mintage	Mint		Collecting Difficulty	References
100	Royal Mint (Melbourne)		Extremely difficult (as a set)	KM-22

Penny				
Composition	Weight	Diameter	Alignment	Edge
Bronze (.970 copper, .025 zinc, .005 tin)	9.45 grams	30.8 mm	Medal	Smooth
Mintage	Mint		Collecting Difficulty	References
100	Royal Mint (Melbourne)		Extremely difficult (as a set)	KM-23

Threepence				
Composition	Weight	Diameter	Alignment	Edge
Sterling silver (.925 silver, .075 copper)	1.32 grams	16.1 mm	Medal	Smooth
Mintage	Mint		Collecting Difficulty	References
100	Royal Mint (Melbourne)		Extremely difficult (as a set)	KM-24

Sixpence				
Composition	Weight	Diameter	Alignment	Edge
Sterling silver (.925 silver, .075 copper)	2.82 grams	19.3 mm	Medal	Reeded
Mintage	Mint		Collecting Difficulty	References
100	Royal Mint (Melbourne)		Extremely difficult (as a set)	KM-25

Shilling				
Composition	Weight	Diameter	Alignment	Edge
Sterling silver (.925 silver, .075 copper)	5.65 grams	24 mm	Medal	Reeded
Mintage	Mint		Collecting Difficulty	References
100	Royal Mint (Melbourne)		Extremely difficult (as a set)	KM-26

Florin (2 Shillings)				
Composition	Weight	Diameter	Alignment	Edge
Sterling silver (.925 silver, .075 copper)	11.31 grams	28.5 mm	Medal	Reeded
Mintage	Mint		Collecting Difficulty	References
100	Royal Mint (Melbourne)		Extremely difficult (as a set)	KM-27

An aerial view of Melbourne in the 1930s.

reverse designs featuring the Australian coat of arms. While the coat of arms design might pass without much notice, the blending of Australia's native emu and red kangaroo with European heraldic elements spurred much debate in Parliament at the time of its adoption (despite the fact that versions of the motif had circulated since the early nineteenth century).

The common obverse design was created by Australian medalist and sculptor Sir Edgar Bertram Mackennal. Most famous for the coins and stamps he designed for George V, Mackennal (1863–1931) was the first Australian artist to earn a knighthood for his service to the monarch.

The reverse of the threepence, sixpence, shilling, and florin was designed by William Henry James Blakemore (1871–1945) at the Royal Mint's main facilities in London. This motif would remain on the sixpence coin through 1963. The threepence, shilling, and florin would bear this design only through 1936.

None of the coins have a mintmark, but then that's hardly unusual for pre-decimal coinage out of the Melbourne branch of the Royal Mint.

Canada's half dollar denomination saw demand in fits and starts throughout its production life in the first two decades of the twentieth century. In 1920, 584,429 half dollar coins were struck. The mint more than halved that total in 1921 but still struck 206,398 coins. At this point, the denomination went into hiatus and no new Canadian half dollars were struck from 1922 through 1928.

Without much in the way of demand, the Royal Mint's stockpile of half dollar coins trickled out into circulation. The *Charlton Catalogue* reports a total emission of about 28,000 pieces. Based on the absolutely rarity of the 1921 issue in any grade, it is safe to assume that nearly all of these coins bore the date 1920.

In 1929, the demand for half dollars was born anew. The mint, faced with the choice of issuing its stockpile of coins minted at the start of the decade or issuing new coins of a contemporary date, chose the latter, thinking the public might be confused if it encountered decade-old silver coins with a brand new appearance.

In total, 480,392 half dollars were melted, including nearly the entire 1921 mintage.

Q. David Bowers, in his fantastic collaboration with Michael Hodder entitled *The Norweb Collection: An American Legacy* (1987), recounts an entertaining story of one specimen:

> One coin purchased by Mrs. Norweb in 1954 has an interesting story connected with it. This was a specimen of the rare Canadian 1921 half dollar. Jerry Eisenberg, who had a coin company on 46th Street in New York City called Royal Athena, owned the coin. His father had bought it while on a trip in Ireland, where he found it among other non-Irish coins in a lot. Eisenberg's father paid sixty cents for the rarity! John Ford bought it from Jerry Eisenberg for $200. The *Charlton Guide to Canadian Coins*, the equivalent to our own *Guide Book*, had just been published, and the 1921 half dollar was listed there at $250. Ford sold the coin to Mrs. Norweb for its catalogue value, $250. Thirty years later the identical specimen was sold at auction for $17,600!

That specimen turned out to be the finest known 1921 Canadian half dollar. Of the 24 examples of the issue that PCGS has graded, it is the sole specimen to earn the grade MS-67. Nearly two decades ago, that coin brought a record price of CA$300,000. At a tick below was the important Bass-Belzberg-Brown example, which brought US$218,500 at a January 2010 Heritage Auctions sale (lot 20312).

One example of the issue is currently recorded in the NGC census. That coin was certified SP-60.

The obverse design was created by Australian medalist and sculptor Sir Edgar Bertram Mackennal. Most famous for the coins and stamps he designed for George V, Mackennal (1863-1931) was well known for his portrait sculptures, monuments, and memorials, as well. The reverse was engraved by William Henry James Blakemore (1871-1945), a medalist and engraver at the Royal Mint's main facilities in London. Blakemore based his design on the Victorian Leaves reverse of British coin designer Leonard C. Wyon.

Ambassador and Mrs. Norweb.

CANADA 1921 50 CENTS

Most lost to the Great Canadian Coin Melt.

Obverse. A bust portrait of King George V. Inscription GEORGIVS V DEI GRA: REX ET IND. IMP. (abbreviated Latin for *GEORGIUS V DEI GRATIA REX ET INDIAE IMPERATOR* ["George V, King by the Grace of God, Emperor of India"]). The designer Mackennal's initials, B.M., appear on the bust truncation. Denticles surround along the rim.
Reverse. Denomination 50 CENTS CANADA. The date, 1921, is beneath a horizontal line. an open wreath of maple leaves is tied with ribbon at the bottom. A royal crown is at the top in the opening of the wreath. Denticles surround along the rim.

Composition	Weight	Diameter	Alignment	Edge
.800 silver, .200 copper	11.66 grams	29.72 mm	Medal	Reeded

Mintage	Mint	Collecting Difficulty	References
584,691	Royal Canadian Mint (Ottawa)	Extremely difficult	KM-25a

CHINA 1916 YUAN SHIKAI "GIORGI" GOLD 10 DOLLARS PATTERN

A political and military master in a changing China.

Obverse. A left-facing bust of Yuan Shikai in military attire, with denticles around the coin's rim.

Reverse. A left-facing five-toed Chinese dragon in flight, holding arrows and a compass. The legend above (right to left) is: 中華帝國 (*Zhōnghuá Dìguó* ["Chinese Empire"]). The inscription below: 拾洪憲紀元圓 (*Shí Hóng Xiàn Jìyuán Yuán* ["Beginning of Hong Xian 10 Yuan"]). To the left is the designer's name: L. GIORGI. Denticles are around the rim.

Composition	Weight	Diameter	Alignment	Edge
Gold	7.05 grams		Medal	Reeded
Mintage	**Mint**		**Collecting Difficulty**	**References**
Unknown	Tientsin Mint		Extremely difficult	K-1515 (unlisted with Giorgi); L&M-1028

Yuan Shikai in military attire, 1915.

Yuan Shikai (袁世凱, *Yuán Shìkǎi*) was born into a wealthy family from the central Chinese province of Henan on September 16, 1859. Given a formal education, he struggled when taking the civil service exam, failing twice. Undeterred, Yuan purchased an official title and landed a post in the Qing Brigade.

In 1895, after befriending the general Li Hongzhang (李鴻章, *Lǐ Hóngzhāng*), Yuan was named commander of a 3,000-man army, the first truly modern army in the Qing dynasty. This assignment gave Yuan ample opportunity to court the favor of the rising officer class, power-hungry politicians, and high-ranking members of the Chinese aristocracy.

During an attempted coup against the Guangxu Emperor (光緒帝, *Guāngxù Dì*) in 1989, Yuan sided with the conservatives and aligned himself with the Empress Dowager Cixi (慈禧太后, *Cíxǐ Tàihòu*). In return for his loyalty, Cixi named Yuan Shikai governor of the eastern Shandong Province (山东省, *Shāndōng Shěng*). During his time as governor, the Boxer Rebellion (1899–1901) erupted across China.

Throughout the conflict, Yuan was sympathetic to those in the imperial court who wanted trade and good relations with the leading foreign powers. This position stood in direct opposition to Cixi's declaration of war against them. The foreign powers seized upon China's political disarray and marshaled a multinational force called the Eight-Nation Alliance to wage war on the isolationists within the Qing dynasty. The combined forces of the United Kingdom, Russia, France, Japan, Germany, the United States, Italy, and Austria-Hungary ultimately proved too much and the allies laid siege to Beijing in August 1901.

In Shandong, Yuan's forces suppressed the Boxers and, at his order, massacred tens of thousands of people in the province of Zhili (直隸, *Zhílì*). Similar massacres were carried out throughout the country.

After the rebellion, Yuan's star continued to rise. In 1902, he was promoted to viceroy of Zhili. In this position, he strengthened his army and modernized the police force. He took control of the railroad system and created ministries of education and police. These reforms led to a period of modernization. The civil service test that Yuan failed twice was replaced with a new system. Yuan sought further reforms, including the creation of a constitutional form of government. After the deaths of both Cixi and the exiled Guangxu Emperor (of arsenic poisoning), Yuan was relieved of his post.

In 1911, after an armed rebellion broke out in Wuchang (武昌, *Wǔchāng*), the Qing dynasty was desperate for Yuan Shikai's help again, and after delaying to secure higher titles of nobility and more power within the imperial cabinet, Yuan waged a military campaign that put him in the position of negotiating for peace with the revolutionaries and the abdication of the four-year-old Xuantong Emperor (宣統帝, *Xuāntǒng Dì*) Pu Yi (溥儀, *Pǔyí*).

With this, Yuan became the president of the Republic of China on February 14, 1912, replacing Sun Yat-sen (孫逸仙, *Sūn Yìxiān*), who was then serving as provisional president.

Efforts were undertaken to establish an independent parliamentary system in the early months of the new republic, but Yuan was strongly opposed to the idea. One of the most vocal agitators for the limiting of presidential power was Song Jiaoren (宋教仁, *Sòng Jiàorén*) of the Kuomintang (國民黨, *Guómíndǎng*). These ideas were put down after Song was assassinated in March 1913. It's widely believed that Yuan Shikai was involved in the plot.

As a result of Yuan's thirst for power, Sun Yat-sen agitated for a second revolution and sought help from Japan. Yuan's forces quelled the rebellion and on January 1914, Parliament was dissolved. Yuan Shikai, now in charge of all aspects of the country's government, began to institute measures that strengthened his power. The result of one of these initiatives was the creation of a national coinage, led by the release of the Yuan Shikai silver dollar.

Ultimately, Yuan Shikai worked towards his goal of naming himself the Hongxian Emperor (洪憲皇帝, *Hóngxiàn Dì*)—a goal he achieved, despite much resistance, on December 12, 1915. His reign spanned barely more than three months.

The Yuan Shikai "Giorgi" 10-dollar gold pattern was struck at the Tientsin Mint in the city if Tientsin (天津, *Tiānjīn*) two years after the facility was sacked by an angry mob during the Xinhai Revolution (辛亥革命, *Xīnhài Gémìng*). One of the most significant issues of the Chinese Republican period (1912–1949), this 10-dollar gold pattern was struck to commemorate Yuan Shikai's ascension to the position of Hongxian Emperor.

The design of this gold coin is probably familiar to collectors of modern world coins, as it also graces one of the most widely issued Chinese silver coins of the modern era, the Yuan Shikai dollar (which started in 1914).

The Yuan Shikai dollar was struck in an attempt to modernize Chinese circulating coinage and to fend off foreign issues. First issued in December, the dollar featured a standardized content of .890 fine silver and was struck by the millions, predominantly at Tientsin but also at the provincial mints. It was the first dollar issued by the Republic, and over the regular series' run (1914–1927) it saw the largest mintage (over one billion pieces) of silver dollars in the world. Nicknamed the Fat Man dollar (or the Big Head dollar in China), the Yuan Shikai dollar was exchanged on par for hundreds of millions of Dragon dollars and foreign silver coins of similar size and weight.

While the 1914 silver dollar is common, the 10-dollar gold pattern signed by Tientsin Mint engraver Luigi Giorgi is extremely rare, with only two pieces certified (both by NGC). According to Chinese coin expert Eduard Kann, the "Giorgi" patterns were "made in very small quantities only and presented to a privileged few of Yuan Shikai's immediate

**Mass tomb for those who died in the
Yuhuatai Battle of the Xinhai Revolution.**

entourage," and the dies were destroyed. The type is unlisted in Friedberg, Krause, and Hsu.

In August 2011, Stack's Bowers and Ponterio sold an NGC-graded AU-58 example (lot 70010) for US$170,000 (including buyer's premium). The finer of the two certified examples (NGC MS-63) brought $282,000 at a Heritage auction in August 2014 (lot 23187)[1].

Illustration showing an attack on Beijing Castle during the Boxer Rebellion, 1900.

GREAT BRITAIN 1954 PENNY

A one-of-a-kind coin.

A later British penny showing the design style of the exceedingly rare 1954.

Obverse. Mary Gillick's portrait of Queen Elizabeth II, facing right. Initials M.G. in the bust's truncation. Starting immediately above Elizabeth's head is the inscription + ELIZABETH * II * DEI * GRATIA * REGINA * F: D: (abbreviated Latin for *ELIZABETH II DEI GRATIA REGINA FIDEI DEFENSOR* ["Elizabeth II, Queen by the Grace of God, Defender of the Faith"]). Dots or beads surround along the rim.

Reverse. Britannia, seated, is facing right, looking out over an ocean. A trident is in her left hand, a Union Flag shield beneath the right. A lighthouse is behind. The denomination ONE PENNY is clockwise around the rim, with Britannia's crested helmet and trident between ONE and PENNY. The date 1954 is in an exergue at the bottom. Dots or beads surround along the rim.

Composition	Weight	Diameter	Alignment	Edge
Bronze (.955 copper, .030 tin, and .015 zinc)	9.6 grams	31 mm	Medal	Smooth

Mintage	Mint	Collecting Difficulty	References
6 (estimated; 1 known)	Royal Mint (London)	Virtually impossible	KM-897

The royal coronation coach, currently held in the Mews, London.

W ith only one specimen in private hands and perhaps as few as six made in total, the 1954 penny is one of the rarest issues of a popular, pre-decimal collectible.

Now ubiquitous, Queen Elizabeth II's portrait first appeared in 1953 after the death of her father, King George VI, and her assumption to the throne late in 1952. English sculptor Mary Gaskell Gillick, OBE (1881–1965), created the queen's first, youthful portrait. However, the postwar economy in the United Kingdom was still suffering, so there was little to no demand for new pennies (a similar situation happened in the early 1930s; see number 10, the 1933 George V bronze penny). But with the queen's coronation in 1953 (the first ever to be televised), the Royal Mint followed tradition and produced 1,308,000 circulation strikes and 40,000 Proofs featuring the new monarch for that year.

So, with another million or so pennies entering circulation at a time when there were already enough for day-to-day commerce, the Mint was confident in its decision not to issue circulation strike pennies in 1954. In fact, regular production of the denomination would not resume until 1961.

Nevertheless, the Royal Mint produced experimental die trials and patterns for this very rare issue (the other five known specimens), presumably in an attempt to deal with the persistent technical issue of "ghosting." The relative size and high relief of the queen's portrait meant the obverse design was being transferred to the reverse die, producing a "ghost" image of the queen over the seated rendition of Britannia on the reverse (created by Mint engraver Charles Walter Coombes). The British Museum has two of these experiments, while the Mint retains the other three. The existence of these trials likely gave rise to the fanciful legend that the bronze coin contains some small amount of gold. Sadly, this is not true.

What is true, however, is that the 1954 penny ended up mixed in with the Mint's stock of 1953 pennies and found its way into circulation, from which an eagle-eyed and incredibly lucky collector pulled it not long after its release. It was in the possession of British numismatist C. Wilson Peck (who, by the way, might possibly have been the first to say some version of "buy the book before the coin") by 1955. The esteemed American numismatist Q. David Bowers owned the coin by 1963. It was then sold for around £10,000 in the late 1960s.

Much later, the only available specimen of the penny sold for over £23,000 (about US$30,500) at a Spink sale in 1991. The latest edition of Krause's *Standard Catalog of World Coins* gives an estimated value of $100,000.

An Australian stamp honoring the coronation of Queen Elizabeth II.

The Qing, who had ruled the Chinese Empire since 1644, was a dynasty of ethnic Manchu, a people from the area of northeastern China known as Manchuria. By 1911, however, the non-Manchu population of imperial China had grown restless, which led to the Xinhai Revolution (辛亥革命, *Xīnhài Gémìng*) and the overthrow of the last Qing ruler, the Xuantong Emperor (宣統帝, *Xuāntǒng Dì*) Pu Yi (溥儀, *Pǔyí*). The precarious political situation led to the rise of provincial warlords, or jun fa (軍閥, *Jūnfá*). Nominally a republic, the actual control and administration of the regions and provinces of China fell to military strongmen.

Chang Tso-lin (張作霖, *Zhāng Zuòlín*) was one such warlord. Poor and illiterate, he became a literal bandit as a young man and soon was leading a small group of other bandits who offered their services as mercenaries and bodyguards to anyone who could pay. When the anti-foreign Boxer Rebellion broke out in 1900, Chang and his gang joined the imperial army, and by 1911 (the official fall of the Qing) he had become the most powerful individual in Manchuria.

Using this power, he maintained stability and control in the region. Yuan Shikai (袁世凱, *Yuán Shìkǎi*), the warlord who had engineered the abdication of Pu Yi and was subsequently made the first president of the Republic after negotiating with Sun Yat-sen (孫逸仙, *Sūn Yìxiān*) and the republican revolutionaries, recognized Chang's importance and made him lieutenant general of the army in Manchuria.

The relationship paid off for both men, as Qing supporter Chang consolidated his power and Yuan pursued his own imperial ambition. Soon, Yuan declared himself emperor of a restored Qing dynasty, but in doing so he lost much of his republican support in the central government. Chang, however, was able to secure the governorship of Manchuria from this same republican government after the fall and demise of Yuan Shikai.

Chang Tso-lin used the region as an economic engine to build his own army—the Fengtien Army, so-named for the province of Fengtien (奉天, *Fèngtiān*), a major part of what is called Manchuria. He used this army to operate as he pleased, invading neighboring territories and fighting with the central government in Beijing (北京, *Běijīng*), despite being legally beholden to it as governor. To further demonstrate his independence, Chang allied himself with the Japanese, who at the time represented a grave threat to the fledgling Republic. He was ultimately defeated by the nationalist forces of Chiang Kai-shek (蔣介石, *Jiǎng jièshí*) in 1928, and thanks to this "failure" on his part (as well as opportunistic raiding of Japanese army supplies), Japanese provocateurs in China assassinated Chang Tso-lin by detonating a bomb on a train he was traveling on that same year.

The 1927 Gold 50 yuan specimen was minted in Tientsin (天津, *Tiānjīn*), a city bordering Beijing, during a period of time in which Chang controlled both. And even though the warlord had seized the very heart of the young republic, the reverse legend ("16th Year of the Republic of China") belies this fact.

The edge is reeded, while each side features a relatively high and sharp wire edge.

It is not known how many of these specimen coins were made, but only two known examples of this gold coin exist. One is graded SP-64+ by PCGS and is held in a Secure Plus holder. It sold for US$525,565 (HK$4,100,000) in a November 12, 2012, Bonham's auction in Hong Kong. In a Bonham's auction held in New York City on December 16, 2011, the same piece, estimated at $650,000 to $750,000, did not sell. This piece was consigned by the direct heirs of Chang Tso-lin himself.

Bonham's states that the Chang family piece is the finer of the two known examples.

These two coins represent the largest denominated gold coins of the Chinese Republic.

CHINA 1927 CHANG TSO-LIN GOLD 50 YUAN, SPECIMEN

Largest gold coin of the Republic.

Obverse. A bust-like portrait of Chang Tso-lin in military dress. An empty field surrounds. The portrait is encircled by a solid ring. There is a decorative register along a thick-looking rim.

Reverse. The national emblem of the Republic of China. Based on the ancient symbols of the Twelve Ornaments, the design features a "phoenix" (鳳凰, *Fènghuáng*) and a dragon perched on an axe blade. A slightly thinner decorative band, similar to that on the obverse, runs along the rim. Legend 中華民國十六年 (*Zhōnghuá Mínguó Shíliù Nián* ["Republic of China, 16th Year"]) is inscribed counterclockwise along the top beneath a decorative band. The denomination (right to left) is 伍拾圓 (*Wǔ Shí Yuán* ["50 Yuan"]) at the bottom. Two floral motifs or "sprays" (one per side) separate the two inscriptions.

Composition	Weight	Diameter	Alignment	Edge
Gold			Medal	Reeded
Mintage	**Mint**		**Collecting Difficulty**	**References**
2 (known)	Tientsin Mint		Virtually impossible	L&M-1031

Portrait of General Chang Tso-lin in Manchuria.

SOUTH AFRICA 1928-SA BRONZE SOVEREIGN PATTERN

A popular coin in an unlikely metal.

Obverse. A large left-facing head of King George V. Initials B.M. in the truncation. Clockwise from the left of the sharp neck truncation is the inscription GEORGIVS V D.G.BRITT:OMN:REX F.D.IND:IMP: (abbreviated Latin for *GEORGIUS V DEI GRATIA BRITANNIARUM OMNIUM REX FIDEI DEFENSOR INDIAE IMPERATOR* ["George V, by the Grace of God, King of all the Britons, Defender of the Faith, Emperor of India"]). Denticles surround along the rim.

Reverse. A muscular rendering of St. George, clad in a crested Roman helmet, a soldier's cloak, and leather boots. Atop his steed, which rears up to trample a European-style dragon, St. George pulls back the reins with his left hand and brandishes a short Roman sword *(gladius)* in his right. His left foot is barely visible under his horse. The point of his spear is broken off in the dragon's side; the spear shaft is on the ground behind the horse. The date 1928 is beneath this tableau. Above the date, in the ground, is the mintmark SA. Above and to the right of the date are the initials B.P.

Composition	Weight	Diameter	Alignment	Edge
Bronze (.955 copper, .030 tin, and .015 zinc)		21 mm	Medal	Reeded

Mintage	Mint	Mintmark	Collecting Difficulty	References
1	Royal Mint (Pretoria)	SA	Virtually impossible	Hern-U14A; not listed in Krause

The 1928 South African gold sovereign has the highest mintage of any of the issues in its series. South African King George V gold sovereigns were struck from 1923 through 1932, and during that 10-year run, millions of examples were coined. While only 655 South African sovereigns were made during their first year of issue, by 1928 production had reached a peak of 18,235,000 pieces. One may wonder why an extremely rare bronze pattern appears seemingly out of the blue for the series in 1928.

Established by the Mint Act of 1919, the South African branch of the British Royal Mint officially opened in Pretoria on January 1, 1923. By the end of that year, it had minted its first coins, including sovereigns. After 1917, the production of modern sovereigns, which originated in Great Britain in 1817, was moved almost entirely to Royal Mint branch facilities located in the Commonwealth nations of South Africa, India, Canada, and Australia. The Royal Mint established operations in the African nation 13 years after the formation of the Union of South Africa in 1910. The British Empire, at the apex of its power in the early twentieth century, fashioned a unified South African nation from a collection of four diverse colonies that had experienced wars between English and Boer (Dutch) settlers, not to mention conflicts between incoming Europeans and native African tribes.

The newly formed branch mint (not the first in Pretoria; then-President Paul Kruger established a mint there in 1892) was denoted by its SA mintmark. It was operating at capacity by the mid-1920s, producing a full range of coins denominated according to British standards.

Control over the Pretoria Mint was relinquished to the South African government by the Royal Mint in 1941, subsequently leading to its renaming as the South African Mint. The production and use of British-standard coinage continued in South Africa until 1961, when the nation withdrew from the Commonwealth under duress and became an independent republic.

While the production of coinage went smoothly at the relatively new mint during its first years of operation, some minor adjustments were made. Most significant, perhaps, was the reduction of King George's bust on the gold sovereign in 1929. By the late '20s, such bust modifications had become commonplace throughout the British Empire as the Royal Mint worked to eliminate "ghosting," or progressive indirect design transfer from the obverse to the reverse. Such was the case with Great Britain's pennies in the '30s and Australian pennies in the '50s, among other coins. This South African bronze pattern, minted during a period of bust modifications, is characteristic of other rare British Commonwealth transitional patterns, including another unique 1928 South African pattern: a sixpence minted in .925 sterling silver rather than the standard .800 fineness.

Heritage Auctions, who called the bronze pattern sovereign "one of the rarest coins we have ever handled," sold the unique specimen for US$184,000 (including buyer's premium) at the New York International Numismatic Convention (NYINC) in 2012. Graded as PF-64 by NGC, it almost quadrupled a high estimate of $50,000.

The obverse was created by Australian medalist and sculptor Sir Edgar Bertram Mackennal (1863-1931), who was knighted into the Royal Victorian Order in 1921 and was well-known for his designs of coins and stamps featuring King George V.

The coin reverse features the *St. George and the Dragon* design by Italian medalist Benedetto Pistrucci that appeared in 1817 on the first gold sovereign and some pattern crowns. St. George was a Christian military officer under the Roman emperor Diocletian (ruled 284–305 CE). In medieval legend, St. George was riding by a lake in Libya that was being

Boer family with a wagon on a farm in South Africa, circa 1900.

A depiction of St. George slaying the dragon.

Gen. J.B.M. Hertzog, prime minister of the Union of South Africa from 1924 to 1939.

poisoned by a dragon. The nearby town was forced to feed the dragon with sheep; when they ran out of sheep, the town's children were supplied according to the drawing of lots. On the day St. George rode by, the king's daughter had been selected. He first attacked with his lance, which wounded the dragon. He then took the princess's girdle and leashed it to the dragon, taming it. The two of them led the dragon back to town, where George offered to kill it if the townspeople converted to Christianity. They did and thus the beast was slain. The well-known *Golden Legend* version of this story, written by Jacobus de Varagine in the 1260s, states that a church was built on the site where the dragon was killed, and water with healing properties flowed from a spring in the church's altar. St. George eventually became the patron saint of England.

Commemorative medal marking the Union of South Africa in 1910.

RUSSIA 1902 GOLD 37 RUBLES, 50 KOPEKS

A French-style presentation piece for Russian VIPs.

Obverse: A left-facing portrait of Czar Nicholas II. Inscription S. M. НИКОЛАЙ II ИМПЕРАТОРZ И САМОДЕРЖЕЦZ ВСЕ РОСС. ("S. M. Nicholas II Emperor and Autocrat of all Russia"). Ornamental denticles wrap around the rim.

Reverse: Center: A double-headed imperial eagle, crowned, displayed (spread out), and langued (with tongue protruding) inside a beaded circle. The denomination is denoted in two ways: along the top, with the inscription 37 РУБЛЕЙ 50 КОПѢЕКЬ. (37 Roubles, 50 Kopecks), next to 1902 Г (Year); and below, 100 ФРАНКОВЬ (100 Francs). Five-petaled flowers divide the top and bottom inscriptions on both sides. Ornamental denticles wrap around a thick rim.

Composition	Weight	Diameter	Alignment	Edge
.900 gold	32.25 grams	33.5 mm	Medal	Lettered†

Mintage	Mint	Collecting Difficulty	References
225	Paris Mint, Monnaie de Paris (* on edge)	Extremely difficult	Bitkin-315; Fr-70; Sev-578; Uzd-4212; Y-B65

† ЧИСТАГО ЗОЛОТА 6 ЗОЛОТНИКОВЬ 77,4 ДОЛИ * ("Pure Gold 6 Zolotniks 77.4 Dolyas")

Czar Nicholas II.

НИКОЛАЙ II 1868·1918

The odd, yet impressive, denomination of 37 rubles and 50 kopeks (or 37.5 rubles) was the largest-denomination gold coin the Russian imperial government ever issued. It was denominated so strangely because the coin was struck in conformity with the standards of the Latin Monetary Union, a treaty organization that made an early attempt to coordinate the monetary systems of Europe into a single currency. Founded in 1865, the original signatories were France, Italy, Switzerland, and Belgium (Greece joined later). The fundamental specifications of the Union were that gold coins be struck with a fineness of .900 (90% pure) and in denominations equivalent to 5, 10, 20, 40, 50, and 100 francs. The 37.5-ruble gold coin was therefore the equivalent of 100 francs, the largest LMU denomination.

Despite the fact that Russia struck coins in harmony with the efforts of the Monetary Union, it did not become a party to the treaty. Indeed, this was a common reaction by other European nations and their colonies, as the utility of such a move was apparent. Besides, the Russians were famous francophiles; the coin was even struck in France at the Paris Mint (as denoted by the asterisk mintmark on the edge).

However, it is doubtful that such a large coin was intended for anything other than bullion (if that). Vladimir Bitkin, an expert in Russian numismatics, describes the gold coins as "donative," intended as gifts that imperial Russian officials could give to foreign emissaries and others whom they wished to impress or from whom they wanted to garner favors. Numismatic researcher S.I. Chizov says 200 pieces out of the mintage of 225 were given to Czar Nicholas II (1868–1918; reigned 1894–1917) himself to give away as presentation pieces; the other 25 were given to famed coin collector Grand Duke George Mikhailovich. Part of the Mikhailovich collection of about 11,400 Russian coins and medals now resides at the Smithsonian Institution's National Museum of American History as part of the National Numismatic Collection.

The obverse of the 1902 37.5-rubles gold coin features a tranquil, left-facing portrait of the czar. The reverse features the Russian imperial eagle and coat of arms; see number 12 on our list for an in-depth description.

In May 2012, Swiss auctioneer Sincona sold an Uncirculated example for about $147,600 US; Krause-Mishler gives estimated values of $60,000 for XF-40 and $100,000 for MS-60. As far as Proof issues go, NGC and PCGS have certified a total of just five grading events altogether. NGC lists impaired Proofs as going for $85,000. A PCGS PR-62 Cameo (one of two tied for finest) pedigreed to the Kiev Collection and the Mortimer Hammel Collection was sold for $199,750 US at a Stack's Bowers Galleries auction in August 2016.

Grand Duke George Mikhailovich. Parts of Mikhailovich's numismatic collection can be seen at the International Numismatic Club Museum in Moscow, the Smithsonian Institution in Washington, D.C., the National Museum in Paris, and in museums and private collections in Russia and Europe.

The coin's motif, often referred to in Western references as the "Dragon and Phoenix," is something of a misnomer. The phoenix is in fact a Chinese mythological being called a fenghuang (鳳凰, *Fènghuáng*), a bird resembling the western phoenix but having its own separate mythology and importance to Chinese culture. A chimera made from a number of different bird species, the anatomy of the fenghuang takes on celestial significance. It often stands as a royal female mate to the azure dragon, a powerful figure in Chinese mythology and imperial culture.

The use of these symbols on this coin is particularly interesting in light of the fact that China's "Last Emperor" was deposed in 1911 and replaced by a republican government that sought to force modernizing reforms, which many generals and intellectuals thought was necessary to preserve China's independence and integrity in an increasingly interconnected world. Writers Lu Xun (魯迅, *Lǔ Xùn*), Qian Daosun (錢稻孫, *Qián Dào Sūn*), and Xu Shoushang (許壽裳, *Xǔ Shòushang*) collaborated to create the new design, which was based on the Twelve Ornaments, auspicious Chinese symbols whose origins can be traced back more than 4,000 years. The design was produced in 1912 and adopted a year later.

The interlocking ribbons on the obverse symbolize unity, something that was very much necessary as the country had faced years of turmoil in the aftermath of the crumbling Qing dynasty.

This ornate imperial design was used on a handful of Chinese Republic coins, starting with the 1923 dollar, and appearing later on the 1926 10- and 20-cent coins, the Shantung Province 10-dollar pattern, the present pattern coin, and the 1927 Chang Tso-lin (*Zhang Zuolin*) 50-yuan gold pattern.

Beyond the origin of the design and the date of manufacture, not much is known about the Shantung 20-dollar pattern coin. It's widely believed that the coin was struck at the Tientsin Mint. The design was not adopted for use in general circulation. The timing of the strike dates the coin to the turbulent period of warlord rule by General Zhang Zongchang (張宗昌, *Zhāng Zōngchāng*) (1881–1932).

It is coveted for its artistry, mystery, and rarity. Examples have been owned by noted students of Chinese numismatics Eduard Kann, R.F. Schermerhorn, and Don C. Keefer.

According to Chinese coin expert and auctioneer Michael Chou, between five and seven examples of this coveted 20-dollar gold coin are known, but none finer than the NGC MS-64 example last sold by Heritage Auctions in 2014 at the World's Fair of Money in Rosemont, Illinois. That coin, part of a 400-plus-lot collection of important world and ancient coins from the Ultima Collection, brought US$176,250 (including buyer's premium). Only one other example has been certified by NGC.

In the seventh edition of their *Illustrated Catalog of Chinese Gold & Silver Coins* (2012), Lin Gwo Ming and Ma Tak Wo (L&M) give values of US$12,000 for a specimen in XF, $40,000 in UNC and $180,000 in BU.

A depiction of a Chinese dragon and phoenix.

CHINA 1926 SHANTUNG DRAGON AND PHOENIX GOLD 20 DOLLARS

A most auspicious gold pattern, shrouded in mystery.

Obverse. Center: The 12-symbol national emblem, Republic of China (1913–1928). A Chinese phoenix to the left, an azure dragon to the right of an ornamented, downward-facing axe blade. The phoenix holds pondweed in its right talon and beak. Three stars are behind its head. Both creatures hold a sacrificial cup. A stylized sun surmounts the design, representing the three-legged crow (三足烏, *sānzúwū*) of Asian legend; interlocking ribbons flow down from the bottom. Denticles border the rim.
Reverse. A wreath inside a beaded circle. Denomination 貳拾圓 (*Èrshí Yuán* ["Twenty Yuan"]) is within. At top is the inscription (right to left) 中華民國十五年 (*Zhōnghuá Mínguó Shíwǔ Nián* ["Republic of China Fifteen Years"]). Bottom: 山東省金幣 (*Shāndōng Shěng Jīnbì* ["Shantung Province Gold Coin"]). Two eight-petaled flowers separate the top and bottom inscriptions. Denticles border the rim.

Composition	Weight	Diameter	Alignment	Edge
Gold			Medal	Reeded
Mintage	**Mint**		**Collecting Difficulty**	**References**
5–7 (known)	Shantung		Virtually impossible	K-1535; KM-Pn9; L&M-1065

Lu Xun (seated left) with Xu Shoushang (standing) and Jiang Yizhi (seated right), circa 1908–1909.

ROMANIA 1940 SIX-COIN GOLD SET

Ostentatious commemoration of a king who courted controversy.

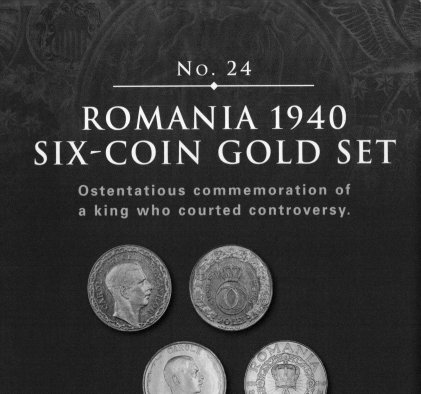

The writing was on the wall, but nevertheless, the Romanian Ministry of Finance must have been in a celebratory mood when it authorized the production of a six-piece set of gold coins to mark the 10th year of the reign of Carol II, the penultimate king of Romania (1893–1953; reigned 1930–1940).

Struck in limited mintage, the set included two 20-lei gold coins, two 100-lei gold coins, and two galden, which were impressively large coins—41 mm in diameter—with a gold value roughly equivalent to 12 ducats. The designs were executed by Romanian engravers E.W. Becker, A. Murnu, and Haralamb Ionescu[1].

The benefit of hindsight allows one to consider the coins in a much different light than was intended upon the issue's release. Offered just weeks before the king's abdication at the beginning of World War II, and at a moment in Romanian history that saw competing hostile powers annex large swaths of its territory, the set should be viewed as the numismatic valedictory of an unpopular monarch in the final days of his failed reign.

In spite of Carol II's failures as a head of state, the popularity of the set has only grown over time.

It is reported that only 346 pieces of each of the 20- and 100-lei coins were struck. For some reason, that number was extended by two for both of the galden issues.

Design-wise, the 100 lei and 20 lei issues feature designs that are fairly standard for the period. The obverses bear the likeness of the monarch, while the reverses carry the royal signet or some variation thereof. Things get very interesting with the larger gold issues, whose obverses feature a depiction of Carol II on horseback, with reverses depicting an ornate scene.

One issue depicts the Roman emperor Trajan, the second-century conqueror of ancient Romania; the other issue depicts Carol II and a peasant woman. The backstory behind this design is quite fascinating.

A Romanian stamp shows a portrait of King Carol II, without inscription, from the series "King Carol II," circa 1935.

20 Lei, Monogram in Circle Obverse. A right-facing bust of King Carol II. Wrapping around the design, just inside rim, is a circular crown of thorns. Inside the crown is the inscription CAROL II REGELE ROMANILOR ("Carol II, King of the Romanians"). Raised rim.

20 Lei, Monogram in Circle Reverse. In the center is the royal cypher of King Carol II, which features two opposite-facing, interlocking letter Cs inside a circle surmounted by a royal crown. To the left of the cypher is the date 8 IUNIE 1930 (8 June 1930); to the right is the date 9 IUNIE 1940. Encircling these motifs is an open wreath, which opens at the bottom of the design, where the denomination 20 LEI is centered. Atop the wreath are six shields representing Wallachia, Moldavia, Dobruja, Transylvania, Oltenia, and the House of Hohenzollern. The artist's name is below the denomination.

20 Lei, Monogram in Thorns Obverse. A right-facing bust of a younger King Carol II. The designer's name, E.W. Becker, is written in small text below the bust truncation (on some examples this name is twice engraved and overlapping). Wrapping around the rim is the following inscription: CAROL II (top), REGELE ROMANILOR (bottom). Separating the two is a vegetal ornament. Raised rim.

20 Lei, Monogram in Thorns Reverse. In the center of the design is the royal cypher of King Carol II, which features two opposite-facing, interlocking letter Cs inside a circle surmounted by a royal crown. From behind is a glory of rays. The cypher is encircled by a crown of thorns that has three flowers: one on the left, one on the right, and one at the top. At the bottom is a twice-bent ribbon that bears the inscription NIHIL SINE DEO ("Nothing without God"). ROMANIA is inscribed in large letters, wrapping around the inside rim at the top. The dual dates 1930 and 1940 bookend both sides of the crown to the left and right. Wrapping around the inside of the rim at the bottom is the date 8 IUNIE (once on the left and once on the right). In the center, at the bottom of the design, is the denomination 20 LEI.

100 Lei, Monogram in Circle Obverse. A right-facing head of King Carol II. Wrapping around the design, just inside the rim, is a circular crown of thorns. Inside the crown is the inscription CAROL II REGELE ROMANILOR ("Carol II, King of the Romanians"). Raised rim.

100 Lei, Monogram in Circle Reverse. In the center of the design is the royal cypher of King Carol II, which features two opposite-facing, interlocking letter Cs inside of a circle surmounted by a royal crown. To the left of the cypher is the date 8 IUNIE 1930 (8 June 1930); to the right is the date 9 IUNIE 1940. Encircling these motifs is an open wreath, which opens at the bottom of the design, where the denomination 100 LEI is centered. Atop the wreath are six shields representing Wallachia, Moldavia, Dobruja, Transylvania, Oltenia, and the House of Hohenzollern. Below the denomination is the artist's name.

100 Lei, Thorns on Reverse, Schaffer-111 Obverse. A right-facing bust of King Carol II. The designer's name, E.W. Becker, is written in small text below the bust truncation (on some examples this name is twice engraved and overlapping). Wrapping around the rim is the following inscription: CAROL II (top), REGELE ROMANILOR (bottom). Separating the two is a vegetal ornament. Raised rim.

100 Lei, Thorns on Reverse, Schaffer-111 Reverse. In the center of the design is the royal cypher of King Carol II, which features two opposite-facing, interlocking letter Cs. From behind is a glory of rays. The cypher is encircled by a crown of thorns that has three flowers, one on the left, one on the right, and one at the top. At the bottom is a twice-bent ribbon that bears the inscription NIHIL SINE DEO ("Nothing without God"). ROMANIA is inscribed in large letters, wrapping around the inside rim at the top. The dual dates 1930 and 1940 bookend both sides of the crown to the left and right. Wrapping around the inside of the rim at the bottom is the date 8 IUNIE (once on the left and once on the right). In the center, at the bottom of the design, is the denomination 100 LEI.

Inside the circle surmounted by a royal crown: To the left of the cypher is the date 8 IUNIE 1930 (8 June 1930) and to the right of it is the date 9 IUNIE 1940. Encircling these motifs is an open wreath, which opens at the bottom of the design, where the denomination 100 LEI is centered. Atop the wreath are six shields representing Wallachia, Moldavia, Dobruja, Transylvania, Oltenia, and the House of Hohenzollern. Below the denomination is the artist's name.

Trajan Galden (12 Ducats), Schaffer-114 Obverse. Facing to the left, King Carol II of Romania is mounted atop a horse. The horse is holding its front left hoof aloft. Wrapping around the top of the design is the inscription CAROL II REGELE ROMANILOR. In the exergue is vegetal scrollwork and the inscription 10 ANI ("10 Years"). On the lower right side is the designer's name: E. W. BECKER.

Trajan Galden (12 Ducats), Schaffer-114 Reverse. A shoulder-up view of right-facing Roman emperor Trajan, conqueror of Dacia (ancient Romania). Trajan is holding a sword in his right hand, propping it up against his shoulder. He holds a royal crown aloft in his left hand. In the background is a field of grain. In the exergue is the dual date 8 IUNIE 1930 and 8 IUNIE 1940.

Carol Galden (12 Ducats), Schaffer-115 Obverse. Facing to the right is King Carol II of Romania, mounted atop a horse. The horse is holding its front left hoof aloft. Wrapping around the top of the design is the inscription CAROL II REGELE ROMANILOR. On the lower left side is the designer's name: E. W. BECKER. Vegetal ornament and interlocking scrollwork are in the exergue.

Carol Galden (12 Ducats), Schaffer-115 Reverse. The sun cresting mountains is in the background. A propeller blade behind the king is on the right.

On June 6, 1930, the future king was on board a Farman F-190 propeller airplane en route to Bucharest, when the plane was forced to make an emergency landing in a wheat field on the outskirts of Vadu Crisului. The assembled townspeople were tasked with helping move the plane from the field to a spot where it could once again embark, while a carriage was sent to pick up fuel for the rest of the journey. One of the villagers, a girl named Maria Mudura, brought Carol II and his crew a jug of water. For her generosity, Maria was awarded three silver bands and honor by sculptor Constantin Baraschi, who erected a statue of the woman in Bucharest. Two days after the event, Carol II would assume the throne.

In an absolute sense, the Jubilee coins were always rare—not too many Romanians would have been able to afford such a set to begin with, and fewer still were the number among those that still supported the crumbling monarchy. Even with that, attrition has taken its toll and the number of surviving examples cannot be ascertained with any degree of precision.

Of the coins that do survive—and we estimate that problem-free, completable sets in Mint State number in the double digits—nearly all show some signs of wear or abuse.

20 Lei				
Composition	Weight	Diameter	Alignment	Edge
.900 gold	6.5 grams	21 mm	Coin	Reeded
Mintage	Mint		Collecting Difficulty	References
346	Bucharest Mint		Difficult	Fr-20; KM-M9, M10

100 Lei				
Composition	Weight	Diameter	Alignment	Edge
.900 gold	32.5 grams	35 mm	Coin	Reeded
Mintage	Mint		Collecting Difficulty	References
346	Bucharest Mint		Extremely difficult	Fr-17, 19; KM-M11, M12

Galden				
Composition	Weight	Diameter	Alignment	Edge
.900 gold	42 grams	41 mm	Coin	Reeded
Mintage	Mint		Collecting Difficulty	References
348	Bucharest Mint		Extremely difficult	

A surviving section of the ancient London Wall, at Tower Hill, with a replica statue of
Roman Emperor Trajan, who is depicted on one of the Romanian galdens in this set.

To illustrate that point, an example of the galden featuring Carol and Mudura brought US$23,500 in an August 2016 Stack's Bowers auction. That coin was one of only three certified by PCGS and graded MS-61 (two in MS-62 are tied for finest). Considerably better, but hardly problem-free, was a PCGS MS-63+ example of the Trajan design, which was the finest of three certified by the service. That example brought $35,250[2].

The same holds true along the other denominations as well.

In August 2016, Heritage Auctions offered the finer of two examples of the Monogram in Circle 100 lei certified by NGC, graded MS-63. That piece brought $42,300[3]. The other 100 lei type, the Thorns on Reverse design, brought $38,187.50 two years earlier. That coin was graded AU-55 by PCGS. To date, only four examples of this type have been certified by that service, none in Mint State. NGC, on the other hand, reports ten grading events of the issue, none finer than MS-62.

The 20 lei issues have evidenced a higher survival rate and more modest prices. NGC has certified 19 examples of each of the two types. Both issues top out at MS-62. One example of the Crown Reverse type brought $4,993.75 at a 2014 Heritage auction[4].

The Fontana Modura statue in Bucharest
celebrates the story of Maria Mudura.

Princess Helen.

CAROL II (OCTOBER 15, 1893–APRIL 4, 1953)

A rebellious and controversial figure even before assuming the throne—a not-uncommon theme running through the pages of this book—the young Carol engaged in a number of open and controversial amorous relationships that the royal court, specifically his father King Ferdinand I, found objectionable.

In 1918, to his family's shock and fury, Carol deserted his military post and eloped with 20-year-old Zizi Lambrino, who was the daughter of a Romanian colonel but still considered a commoner. Seven months later, after several attempts to separate the two, the marriage was annulled. Despite this, Carol continued to cohabitate with Lambrino, who bore a son a year and a half later and was forced to take the child with her to live in exile in France.

A year later, an arranged marriage with Princess Helen of Greece and Denmark bore an acceptable heir to the throne, Prince Michael. Despite the marriage, Carol continued to cavort openly with other women, leaving his marriage in ruins and further diminishing his esteem with his father. After taking up a relationship with Magda Lupescu, a married woman whose Jewish ancestry sparked outrage amongst the public and members of Parliament, Ferdinand I forced Carol to renounce his right to the throne. In his place, the line of succession would proceed to his son from his "legitimate" marriage, Michael.

Michael's time came in short order, as Ferdinand died when he was five years old. A regency was established to oversee government affairs, but its tenure proved short and unsuccessful. Agitation in Parliament breathed life into Carol II's royal claim, and a coup d'état in 1930 deposed the son in order to install the father. In the aftermath, the boy king was not exiled but rather given a new title, the Grand Voivode of Alba-Iulia. His time would come again.

As monarch, Carol II was determined to strengthen the power of the monarchy, which had been stripped of much of its power following the country's disastrous showing in World War I. He sought to establish a cult of personality around himself, drawing parallels for his rule to the Roman emperor Trajan. Across Europe, Carol II became known as the "Dictator King."

The headwinds of history would temper his ambitions. As the specter of world war began to enshroud the continent, the very survival of the Romanian monarchy came under direct threat from internal pressures brought about by the rise of far-right nationalism, far-left populism, and Carol's dissatisfaction with democratic political solutions. In truth, he faced a prisoner's dilemma. Already in disarray, Romania entered a period of political crisis after Prime Minister Armand Călinescu was assassinated on September 21, 1939, by an Iron Guard death squad, the group led by militant Christian extremist Corneliu Codreanu. Sadly, it was just one of many violent acts carried out by the group under Carol's reign.

External issues compounded his problems. Within days of France's surrender to Germany on June 22, 1940, Carol began to cede blocks of Romanian territory to the Soviet Union and Northern Transylvania to Hungary. His hope was that these appeasements would stave off further interference or, worse, invasion, and thus preserve his government, but it had the opposite effect.

With collapsing public support, a government in disarray, and a military unwilling to follow his orders, Carol II was forced to abdicate his throne on September 6 and flee to Mexico with Lupescu, whom he later married. Carol died in 1953.

Crown Prince Carol II (1893–1953) who reigned as king of Romania from 1930 to 1940. Photo circa 1915–1920.

SAXONY 1913-E ALBERTINE 3 MARKS, MATTE PROOF

Commemorating the Battle of the Nations, right before a world war.

Obverse. A frontal view of the monument to the Battle of Leipzig, from the reflecting pool. The inscriptions include 18. OKTOBER *1813=1913. The mintmark E is at the bottom.

Reverse. A German imperial single-headed (Prussian) eagle is displayed (spread out) and langued (with tongue protruding), with the crown of Charlemagne (with bows to either side) above the head. the shield on its breast features a Prussian eagle with the escutcheon of the House of Hohenzollern on its breast; together the design is the lesser arms of the German emperor. Clockwise along the top of the rim is the inscription DEUTSCHES REICH 1913. Counterclockwise along the bottom is the denomination DREI MARK (three marks). A five-pointed star is on each side, between the top and bottom inscriptions. Beads or dots encircle the design.

Composition	Weight	Diameter	Alignment	Edge
.900 silver	16.6670 grams	33 mm	Medal	Lettered†

Mintage	Mint	Collecting Difficulty	References
150	Muldenhütten Mint (Dresden)‡	Difficult	Jaeger-140; KM-1275

† GOTT MIT UNS ("God With Us") ‡Mintmark: E

A 2013 Russian stamp honoring the 200th anniversary of the victory of the allied armies in the Battle of Leipzig.

Н «АТАКА ЛЕЙБ-КАЗАКОВ ПОД ЛЕЙПЦИГОМ 4 ОКТЯБРЯ 1813 ГОДА». 1845
НОВОЧЕРКАССКИЙ МУЗЕЙ ИСТОРИИ ДОНСКОГО КАЗАЧЕСТВА

The Battle of Leipzig—also known as the Battle of the Nations—was the largest single battle fought on European soil until World War I (1914–1918). It was the first defeat of French emperor and military genius Napoleon Bonaparte on the battlefield, as armies from Russia, Austria, Prussia, and Sweden met Napoleon's forces at Leipzig in the eastern German state of Saxony on October 16–19, 1813. The battle was the climax of an allied effort to free the German states from French rule, and as such the 1913-E 3-mark circulating commemorative coin celebrates not just an important and proud event in German history but also independence from foreign domination. A fitting commemoration of nationalism considering the conflagration that was about to begin the very next year.

The Monument to the Battle of the Nations (Völkerschlachtdenkmal) was completed in 1913 at an expense of six million gold marks; the coin therefore is one aspect of the centennial commemoration. Supposedly, the monument was built on the spot of some of the most intense fighting and where Napoleon ordered the retreat of his forces. The project was headed by architect Bruno Schmitz, with help from sculptors Christian Behrens and Franz Metzner. Standing 299 feet (91 meters) tall, it is one of the tallest memorials in Europe.

The coin was designed by Friedrich Wilhelm Hörnlein (1873–1945), a respected medalist and engraver from Saxony who was also responsible for the 1917 3-mark commemorative celebrating the 400th anniversary of the Reformation. The circulating issue of the 1913-E 3 marks saw a mintage of 999,999 pieces, while a regular Proof version saw a mintage of 17,000.

Much rarer are the Matte Proofs, of which only 150 were struck.

Frederick Augustus III (1865–1932; ruled 1904–1918) was the last king of Saxony. A popular sovereign, he abdicated upon the defeat of Germany in WWI (like other kings of German states; see number 46) and the proclamation of the new Weimar Republic.

The Völkerschlachtdenkmal monument to the Battle of Leipzig, built in 1913 in Leipzig, Saxony, Germany.

As stated earlier, Edward VIII (1894–1972; reigned January 20–December 11, 1936) ascended to the British throne following the death of his father, King George V. This necessitated new designs for British coinage, but the Royal Mint had time to produce only a few pattern sets bearing Humphrey Paget's portrait of Edward VIII before the king abdicated to marry the American divorcée Wallis Simpson (handing the throne over to his brother Albert, now King George VI, in the process). Number 6 in our list considered the gold sovereign on its own; here, we discuss the set as a whole.

The 1937 Edward VIII Proof set consists of 13 coins (from smallest to largest denominations): the bronze farthing, half penny, and penny; two threepence coins (in silver and nickel-brass); the silver sixpence, shilling,

florin, half crown, and crown; and the gold sovereign, 2-pound, and 5-pound coins. All the coins in the set are considered pattern coins because no Royal Proclamation authorizing them (making them legal tender) was issued before Edward's abdication in December 1936. No plans were made to strike the gold half sovereign for Edward VIII.

Another interesting aspect of the Proof set is the inclusion of a 12-sided, nickel-brass version of the threepence. The general public had been unhappy with the small, unwieldy silver threepence for some time before the 326 days of Edward's reign as king. It just so happened that the Royal Mint's experiments with a thicker, easier-to-use base metal threepence came to fruition for this rarest of rare sets. Lord Kitchener's niece, artist Frances Madge Kitchener (1889–1977), designed the brass threepence, inspired by the "native flora and fauna" concept of the 1928 coinage of the Irish Free State. The 1937 nickel-brass threepence was the first dodecagonal coin struck by the Royal Mint, as well as the first UK coin minted in nickel-brass.

Also, some of the Edward VIII Proofs were struck in a matte finish for official photography. These are likely unique for their respective types.

The wren on the farthing was designed by English sculptor and medalist Harold Wilson Parker (1896–1980). The design made its debut in the Edward VIII set and was adapted for use later during the reigns of both George VI and Queen Elizabeth II.

The galleon on the back of the half penny was designed by the man whose portrait was personally selected by Edward VIII for use on his coinage, Thomas Humphrey Paget, OBE (1893–1974). It is based on Sir

GREAT BRITAIN 1937 KING EDWARD VIII 13-COIN PROOF SET

Coins for a king who was never crowned.

Recreation of Sir Francis Drake's *Golden Hind* galleon, located in London.

Common Obverse. A portrait of King Edward VIII, facing left. Clockwise from the left along the top rim are various inscriptions in abbreviated Latin for EDWARDUS VIII DEI GRATIA BRITANNIARUM OMNIUM REX FIDEI DEFENSOR INDIAE IMPERATOR ("Edward VIII, by the Grace of God, King of All Britain, Defender of the Faith, Emperor of India") or EDWARDUS VIII DEI GRATIA BRITANNIARUM OMNIUM REX ("Edward VIII, by the Grace of God, King of All Britain"). The designer's initials, H.P., are under the truncation of the neck. An enclosed ring of denticles encircles the entire design.

Farthing Reverse. A wren, perched close to the ground, facing left. Above, the date 1937. Below, the denomination FARTHING. A ring of squat denticles surrounds along the rim.

Half Penny Reverse. A galleon sailing left in wavy seas, flags and pennant atop its masts. The designer's initials, H.P., are to the right of the ship. Above is the denomination HALF PENNY. Below the water is the date 1937. Sharp tilde ornaments are to either side of the date. an enclosed ring of denticles encircles the entire design.

Penny Reverse. Britannia is seated with a crested helmet. A trident is in her left arm, touching the rim. her right arm steadies a shield with a Union Jack design. her right foot is in a sandal. Stylized waves are beneath her seat. there is open water in the background, with a lighthouse on the left. Clockwise from the left is the denomination, with Britannia situated between the words: ONE PENNY. The date 1937 is in the exergue. an enclosed ring of denticles encircles the entire design.

Threepence (Silver) Reverse. In the center are three interlinked rings of St. Edmund. Clockwise around the top half, from left, is the inscription FID: DEF: IND: IMP (abbreviated Latin for FIDEI DEFENSOR INDIAE IMPERATOR ["Defender of the Faith, Emperor of India"]). The denomination THREE * PENCE is at the bottom. the designer's initials, K.G., are beneath the rings. an enclosed ring of denticles surrounds the entire design. Relatively thick rim.

Threepence (Nickel-Brass) Reverse. In the center is a three-flowered thrift plant. The denomination THREE PENCE runs clockwise from the left around the rim. The date, 1937, is at the bottom. Relatively thick rim.

Sixpence Reverse. In the center are six interlocking signet rings. an enclosed ring of denticles encircles the entire design. Clockwise around the top half from the left is the inscription FID: DEF: IND: IMP (abbreviated Latin for FIDEI DEFENSOR INDIAE IMPERATOR ["Defender of the Faith, Emperor of India"]). The denomination SIXPENCE is at bottom. the designer's initials, K and G, are to the left and right of the bottom ring, respectively. an enclosed ring of denticles surrounds the entire design.

Shilling Reverse. Head-on in the center, a crowned lion with a ruffle collar, holding a scepter in its left paw and a sword in its right, is seated on its back legs on a royal crown. Clockwise around the top half, from left, is the inscription FID: DEF: IND: IMP (abbreviated Latin for FIDEI DEFENSOR INDIAE IMPERATOR ["Defender of the Faith, Emperor of India"]). The numerals 19 and 37 are on the left and right of the lion, respectively. A dot is to the right of the 7. A shield with a cross of St. Andrew is beneath the 19; a shield with the Scottish thistle is beneath 37. The designer's initial, K, is beneath the sword; and the initial G is beneath the scepter. Along the bottom is the denomination ONE * SHILLING. an enclosed ring of denticles encircles the entire design.

Florin Reverse. In the center is a rose with a crown and a thornless stem with leaves to both sides. A thistle to the left, a shamrock to the right. The letter E is beneath the thistle, and R beneath the shamrock. Clockwise around the top half, from left, is the inscription FID: DEF: IND: IMP: (abbreviated Latin for FIDEI DEFENSOR INDIAE IMPERATOR ["Defender of the Faith, Emperor of India"]). Along the bottom is the inscription TWO SHILLINGS 1937. the designer's initials, K and G, are beneath the left and right leaves, respectively. an enclosed ring of denticles encircles the entire design.

Half Crown Reverse. In the center is a royal standard (flag). The first and fourth quadrants, with three lions passant guardant on a field, represent the Kingdom of England. the second quadrant, with a lion rampant, represents Scotland. I third quadrant has an Irish harp. Crowned double-E monograms are to either side. Clockwise around the top half, from left, is the inscription FID: DEF: IND: IMP (abbreviated Latin for FIDEI DEFENSOR INDIAE IMPERATOR ["Defender of the Faith, Emperor of India"]). Along the bottom is the inscription HALF * CROWN * 1937. The designer's initials, K.G., are beneath the standard. An enclosed ring of denticles encircles the entire design.

Crown Reverse. In the center is the royal coat of arms. The first and fourth quadrants of the shield, with three lions passant guardant on a field, represent the Kingdom of England. The second quadrant, with a lion rampant, represents Scotland. The third quadrant has an Irish harp. A lion supporter is on the left and a unicorn on the right. Beneath the shield is a scroll with the motto DIEU ET MON DROIT ("God and My Right"). Clockwise around the top half, from left, is the inscription FID: DEF: IND: IMP (abbreviated Latin for FIDEI DEFENSOR INDIAE IMPERATOR ["Defender of the Faith, Emperor of India"]). Along the bottom is the denomination and date: CROWN : 1937. The designer's initial K is beneath the lion and G is beneath the unicorn. An enclosed ring of denticles encircles the entire design.

Common Reverse (Sovereign, 2 Pounds, 5 Pounds). A muscular rendering of St. George, clad in a crested Roman helmet, a soldier's cloak, and leather boots, atop a horse trampling a European-style dragon. St. George pulls back the reins with his left hand, brandishing a short Roman sword (*gladius*) in his right. His left foot is barely visible under the horse. The point of his spear is broken off in the dragon's side; the spear shaft is on the ground behind the horse. The date 1937 is beneath this tableau. Above and to the right of the date are the designer's initials, B.P.

Francis Drake's famous ship, *Golden Hind,* and the design was used for the coinage of George VI and beyond.

The penny reverse features an adaptation of Leonard Charles Wyon's (1826–1891) seated Britannia design, first created in 1860. Mint sculptor Charles Walter Coombes was responsible for the new engraving.

The silver threepence, sixpence, shilling, florin, and half crown reverses use designs created in 1927 by artist and prolific coin designer George Kruger Gray (1880–1943). These designs continued to be used through 1948 and were utilized in modified form from 1949 through 1952. The only major difference here is that the Edward VIII half crown employs a flag, while the George VI version uses a shield. Otherwise, they are the same designs. Gray is also responsible for the crown reverse, which was used for the 1937 George VI crown as well.

The reverses of the gold coins feature the famous *St. George and the Dragon* design by Royal Mint Chief Engraver Benedetto Pistrucci (1783–1855), first used on the sovereign in 1817.

Only a few Edward VIII Proof sets were ever struck. Not even the former king himself received one (his own brother, George VI, turned down his request from the Mint). Including the individual coins in the Proof sets, the Mint struck a mere six Edward VIII gold sovereigns dated 1937, and in order to spare the royal family any awkward feelings, the Royal Mint hid the coins away until 1970, when a cardboard box was pulled from the safe of retiring Deputy Master of the Royal Mint (1957–1970) Sir Jack James (though according to A.H. Baldwin and Sons, the Mint took an inventory of the contents of the box in 1950). Contained within were the six gold sovereigns, along with 43 other coins and patterns featuring Edward.

Out of those few Proof sets, only one complete set made it into private hands. Ira and Larry Goldberg Auctioneers of Long Beach, California, acquired it on behalf of the anonymous collector of the Tyrant Collection in 2010 from Spink for US$2.2 million. The set was recently on display at the 2018 Long Beach Expo.

Farthing				
Composition	Weight	Diameter	Alignment	Edge
Bronze (.955 copper, .030 tin, .015 zinc)	2.86 grams	20.2 mm	Medal	Smooth
Mintage	Mint		Collecting Difficulty	References
Unknown	Royal Mint (London)		Extremely difficult	KM-Pn122

Half Penny				
Composition	Weight	Diameter	Alignment	Edge
Bronze (.955 copper, .030 tin, .015 zinc)	5.69 grams	25.48 mm	Medal	Smooth
Mintage	Mint		Collecting Difficulty	References
Unknown	Royal Mint (London)		Extremely difficult	KM-Pn123

Penny				
Composition	Weight	Diameter	Alignment	Edge
Bronze (.955 copper, .030 tin, .015 zinc)	9.4 grams	31 mm	Medal	Smooth
Mintage	Mint		Collecting Difficulty	References
Unknown	Royal Mint (London)		Extremely difficult	KM-Pn124

Threepence (Silver)				
Composition	Weight	Diameter	Alignment	Edge
.500 silver, .400 copper, .050 nickel, .050 zinc	1.4 grams	16.3 mm	Medal	Smooth
Mintage	Mint		Collecting Difficulty	References
Unknown	Royal Mint (London)		Extremely difficult	KM-Pn125

Threepence (Nickel-Brass)				
Composition	Weight	Diameter	Alignment	Edge
Nickel-brass (.790 copper, .200 zinc, .010 nickel)	6.8 grams	21 mm side to side, 21.6 mm corner to corner	Medal	Smooth
Mintage	Mint		Collecting Difficulty	References
Unknown	Royal Mint (London)		Extremely difficult	KM-Pn126

Sixpence				
Composition	Weight	Diameter	Alignment	Edge
.500 silver, .400 copper, .050 nickel, .050 zinc	28 grams	19 mm	Medal	Reeded
Mintage	Mint		Collecting Difficulty	References
Unknown	Royal Mint (London)		Extremely Difficult	KM-Pn127

Shilling				
Composition	Weight	Diameter	Alignment	Edge
.500 silver, .400 copper, .050 nickel, .050 zinc	5.64 grams	23.7 mm	Medal	Reeded
Mintage	Mint		Collecting Difficulty	References
Unknown	Royal Mint (London)		Extremely difficult	KM-Pn128

Florin (2 Shillings)				
Composition	Weight	Diameter	Alignment	Edge
.500 silver, .400 copper, .050 nickel, .050 zinc	11.39 grams	28.5 mm	Medal	Reeded
Mintage	Mint		Collecting Difficulty	References
Unknown	Royal Mint (London)		Extremely difficult	KM-Pn129

Half Crown				
Composition	Weight	Diameter	Alignment	Edge
.500 silver, .400 copper, .050 nickel, .050 zinc	14.09 grams	32.2 mm	Medal	Reeded
Mintage	Mint		Collecting Difficulty	References
Unknown	Royal Mint (London)		Extremely difficult	KM-Pn130

Crown				
Composition	Weight	Diameter	Alignment	Edge
.500 silver, .400 copper, .050 nickel, .050 zinc	28.27 grams	38.61 mm	Medal	Reeded
Mintage	Mint		Collecting Difficulty	References
Unknown	Royal Mint (London)		Extremely difficult	KM-Pn131

Sovereign				
Composition	Weight	Diameter	Alignment	Edge
.9167 gold	7.98 grams	22.05 mm	Medal	Reeded
Mintage	Mint		Collecting Difficulty	References
6 (per Krause)	Royal Mint (London)		Virtually impossible	KM-Pn132

2 Pounds				
Composition	Weight	Diameter	Alignment	Edge
.9167 gold	16 grams	28 mm	Medal	Reeded
Mintage	Mint		Collecting Difficulty	References
Unknown	Royal Mint (London)		Virtually impossible	KM-Pn133

5 Pounds				
Composition	Weight	Diameter	Alignment	Edge
.9167 gold	40 grams	37 mm	Medal	Reeded
Mintage	Mint		Collecting Difficulty	References
Unknown	Royal Mint (London)		Virtually impossible	KM-Pn134

Edward, Prince of Wales, in a portrait by Arthur Stockdale Cope, circa 1911–1912.

King Edward VIII and Mrs. Simpson on vacation in Yugoslavia, 1936.

No. 27

PHILIPPINES 1907-S PESO, PROOFS (LARGE SIZE AND REDUCED SIZE)

The only unique currency system among U.S. territories.

Obverse. A full-figured woman in a flowing dress, facing left and striking an anvil with a hammer in her right hand. In her left hand is an olive branch. Behind is the erupting volcano Mt. Mayon. The flat space between the ground and volcano presents an illusion of water separating two islands. Encircling the design is the inscription ONE PESO FILIPINAS. The rim is beaded.

Reverse. In the center is the United States federal shield, surmounted by a bald eagle holding an olive branch and three arrows. The legend UNITED STATES OF AMERICA encircles the design clockwise from left. Two dots separate the legend from the date, which is located below the shield. The S mintmark is below the left dot. The rim is beaded.

Large Size

Composition	Weight	Diameter	Alignment	Edge
.900 silver, .100 copper	26.95 grams	38 mm	Coin	Reeded

Mintage	Mint	Collecting Difficulty	References
1	United States Mint (San Francisco)†	Impossible	KM-168

† Mintmark: S

Reduced Size

Composition	Weight	Diameter	Alignment	Edge
.800 silver, .200 copper	20 grams	35 mm	Coin	Reeded

Mintage	Mint	Collecting Difficulty	References
1	United States Mint (San Francisco)†	Virtually impossible	KM-172

† Mintmark: S

On March 2, 1903, less than a year after the conclusion of the Philippine-American War (1899–1902), the United States Congress authorized an act that called for the creation of a standard of value for coinage for the Philippine Islands. Most American collectors are aware that the United States acquired the islands from Spain at the conclusion of the Spanish-American War (1898), after paying Spain a total of $20 million for control of the islands. The Philippine Islands number in excess of 7,000, but only 2,000 of them are occupied. The people of the islands are from a diverse array of ethnic groups, many with their own unique languages and cultures.

Considered too impoverished to support the circulation of the American dollar, the Philippines became the only U.S. territory to receive its own coinage and monetary system. The coins would be known as the Conant series, named for U.S. journalist and banking expert Charles Arthur Conant (1861–1915), who had been sent to the Philippines in 1901–1902 to investigate the currency. The silver peso of the Philippines would be struck on a .900 fine planchet set to the weight of a United States silver dollar but would only be worth half that. This arrangement lasted until 1906, by which time administrators had noticed people were hoarding the new pesos because the bullion value exceeded the coin's legal tender face value. A new .800 fine silver peso was introduced into circulation in 1908 and was issued through 1912.

However, two unique patterns were struck in 1907 that few, if any, numismatic references knew existed. One was made to the prior .900 standard, while the other was produced according to the new debased standard. Both were Proofs struck at the San Francisco Mint.

According to Ron Guth, the .900 silver peso is impounded in a museum in the Philippines. The .800 silver, graded PCGS PR-65 (the only example certified by any third party grading service), was offered at a Lyn Knight auction in June 2012 as part of the Dr. Greg Pineda Collection of Philippines coins and paper money, where it sold for US$193,875 (including buyer's premium).

The obverse and reverse were designed by Filipino artist Melecio Figueroa (1842–1903). Educated in Spain, Figueroa returned to his homeland and taught the art of engraving at the Escuela de Pintura, Escultura y Grabado. He also worked as an engraver for the Spanish colonial mint (Casa Moneda) in Manila. Outside of his engraving work, Figueroa also participated as a delegate in the Malolos Revolutionary Congress and taught at Liceo de Manila, now Manila Central University.

Illustration of the battle of Malate, Manila, Philippines, night of July 31, 1898.

(Left) Mount Mayon in eruption on July 21, 1928.

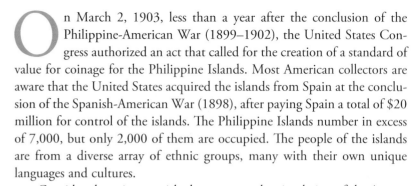

In republican China, Sun Yat-sen is considered the father of his country, much like George Washington in the United States.

A revered figure in both communist China and nationalist Taiwan, Dr. Sun Yat-sen (孫逸仙, *Sūn Yìxiān*, his art name, or the popular 孫中山, which is transliterated to *Sūn Zhōngshān*) was the first president of the fledgling Republic of China. With the Republican revolution came an end to many of the old ways, including the modernization of styles of dress. Besides being notable that on a coin of this period he is not dressed in a military uniform, laden with decorations and epaulets, Sun is depicted in a Westernized overcoat (which came to be called a Sun Yat-sen jacket, or *Zhōngshān fu*), a high-collar shirt, and a tie—as copied from a famous photograph. The new style of clothing he introduced to the Republic was a combination of Western, Meiji Japanese, and Chinese military influences.

The central motif on the reverse of this coin consists of two flags bound together with a lengthy ribbon over the upper portion of a globe. The flag on the viewer's left is that of the Kuomintang (國民黨, *Guómíndǎng*), or Nationalist Party of China, which ruled China from 1928 to 1949. The flag on the viewer's right is the flag of the Republic of China and features the same white sun on a blue field as seen on the Kuomintang flag (which itself was the flag of the resistance movement founded by Sun and others against the Qing dynasty). The globe presents Europe, Asia, and a large portion of Africa to the viewer, with an overlay of latitude and longitude lines.

An English inscription that reads "The Republic of China" arcs around the top of the reverse. At the bottom of the coin and superimposed over the globe is the inscription 壹圓, which means "One Yuan" or "One Dollar." The numeral 壹 is used in financial and official records for the number one (*yī*) to avoid possible confusion with other Chinese numerals, and "圓" is an alternative form of the now-more-common symbol for yuan, 元.

Sun was educated at a British Anglican school in Hawaii, where he learned English and science, among other subjects. It is here that Christianity came to have a big influence on his beliefs. When Sun returned to China, his newfound beliefs alienated the locals, causing him to flee to Hong Kong, where he was baptized and learned Western medicine. He then became dissatisfied with what he viewed as the overly traditional Qing dynasty and its reluctance to adopt modern Western ways, so he quit his practice to become a political reformist. Sun joined up with a friend in a group advocating the overthrow of the Qing and he wrote a lengthy petition to the imperial government with suggestions for modernizing China.

He was not, however, granted an audience to present the petition. This confirmed Sun in his views and so he went back to Hawaii to found his own revolutionary group, which eventually fused with the Hong Kong group of his friends.

The defeat of the Qing in the First Sino-Japanese War (1894–1895) led to a much more urgent feeling for modernization. Non-revolutionary reformists carried the day, but their reforms were unsuccessful. Sun was part of a faction that advocated replacing the rule of the Qing with a modern republic. This faction was responsible for a failed uprising in Canton (广州, *Guǎngzhōu*) in 1895, which resulted in Sun's exile.

During this time, he lived in Japan and befriended similarly-minded democratic revolutionaries in that country, receiving the name "Zhongshan" (孫中山, *Sūn Zhōngshān*)—the name he is perhaps best known by in China. He also helped funnel arms to Filipino resistance fighters in the Philippine-American War (1899–1902). In 1900, Sun led the Huizhou Uprising (惠州, *Huìzhōu*), which also failed. He returned to exile in Japan and traveled around the world.

Dr. Sun Yat-sen.

CHINA 1929 SUN YAT-SEN FLAG AND GLOBE SILVER DOLLAR PATTERN

An unusual tribute to the Father of Modern China

Obverse. An effigy of Sun Yat-sen in a Westernized overcoat, high-collar shirt, and tie. Above the effigy is the legend 中華民國十八年 (*Zhōnghuá Mínguó Shíbā Nián* ["Republic of China Year 18"]) inscribed counterclockwise between Dr. Sun's portrait and a ring of denticles. Relatively thick rim.

Reverse. In the center, two flags are bound together with ribbon over the upper portion of a globe presenting Europe, Asia, and part of Africa, with an overlay of latitude and longitude lines. The flag on the viewer's left represents the Kuomintang; to the viewer's right is the flag of the Republic of China. On top is the English inscription "The Republic of China." At the bottom (superimposed over globe) is the inscription 壹圓 (*Yī Yuán* ["One Dollar"]). A ring of denticles surrounds the reverse design.

Composition	Weight	Diameter	Alignment	Edge
Silver	26.73 grams		Medal	Reeded
Mintage	**Mint**		**Collecting Difficulty**	**References**
Unknown (possibly unique)	Tientsin Mint		Virtually impossible	Kann-61; KM-Pn99; L&M-94

By 1904, Sun had developed and refined his Three Principles of nationalism, modernism, and welfare. The next year saw the formation of the Tongmenghui (同盟會, *Tóngménghuì* ["The United League"]) in Tokyo from among his fellow revolutionary Chinese students—a secret society that would eventually give way to the nationalist Kuomintang. The Tongmenghui began a series of further uprisings in China over the next decade (including a second uprising in Canton), all of which failed. This caused some in the Tongmenghui to question Sun's leadership, and the alliance split into different factions. While Sun was in the United States, the Tongmenghui-led 1911 uprising in Wuchang (武昌, *Wǔchāng*) against Yuan Shikai (袁世凱, *Yuán Shìkǎi*) was successful. Sun returned to China from the United States to help lead what would become the Xinhai Revolution (辛亥革命, *Xīnhài Gémìng*) that overthrew the Qing.

Sun was elected the provisional president at a meeting of provincial revolutionaries, but the general Yuan Shikai offered the revolutionaries a deal. If they would designate him as president, then he would make the Xuantong Emperor (宣統帝, *Xuāntǒng Dì*) Pu Yi (溥儀, *Pǔyí*)—the last of the Qing—abdicate. Once Pu Yi descended from the throne, Sun resigned and Yuan became the president.

Yuan proved himself no ally of republican sentiment, which led to a second revolution in 1913 that ultimately failed. Once again, Sun fled to Japan. In 1915, Yuan declared himself emperor, which lost him the support of his generals. Sun joined in this larger coalition that succeeded in Yuan's overthrow, and he became provisional president one more time.

Unfortunately, this did not herald the beginning of a new republic but instead ushered in the Warlord Era (1916–1928; 軍閥時代, *Jūnfá Shídài*), during which China was effectively controlled by regional armies and strongmen. Numismatically, the era is known for several interesting provincial issues, such as the 1949 Kweichow 50 cents (number 15 in our list) and the 1928 Auto Dollar (number 59).

As early as 1917, Sun was advocating for the reunification of China. A military government was set up in Canton to serve as a base of operations for the conquest of the rest of the country. Already a socialist and admirer of Vladimir Lenin (the feeling was mutual), Sun cooperated with the Communist Party of China to achieve this slow takeover. Future Nationalist leader Chiang Kai-shek (蔣介石, *Jiǎng Jièshí*) was chosen to lead the Nationalist forces in this endeavor.

As a side note but no less important to national unity, Sun established the Canton Central Bank in 1924—the first central bank in Chinese history.

Dr. Sun Yat-sen died of liver cancer on January 26, 1925.

As for the 1929 Flag and Globe pattern, Michael Chou of Champion Auctions called it "one of the most imaginative designs ever used on a Chinese coin" and says it is the first design on Chinese coinage to feature a rendering of the world as a map or globe (the first to reach circulation being the 1932 Chinese Soviet dollar and 20-cent pieces). This is because the Sun Yat-sen Flag and Globe dollar was one of many patterns created that year, which included other dollars and fractional denominations.

The seventh edition of Lin Gwo Ming and Ma Tak Wo's (L&M) *Illustrated Catalog of Chinese Gold & Silver Coins* (2012) states that the coin sells for US$200,000 in Uncirculated condition, and $650,000 in Brilliant Uncirculated. The 2014 *Standard Catalog of World Coins* gives this pattern a market value of $50,000.

Sun Yat-sen as provisional president of the Republic of China, 1912, after the Xinhai Revolution.

The Sun Yat-sen Memorial Hall in Taipei.

The coinage of South Africa is a complex yet well-traveled field of study. There may be some mysteries here and there, some unknowns, or some controversies still left to parse, but students of the specialty are more or less confident about their understanding of the terrain.

The time for surprises had surely passed.

That is, until about 10 years ago, when a coin long thought not to exist was discovered and its authenticity confirmed.

A subtype of the South African George V sixpence was struck from 1925 through 1930 that features the denomination written out as "6PENCE" on the coin's reverse. This was abbreviated to "6ᵈ" in 1932, but otherwise the design—which features the national flower of South Africa, the king protea *(Protea cynaroides)*—continued to occupy the reverse until the end of the silver denomination's run in 1960.

Interestingly, there was a gap year in the 1925–1930 subtype. *Hern's Handbook on South African Coins & Patterns* listed "None Minted" for 1928, and Krause's *Standard Catalog of World Coins* didn't even list the date under the type's reference number.

But in 2009, a coin appeared at a September London Coins Limited auction (lot 571) that did indeed bear the year 1928 on its reverse. The piece, listed as "toned" and "GEF" (the British numismatic grade of "Good Extremely Fine"), sold for £4,200, or about US$5,480. Not only was it deemed authentic by experts in South Africa, but it was also found to consist of .925 fine sterling silver (a throwback to the original South African sixpence, featuring President Paul Kruger), whereas other coins of the type contained .800 silver. This and other aspects of the specimen (the mirrored low-relief fields, the squared rims, the quality of the strike, etc.) led numismatists to conclude that the startling new discovery had been struck as a presentation piece at the Royal Mint in London and was not intended for circulation.

The unique coin was then sent to Numismatic Guaranty Corporation (NGC) for certification and encapsulation, where it received a grade of SP-63. In August 2010, the specimen sold for US$155,250 (including buyer's premium) at a Heritage Auctions sale.

Australian medalist and sculptor Sir Edgar Bertram Mackennal (1863–1931) is responsible for the obverse. The artist was most famous for the coins and stamps he designed for George V, though his sculptures and monumental works are found throughout the Commonwealth and he earned a knighthood in 1921 in recognition of his service to the Crown. The prolific English artist George Kruger Gray (1880–1943) designed the reverse. Gray is notable for a number of coins he designed for countries around the world.

When it comes to elusive South African coins, the 1928 sixpence is in good company. One of the most famous rare coins from South Africa happens to be another unique coin from 1928: number 21 in our list, a bronze George V sovereign.

King George V, circa 1923.

The king protea flower, the national flower of South Africa, at the beginning of blooming.

SOUTH AFRICA 1928 STERLING SILVER SIXPENCE, SPECIMEN

A surprise discovery.

Obverse. A crowned bust portrait of King George V, facing left. The designer's initials B.M. are in the truncation of the neck. Clockwise from left along the top is the inscription GEORGIVS V REX IMPERATOR ("George V King Emperor"). Denticles surround the entire design along the rim.
Reverse. In the center, a king protea flower with stem and leaves. Six bundles of four rods each, bound with crosswise straps, surround the flower. The inscription, clockwise from left around the top: SOUTH AFRICA 1928 ZUID AFRIKA. The denomination 6PENCE is at the bottom, with lozenges to either side. The initials K.G. are under the right leaf of the flower. Denticles surround the entire design along the rim.

Composition	Weight	Diameter	Alignment	Edge
Sterling silver (.925 silver, .075 copper)	2.83 grams	19.35 mm	Medal	Reeded

Mintage	Mint	Collecting Difficulty	References
1 (known)	Royal Mint (London)	Extremely difficult	Hern-S165 ("None Minted"); KM-16.1 (unlisted date)

SWITZERLAND 1925-B GOLD 100 FRANCS, SPECIMEN

Beautiful Swiss artistry minted in gold.

Obverse. The head of Helvetia, the personification of Switzerland, with braided hair in back, facing left. There are edelweiss flowers on her left shoulder and mountains in the far background, representative of the Swiss Alps. HELVETIA, the Latin name for Switzerland, is inscribed clockwise at the top. The designer's signature, F. LANDRY, is found counterclockwise on the left side near the bottom. A ring of dots along the rim surrounds the design.

Reverse. A radiant Swiss cross with the denomination 100 FR below. The date, centered, is below the denomination: 1925. A floral arrangement wraps around the bottom of the design. The mintmark B is located below the flowers. Small beads encircle the design along the rim.

Composition	Weight	Diameter	Alignment	Edge
.900 gold	32.2581 grams	36 mm	Coin	Lettered†
Mintage	**Mint**		**Collecting Difficulty**	**References**
Unknown (exceedingly rare)	Banque Nationale Suisse (Bern)‡		Virtually impossible	Fr-502; HMZ-21193a; KM-39; Schön-34

† DOMINUS PROVIDEBIT ("The Lord Will Provide") ‡ Mintmark: B

Edelweiss in the Swiss Alps.

I n 1925, Switzerland set out to introduce a 100-franc gold coin denomination for circulation. In total 5,000 pieces were struck, but the Swiss National Bank was unable to distribute the entire mintage. As a result, some 1,200 pieces were melted down.

While not making a major impact in Swiss commerce, the large 36 mm coin is revered by collectors. Its design is the ultimate presentation of engraver Fritz Ulisse Landry's "Vreneli," which had been in use since 1897 on the Swiss 10- and 20-franc gold coins. While attractive on the smaller denominations, the design's detail and craftsmanship is amplified on the larger canvas.

When judged against the backdrop of other European issues of the Latin Monetary Union, Landry's design signals the coming change of coin and medal design that would overtake the continent in the ensuing decades. It's hard to imagine that Landry wasn't inspired by the same French movement that inspired the likes of American artists Augustus Saint Gaudens and James Earle Fraser.

In the design, Landry depicts the mythical Helvetia as a young woman set against the backdrop of the Swiss Alps. She is depicted in a natural style, and her facial features and hair are elegant and detailed. The design stands in sharp contrast to the figures cut by Swiss engraver Karl Friedrich Voigt, whose coin designs immediately preceded the Vreneli series.

For fans of the design, the size of the 100-franc coin offers the best opportunity to see every detail of Landry's work. But because of the issue's scarcity, only the most well-heeled collector of Swiss coins ever gets a chance at owning one of the few hundred surviving circulation strikes. Those that survive in Gem quality condition number even fewer and routinely sell for about US$30,000.

Adding to the complexity of the issue are essais and specimens. Essai pieces reported in Krause-Mishler and other references were struck in bronze and offer a more affordable option for collectors. If these coins were struck in gold, they would likely sell for prices in excess of those realized by circulation strike examples.

Beyond these pieces is a mysterious Specimen strike that turned up in a European auction in recent years. American dealer James Ricks purchased the coin and we featured it in a 2016 CoinWeek "Cool Coins!" segment, where Ricks talked about how he found the coin. Subsequently, the piece was offered for sale at Heritage Auctions, where it sold for US$58,750. In Heritage's lot description, the cataloger remarked that he had never seen a 1925-B struck in such a quality. The piece is truly remarkable and has the appearance of a Proof, complete with mirrored fields and frosty cameo devices. It was certified SP-64 by NGC.

A photochrome print of Lake Geneva in Switzerland.

It might surprise some to learn that colonial India wasn't ruled by the British Crown until 1858. For a century prior to the Government of India Act, the subcontinent was controlled by the British East India Company. The Rebellion of 1857 forced the crown to take direct control, and the East India Company slowly withered until it was officially dissolved in 1874. Queen Victoria (reigned 1837–1901) took on the title empress of India two years later, and the crown retained this position until India became an independent member of the Commonwealth in 1947 under King George VI.

Consequently, a new coinage was created for India. At first, the coins were still representative of the East India Company, but new designs featuring Victoria were released in 1862. Over the 90 years of British control, denominations included the pie, the pice (three pies), the anna (four pice), and the rupee (16 anna). Indian gold sovereigns were first struck in 1918. The mohur, a native gold coin worth about 15 rupees, was produced irregularly.

As with much of the world, the economic effects of World War I were felt across the empire. Great Britain stopped production of silver rupees in 1923 and did not resume it until 1938. It is sadly ironic that the beginning of a new world war helped the economy recover from the end of the last one.

This is where the numbers, whether dates or mintage figures, don't tell the real story.

According to Major Fred Pridmore's *Coins of the British Commonwealth of Nations*, a "small quantity" of 1938-dated 1-rupee coins was struck in Bombay (modern Mumbai) in late 1939, leaving the majority of 1938-dated production for 1940. This production stopped in mid- to late July 1940, and the Bombay Mint began producing rupees dated 1939.

There was, however, significant hoarding of the 1938 issue for its precious metal content, sparked by public fears of a bullion shortage as the British entered World War II. A similar scenario played out in 1918 that spurred the Pittman Act, which saw the United States melt 270 million silver dollars and sell the bullion to the British government for $1 per troy ounce so Great Britain could back payments for critical wartime goods and services from India.

Monetary reforms to prevent this widespread hoarding started taking shape in mid-1940, just as Bombay began striking 1939-dated rupees consisting of .917 fine silver. Presumably, the run of 1939 rupee coins was halted following a July 24 order to reduce the silver fineness to .500—not to mention the implementation of an ordinance that called for the production of rupee paper notes (a tough sell in a nation whose citizens value hard assets much more than fiat currency).

This means the production period for 1939-dated, .917-fine silver rupee coins may have been extremely short, possibly not more than one or two days. Did the Mint really strike almost 2.5 million 1939-B rupees in that amount of time?

Collectors know the coin is rare, and nothing is known to have occurred that could so dramatically reduce the issue's survival rate. So, what happened? Perhaps the answer lies in the Bombay Mint's then-practice of releasing "proposed" mintage figures instead of actual production numbers.

Numismatist Sanjay C. Gandhi estimated in 2012 that perhaps 7,500 to 10,000 of the 0.9710-fine 1939-B rupees, bearing a reeded edge, were struck and the survival rate may be as low as just two percent. As of 2017, the Professional Coin Grading Service (PCGS) states a population of seven reeded-edge pieces in various circulated and Uncirculated grades, whereas Numismatic Guaranty Corporation (NGC) reports 20.

Indian soldiers serve in France during World War I (photo circa 1914–1915).

INDIA 1939-B RUPEE

When the numbers lie.

Obverse. A crowned portrait of King George VI, facing left. Clockwise from left around the top is the inscription GEORGE VI KING EMPEROR. There is a small dot beneath the truncation of the neck. Alternating large and small decorative denticles surround along the raised rim.

Reverse. In the center is the inscription * ONE * * RUPEE * * INDIA * ~ 1939 ~ کی یپور یک (*Yek Rupiya* ["One Rupee"]) in five lines. There is a solid ring around the inscription. A saracen scroll of flowers representing the realms of the British Empire (from top to bottom): a closed lotus (India); a rose (England); a shamrock (Ireland); a three-flowered thistle (Scotland); and an open lotus (India). There is a small dot beneath the bottom lotus representing the Bombay Mint. Alternating large and small decorative denticles surround along the raised rim.

Composition	Weight	Diameter	Alignment	Edge
.917 silver	11.58 grams	30.5 mm	Medal	Reeded

Mintage	Mint	Collecting Difficulty	References
2,450,000 (unknown surviving)	Royal Mint (Bombay)†	Difficult	KM-555

† Mintmark: Dot

Additionally, Pridmore's research revealed that five specimens of a 0.500-fine security edge variety were also minted. Just one example is known today, according to NGC records.

To date, the record price paid for a 1939-B reeded-edge rupee coin goes to an NGC MS-62 specimen sold by Heritage Auctions in August 2014 for US$16,450 (including a 17.5 percent buyer's premium).

The coin was designed by English artist and Royal Mint engraver Percy Metcalfe, CVO (1895–1970), who produced royal portraits (usually crowned) and coin designs for Britain's foreign coinage. He is perhaps best known for the first coinage of the Irish Free State in 1928 (the famous "Barnyard Collection").

(Right) British East India Company painting of a company official, circa 1760–1764.

(Below) Indian lotus flowers in Madurai. The lotus was used to represent India as part of the British Empire.

The 1940-R Italian 100 lire is the rare final gold coin emission of the Italian Empire. Not released for circulation, the issue was reportedly made at the behest of Bank of Italy head Vincenzo Azzolini, who wished to see a 1940 emission to celebrate the 40th year of the reign of Victor Emmanuel III and Italy's victory in Ethiopia. Unfortunately, the Ethiopian situation grew more complex as the year dragged on, and only two examples of this coin are known to have escaped mint custody. Other examples reportedly exist, locked away in the vault of Italy's Ministry of Finance, but the exact disposition of this rumored cache is unknown.

The coin bears the same design as the 1937 issue of the same type. That coin marked a new (smaller) size and weight for the denomination and marked Emmanuel's shift in title from king to emperor.

Due to its rarity, auction records for the issue are few and far between. The most recent instance of a 1940-R 100 lire coming to market occurred in 2013, where the coin realized €187,200 (US$214,572) at a Roma Numismatics auction. It's possible that the other example sold in 2000, when the collection of Mario D'Incerti was offered for sale.

As an organization, the National Fascist Party (*Partito Nazionale Fascista*, or PNF) was founded in 1921 by Benito Mussolini but has its roots in the politics of nineteenth-century Italy and the nationalist reaction to World War I. The party came to power after the fascist March on Rome on October 28, 1922, which King Victor Emmanuel III allowed to happen without military opposition. In fact, the king made Mussolini prime minister the day after the march.

ITALY 1940-R GOLD 100 LIRE

Coniatura di due.

Obverse. The bald head of King Victor Emmanuel III, facing right. Starting beneath the truncation going clockwise is the inscription VITTORIO * EMANVELE * III * RE * E * IMP * (abbreviated Italian for Vittorio Emanuele III Re e Imperatore ["Victor Emmanuel III King and Emperor"]) in serif font. The designer's signature, G.ROMAGNOLI, runs counterclockwise in small letters in the gap between the beginning and end of the inscription at the bottom right. The rim is thick.

Reverse. A youthful *lictor* carries *fasces* on his right shoulder; in his left hand, the statue of Victory holds a laurel branch aloft. The lictor is wearing a tunic, cloak, and Roman sandals. Counterclockwise along the top half is the legend ITALIA. The lictor is standing on a thick bar; to either side are different representations of the date: the Arabic numerals 1940 (left) and the Roman numerals XVIII (right). The coat of arms of the Kingdom of Italy is in exergue. To the left of the shield is the word LIRE; to the right is the numeral "100." The rim is thick.

Composition	Weight	Diameter	Alignment	Edge
.900 gold	5.19 grams	20.7 mm	Coin	Reeded

Mintage	Mint	Collecting Difficulty	References
2 (per Krause; possibly more)	Istituto Polografica e Zecca dello Stato (Rome)†	Virtually impossible	KM-84

† Mintmark: R

Crown Prince Umberto.

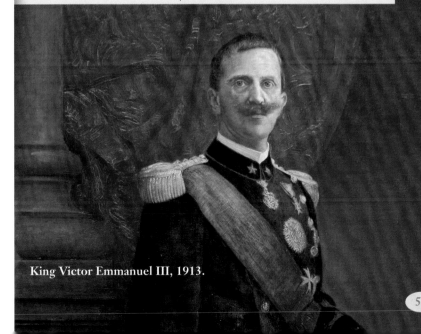

King Victor Emmanuel III, 1913.

Under the fascists, Italian coinage took on a new character. While the king maintained a prominent place on the obverse, the reverses of the Italian coins of this period were repurposed to promote the militaristic and cultural ambitions of the new government. This was done by co-opting historic symbols and placing them into a contemporary political context.

Take for instance the reverse of the present type, the gold 100 lire. On the reverse of this coin is the full-bodied depiction of a Roman lictor, who in ancient Rome served as a bodyguard of sorts to those Roman politicians who possessed a special political authority known as *imperium,* or the power to command the Roman army. Depending on the rank of their office, a Roman politician could have been eligible to be accompanied by anywhere from one to 12 or even 24 lictors. Often members of the plebeian class or centurions in the military, lictors wore a tunic of a less refined variety than the politicians they accompanied.

The most noticeable job of the lictor was to carry the *fasces,* a bundle of wooden rods bound with leather straps and often surrounding an axe. The fasces was a prop representing the authority of government as derived from the unity of the people; each stick or rod by itself could be broken, but together they could not (or so the story goes). On a literal level, the fasces represented the power of the state over the life and death of its subjects. For this reason, plus its roots in classical antiquity, the Fascist Party of Italy adopted the fasces as a primary symbol.

The March on Rome, 1922.

At a crossroads between east and west, Polish history is marked by frequent invasions. Over the centuries, the territory of what we know as modern Poland has changed and shifted many times, with several countries laying claim to great swaths of the country or exerting dominance over the entire Polish nation outright.

During World War I, different parts of Poland had been controlled by Germany, Russia, and the Austro-Hungarian Empire. With the Allied victory in 1918 and the Treaty of Versailles with Germany in 1919, the newly independent Second Polish Republic was born. A preliminary constitution, written in 1919 and amended in 1920, established the basic parliamentary architecture of the state. Then, in March 1921, the republic adopted what came to be known as the "March Constitution." Incorporating democratic influences from the Third French Republic (and perhaps inspired by the "Fourteen Points" of American President Woodrow Wilson), it attempted to produce a more egalitarian Polish society by eliminating royal titles, outlawing discrimination (both religious and racial), and elevating the role of Parliament.

While the March Constitution was celebrated for its idealism (as on the 5-złotych silver commemorative coin of 1925 and the gold patterns discussed here), ultimately it did not prove to be sturdy enough to resist the 1926 coup that brought dictator Józef Piłsudski—one of the heroes of the Second Polish Republic—to power.

The March Constitution was replaced by the April Constitution of 1935, which empowered the president of Poland above all other government authorities. The country lost its independence once more when Nazi Germany invaded in 1939, marking the official beginning of World War II and ending the Second Republic.

The era of the Second Republic is especially important for numismatists because the Warsaw Mint was reactivated in April 1924, almost 60 years after it had been shut down by the Russians. Shortly over a month later, Treasury Minister (and Prime Minister) Władysław Grabski—who had founded the Bank of Poland in 1920 and reintroduced the gold złoty as the national currency in 1924 to combat post-war hyperinflation—introduced the Second Republic's first coin patterns in a special decree.

The design of the 5-złoty gold pattern was created by Polish sculptor and medalist Stanisław Roman Lewandowski (1859–1940). Lewandowski began his career studying at the Cracow School of Fine Arts and the Vienna Academy, and over time he instructed other artists in sculpture and published art criticism. His style changed over the years, going from realistic portraiture to symbolism and secessionism by the turn of the twentieth century.

The obverse features Polonia, the female personification of Poland, seated in a throne and elaborately dressed. This is quite a statement of pride and independence, as the depiction of Polonia historically reflects the status of the Polish nation. A common motif during times of occupation was to depict her in chains or in all black, as if in mourning.

The heraldic Polish eagle on the reverse goes back possibly to the first king of Poland, Boleslaw I (ruled 1025), with a precursor of the eagle appearing on one of his silver denarii. And while not quite as old, the use of the word "złoty" (meaning "golden") as a monetary unit goes back to the Middle Ages, when it was applied to all (foreign) gold coins circulating in Polish realms.

According to numismatist Janusz Parchimowicz, only four of the gold patterns were struck. Of those four, there are three varieties: arrow, no arrow, and arrow with 81 pearls. Ponterio sold an 81-pearl variety specimen that had belonged to King Farouk of Egypt and was part of the Sid and Alicia Belzberg Collection in April 2009 at the Chicago International Coin Fair. The specimen is reputedly the only one in private hands.

POLAND 1925 GOLD 5 ZLOTYCH

A golden opportunity for a newly independent nation.

Obverse. In the center is the seated Polonia. Her left arm points to KONSTYTUCIA ("Constitution"), held by a page boy on the right. Polonia's right arm rests on a shield featuring the Polish eagle. Below the shield is a scythe and a bushel of wheat. In exergue is the denomination PIĘĆ 5 ZŁOTYCH 5. A ring of connected pearls is along the rim.

Reverse. In the center is the Polish eagle crowned and displayed (wings and talons spread). Clockwise from left is the inscription RZECZPOSPOLITA POLSKA ("Polish Republic") in large letters. Counterclockwise beneath the eagle is the date 1925. One variety of the pattern (Y-17.3a) features a thin, almost stick-figure arrow monogram with a perpendicular crossbar between the date and the "A" in "POLSKA," but no mintmark; this variety is similar to the circulating silver 5 złoty coin (Y-17.3). A second variety of the gold pattern (Y-17.4) lacks the monogram but features the mintmark of the Warsaw Mint.

Composition	Weight	Diameter	Alignment	Edge
.900 gold	43.33 grams	37 mm	Medal	Lettered†
Mintage	**Mint**		**Collecting Difficulty**	**References**
4 (per Parchimowicz)	Warsaw		Extremely difficult	Y–17.3a, 17.4

† SALUS REIPUBLICAE SUPREMA LEX ("The Strength of the Republic the Supreme Law")

Polish stateman Józef Klemens Piłsudski.

JAPAN 1903 MEIJI GOLD 20 YEN

An exceedingly rare relic of the Meiji Restoration.

Artist's rendering of the 1903 20 yen.

Obverse. Wrapping clockwise from the left, around an eight-foil shape with a sunburst and rays in the center, is the inscription * 大日本 * 明 治 四十四年 * 圓十二 * (* Dai Nihon * Meiji Shi Jū Shi Nen * 20 en * ["Great Japan, Meiji Year 44, 20 Yen"]). Beaded denticles circle the inside of the rim.

Reverse. In the center of the design, the denomination 二十 圓 ("20 Yen") is surrounded by an open wreath. The chrysanthemum imperial seal is at the top. Beaded denticles circle the inside of the rim.

Composition	Weight	Diameter	Alignment	Edge
.900 gold	16.666 grams	28.78 mm	Medal	Reeded

Mintage	Mint	Collecting Difficulty	References
Unknown	Japan Mint (Osaka)	Virtually impossible	JNDA-01-6; Y-34

The 20-yen gold coin of the type that bore the rare 1903 issue first entered production in 1897. Its release marked a shrinking of the 20-yen denomination, which since the launch of decimal coinage had weighed 33.333 grams. The new tenor of 16.666 grams, authorized by the Coinage Act of Meiji 30, represented a significant decline in value for the Japanese yen.

After an initial mintage of 1,861,000 pieces, production of the new 20-yen coin ceased and would not resume in earnest until 1904, when the Osaka Mint struck 2,759,470. A year before, Japan struck an indeterminate number of one of its great twentieth-century rarities, the 1903 (Meiji 36) 20 yen.

So rare was the 1903 issue that Dr. Norman Jacobs and Dr. Cornelius Vermeule provide only the following mention in their landmark 1953 English language reference *Japanese Coinage*: "A coin inscribed Meiji 36 (1903) in Proof condition exists. It was probably minted for exhibition purposes only."

One example, described as Uncirculated and Choice, sold at the January 1974 Stack's sale of the Winter Collection of United States ancient and foreign coins (lot 390), where it brought $1,950, an astonishing sum considering the coin carried a presale estimate of $3,000.

While certified populations and American auction records are not necessarily true indications of a coin's rarity, know this: to date, not one single example of the 1903 20 yen has been certified by either PCGS or NGC. Given that a specimen in Choice or Gem Uncirculated could bring hundreds of thousands of dollars at auction, this absence speaks volumes.

THE MEIJI RESTORATION

When Mutsohito (better known as Emperor Meiji), the 15-year-old son of Emperor Kōmei, ascended to the throne on February 3, 1867, there was little reason to expect the young student of poetry and literature would end his reign as one of the most consequential rulers in modern Asian history.

But under his rule, Japanese society was transformed.

Japan's antiquated feudal system, which had been in decline for more than a century under the military rule of the Tokugawa shogunate, was replaced with a new imperial system that provided ruling authority to the emperor but also allowed for the creation of a bicameral legislature and an independent judiciary.

While participation in elected offices and voting was limited to Japan's elite classes, in many respects the Meiji reformation mirrored European best practices.

It placed priority on education, infrastructure, industry, militarization, and the expansion of trade and international influence, especially among its Asian competitors. With a focus on education and technology, Japan's workforce and industry modernized. This increased the country's regional power but also drew the attention of would-be rivals China and Russia. Both tested Japanese military power and were stung by humiliating defeats.

U.S. president Theodore Roosevelt, himself an imperialist, saw in the resurgent Japanese Empire much to admire, telling a group of constituents gathered at the San Francisco Mechanics' Pavilion in May 1903 that "Japan, shaking off the lethargy of centuries, has taken her rank among the civilized, modern powers."

Emperor Meiji of Japan.

King George VI died on February 6, 1952, following a period of declining health. He had led Great Britain through World War II and through the transition from empire to commonwealth. Upon George's death, his daughter Elizabeth ascended to the throne and became queen, with her coronation being held more than a year later on June 2, 1953.

One of the very last coins to depict King George VI from his reign is the 1952 half crown. English medalist Thomas Humphrey Paget, OBE (1893–1974), designed the bareheaded royal portrait of George VI (having also designed the portrait of Edward VIII used on his pattern coinage; see number 26 on this list). The prolific English artist George Kruger Gray (1880–1943) designed the reverse. Gray is notable for a number of coins he designed for countries around the world.

For the remainder of 1952, Paget's George VI portrait would continue to appear on all official British coins; Queen Elizabeth II first appears on 1953-dated coins (see number 9). Earlier in his reign, in 1947, the composition of the traditionally silver denomination (in existence since for over 400 years) was changed to a copper-nickel alloy.

The production of several British coins had temporarily been suspended throughout the twentieth century, most often due to an abundance of a given denomination in circulation. This was the case, for example, with Great Britain's penny from 1923 through 1925, 1933, and throughout much of the 1950s.

But even though there were plenty of half crowns to go around (28,273,000 circulation strikes were minted in 1949, another 28,336,000 in 1950, and 9,004,000 in 1951), this wasn't necessarily why the Royal Mint curtailed its mintage in 1952.

The reason the Mint suspended production of the nickel-bearing half crown was to save the critical metal for the Korean War effort. This is not unlike the situation in Canada, where Royal Canadian Mint officials substituted the metal in the nation's 5-cent coin for a chromium-and-nickel-plated steel composition. But instead of replacing the cupro-nickel composition of the British half crown with an alternative metal, the British Royal Mint ceased circulation-strike production altogether in 1952.

Only one VIP Proof specimen was produced, and this piece currently resides in the Royal Mint Collection. The 1952 half crown specimen was long known as unique until 1967, when a suspected second issue turned up in pocket change.

Mint employee Graham Dyer was among the experts who inspected the circulated 1952 half crown in 1967. However, busy Mint officials had little time to subject the coin to thorough investigation and, while proclaiming the coin genuine, could not determine its origin. Officials suspected it was a die trial that had mistakenly escaped the Mint.

In 2003, Dyer inspected the coin again following a discussion about the 1952 half crown at a numismatic society event. He made a lengthy in-hand evaluation and once again, some 35 years after his initial inspection, determined it genuine.

Among the diagnostics Dyer considered was the coin's composition, which was confirmed by X-ray fluorescence spectrometry to be 75 percent copper and 25 percent nickel. The coin's weight of 14.118 grams is within standard tolerance, and the reeding matches standard issue specifications for 1949–1951 half crowns. Furthermore, Dyer confirmed that the shape of the date and other aspects of the design matched the appearance of those same elements on the 1952 half crown contained in the Royal Mint collection, and that no suspicious surface markings existed to suggest the coin was altered.

Numismatic Guaranty Corporation (NGC) and Krause's *Standard Catalog of World Coins* estimate that the circulated 1952 half crown is worth around US$80,000; the Proof, meanwhile, is valued at $100,000.

GREAT BRITAIN 1952 KING GEORGE VI HALF CROWN

Korean War brings metal scarcity for Royal Mint.

Obverse. The center is a bare portrait of King George VI, facing left. Clockwise from left, the inscription: GEORGIVS VI D: G: BR: OMN: REX (abbreviated Latin for *GEORGIUS VI DEI GRATIA BRITANNIARUM OMNIUM REX* ["George VI, By the Grace of God, King of All the Britons"]). The designer's initials H.P. are beneath the neck truncation. Denticles surround along the rim.

Reverse. Hanging from a ribbon attached to a ring is a shield with concave vertical sides featuring the royal coat of arms. The first and fourth quadrants, with three lions passant guardant on a field, represent the Kingdom of England. the second quadrant, with a lion rampant, represents Scotland. The third quadrant features an Irish harp. There are crowned double-G monograms to either side. Clockwise around the top half from the left is the inscription * FID * * DEF * (abbreviated Latin for *FIDEI DEFENSOR* ["Defender of the Faith"]). Counterclockwise along the bottom is the inscription HALF CROWN 1952. Denticles surround along the rim.

Composition	Weight	Diameter	Alignment	Edge
Copper-nickel	14.138 grams	32.3 mm	Medal	Reeded
Mintage	**Mint**		**Collecting Difficulty**	**References**
2 (estimated)	Royal Mint (London)		Virtually impossible	KM-879

Sandringham House, Norfolk, where King George VI died.

IRELAND 1938 SILVER HALF CROWN PATTERN

New name, new currency.

A later-date half crown showing the style of the 1938 pattern.

Obverse. A Celtic harp in the center. The inscription ÉIRE ("Ireland") on the left and date 1938 on the right. Denticles or beading surround along the rim.

Reverse. An Irish sport horse stands on a thick line, facing left. The clockwise denomination LEATH ("Half") is to the left of the horse and CHORÓIN ("Crown") above. The denomination "2ˢ6ᵈ" is in exergue. Denticles or beading surround along the rim.

Composition	Weight	Diameter	Alignment	Edge
.750 silver, .250 copper	14.138 grams	32.3 mm	Medal	Reeded

Mintage	Mint	Collecting Difficulty	References
1 (estimated)	Royal Mint (London)	Impossible	KM-Pn2

On December 6, 1921, the Irish Free State was established following a five-year struggle for independence from Great Britain. By 1926, the new state established a committee to create a new coinage system for Ireland. While the sterling pound system was established as the nation's currency standard, members of the committee, headed by Irish poet William Butler Yeats, were tasked to choose designs for Ireland's coins.

The committee decided on the Irish harp as the national symbol to be depicted on the obverse of the coins (as had been the case since the 1530s) and chose Ireland's agricultural animals—known collectively as the "Barnyard Collection"—as subjects for the reverses. They also established a contest to design the new coins, eventually selecting English artist and sculptor Percy Metcalfe for the role.

The first modern coins of an independent Ireland were released in 1928 and included the farthing, the half penny, the penny, the threepence, the sixpence, the shilling, the florin, and the half crown.

Nine years later, the 1937 constitution renamed the country Ireland and replaced the government agreement which created the Irish Free State. Inscriptions on Irish coins subsequently reflected this constitutional change, and beginning in 1939, the legend SAORSTAT EIREANN (IRISH FREE STATE) was replaced with the simple inscription EIRE.

Following the production of patterns in 1938, the newly modified Irish coinage entered circulation in 1939.

The patterns of 1938 addressed another key issue aside from the country's name: the weakened appearance of the obverse harp due to metal flow during striking, particularly on the penny and half crown. Metcalfe sharpened the harp design on all the Irish denominations in an attempt to correct the issue. Patterns reflecting the new changes were made in extremely limited numbers, with just two 1938 pennies and only one 1938 half crown known to exist.

Metcalfe presented examples of the redesigned penny and half crown to the Department of Finance in November 1938. They would not resurface until their rediscovery in a vault over six decades later. On July 10, 2000, finance officials presented the coins to the National Museum of Ireland.

The sole 1938 half crown securely resides at the National Museum of Ireland, and while it is presently considered unique by numismatic standards, it's possible that another specimen (or perhaps several more) could someday reappear. For this reason, Irish numismatic researcher John Stafford-Langan ascribed a catalog price to the 1938 half crown pattern, determining one to potentially sell for €40,000 (approximately US$45,000).

One 1938 penny wound up in private hands years earlier and was graded by Numismatic Guaranty Corporation (NGC) as a Brown SP-66, bearing greater details and surface quality than circulation strikes. This great national rarity became arguably the most challenging of all pre-decimal Irish coins struck between 1928 and 1970 for collectors to acquire. More could potentially be discovered, and they are presently valued at between $15,000 and $40,000. Beware of fakes with altered dates.

(Right) William Butler Yeats, circa 1933.

(Left) National Museum of Ireland in Dublin.

Czar Nicholas II came to power in 1894, at the age of 26. His father Alexander III had been an extremely conservative autocrat, and with his death came some hope among the poor peasantry and working classes that the new czar might implement longed-for land and governmental reforms. However, Nicholas embraced the authoritarian attitudes of his father and refused to change anything about the imperial system. He would eventually pay for this choice.

Over the years of his reign, the new czar earned the nickname "Nicholas the Bloody" from his political adversaries in Russia. This was due to his role, actual or perceived, in the deaths of millions of Russians due to war and suppressed rebellion. In February 1904, the Russo-Japanese War began; Nicholas was rightly blamed for this, as well as for Russia's shocking defeat by Japanese imperial forces just one year later.

In 1903, the first of multiple attacks on the Jewish community of Kishinev in Bessarabia (located in a portion of modern-day Moldova and Ukraine) was instigated with government funds. Nicholas II viewed such anti-Semitic violence as politically useful, though publicly he disavowed the terror.

In 1905, a worker's march on the Winter Palace in St. Petersburg to petition for redress of grievances turned into the massacre known as "Bloody Sunday," as soldiers opened fire on the crowds (a sequence dramatized in Sergei Eisenstein's magnificent 1925 film *Battleship Potemkin*). This was the spark that set off the Revolution of 1905, which forced the czar to invest some of his power in the Duma, or legislative assembly.

Blind to the inevitability of change, as historical figures often are, Nicholas II stumbled along, insisting in his sole authority while being peculiarly cut off from what was really going on around him in Russian society. It was also around this time that the czar welcomed the controversial Rasputin into his household, further scandalizing the Russian people and caring not a whit.

Then came June 28, 1914. Serbian assassin Gavrilo Princip shot Archduke Franz Ferdinand of Austria-Hungary as the archduke's carriage traveled the streets of Sarajevo. The pre-existing tangle of alliances led to a cascade of declarations of war, until Russia found itself on the side of France and the United Kingdom in World War I. Russia suffered horribly, and political unrest—answered with extreme force—continued during wartime. The situation was such that even the czar's soldiers and generals began to desert him.

Nicholas II, "Emperor and Autocrat of All the Russias," abdicated in March 1917. The new government quickly left the war, conceding large amounts of territory for peace. Conditions for Nicholas and the Romanovs slowly deteriorated, until the rise of Vladimir Lenin and the Bolsheviks in October virtually ensured the royal family would meet a bad end.

RUSSIA 1904 5 KOPEKS

"One of the great rarities of twentieth-century Russian numismatics."

Obverse. In the center is a double-headed imperial eagle and the lesser coat of arms of the Russian Empire (see inset number 12 for a more complete description). The Cyrillic initials A and P are on either side of the eagle's talons, which transliterate to AR. Stylized tail feathers are at the bottom. A ring of small denticles surrounds along the relatively thick rim.

Reverse. The denomination 5 КОПѢЕКЪ ("Five Kopeks"), with six-pointed stars flanking the numeral 5 and an imperial crown above. The date 1904 is beneath a decorative element (spear points with four dots surrounding a lozenge separating them). Beneath the date is the mintmark С.П.Б. (St. Petersburg Mint). The design is surrounded by a wreath of laurel (left) and oak (right), tied together with a ribbon at the bottom. Denticles encircle the entire design.

Composition	Weight	Diameter	Alignment	Edge
.500 silver	0.8998 grams	15 mm	Medal	Reeded

Mintage	Mint	Collecting Difficulty	References
9 (per Krause); 10 (per HA.com); 20 (per Kosinski)	St. Petersburg Mint†	Extremely difficult	Bitkin-181; KM-Y59a.1

† Mintmark: С.П.Б.

Bloody Sunday, 1905.

St. Petersburg Mint.

Struck under the authority of St. Petersburg Mint official Alexander Redko (A.R.), who was in charge from 1901 through 1905, the 1904 5-kopek silver coin betrays no hint of the chaos or unrest of the times. In the first half of the twentieth century, it seems that world mints were freer to strike or not strike new coinage each year as they deemed necessary for circulation. This would have been such a year for the precious metal 5 kopeks, with far less than 100 pieces produced in 1904.

Russian coin expert Vladimir Bitkin estimates that around 20 pieces were minted. Krause, however, lowers that to nine, and Heritage Auctions isn't much different at 10. To complicate the matter, Krause says mintages for Russian imperial coins struck after 1885 are for fiscal years, and true rarity may not be represented. Krause gives estimated values of US$9,000 for VF(20) and $37,500 for XF(40); numismatist Tomasz Kosinski in his *Coins of Europe* catalog offers values of $5,000 and $20,000 for the same grades[1].

An NGC PR-62 specimen—the only example certified by either NGC or PCGS, regardless of grade—sold as lot 3037 at the January 5, 2015, NYINC World Coins & Ancient Coins Signature Auction for US$76,375 (including a 17.5 percent buyer's premium). Heritage noted that it could not find any auction records for the issue having taken place between the 2015 sale and the 2002 sale of the Antonin Prokop Collection conducted by Russian dealer Aurea Numismatika (lot 383, a worn circulated example), calling it "[u]ndoubtedly, one of the great rarities of twentieth-century Russian numismatics."

Monument to the Revolution of 1905.

D
r. Sun Yat-sen (孫逸仙, *Sūn Yìxiān*, or 孫中山, *Sūn Zhōngshān*; 1866–1925) was a revolutionary reformer and the first president of the fledgling Republic of China. As such, he is a revered figure both in Taiwan and the People's Republic of China.

In 1904, Sun had developed and refined his Three Principles of nationalism, modernism, and welfare. The next year saw the formation of the Tongmenghui (同盟會, *Tóngménghuì* ["The United League"]) in Tokyo from among fellow revolutionary Chinese students—a secret society that would eventually give way to the nationalist Kuomintang (國民黨, *Guómíndǎng*).

The Tongmenghui began a series of uprisings in China over the next decade, all of which failed. While Sun was in the United States, the Tongmenghui-led 1911 uprising in Wuchang (武昌, *Wǔchāng*) against Yuan Shikai (袁世凱, *Yuán Shìkǎi*) was successful. Sun returned to China to help lead what became the Xinhai Revolution (辛亥革命, *Xīnhài Gémìng*) that overthrew the Qing dynasty, and he was elected the provisional president of the new republic at a meeting of provincial revolutionaries.

Of course, the story didn't quite end there; see number 28, the 1929 Sun Yat-sen Flag & Globe Dollar Silver Pattern, for more information about Sun's life and work.

The first dollar featuring the profile of Sun Yat-sen minted by the nascent republic actually was struck as a gold presentation piece, though the same design was used on silver coins. This issue commemorates the first anniversary of the founding of the republic in 1911, yet there is no date given on the coin. There are two known types of the silver dollar; the coin in this list has stars low on the reverse, which associates it with the "Low Star" variety (as opposed to the "High Star").

On the obverse, Dr. Sun is wearing a "Sun Yat-sen jacket" (or *Zhōngshān fú*), a mode of dress that he made famous. The new style of clothing Sun introduced to the republic was a combination of Western, Meiji Japanese, and Chinese military influences.

As seen on the reverse, the numeral 壹 is used in financial and official records for the number one (*yī*) to avoid possible confusion with other Chinese numerals. The character 圓 is an alternative form of the now-more-common symbol for yuan, 元.

Sotheby's sold a specimen to an unnamed English collector in London in May 1951. In the era of third-party grading, only one example has been certified by either NGC or PCGS. The most recent auction record on Heritage Auctions' website is from August 8, 2014, at the ANA World & Ancient Coins Platinum Night Auction; this specimen is graded NGC MS-64 and pedigreed to the Liu/Ultima Collection. It sold for US$94,000 (including a 17.5 percent buyer's premium). The Krause *Standard Catalog of World Coins: 1901–2000* gives the coin an estimated market value of $20,000, regardless of condition.

CHINA 1912 GOLD DOLLAR

Celebrating the creation of a Chinese Republic.

Obverse. Within a solid circle and outer ring of beads, Sun Yat-sen in his eponymous jacket in the center, facing left. Reading from right to left at top is the inscription 中華民國 (*Zhōnghuá Mínguó* ["Republic of China"]). Right to left at bottom: 開國紀念幣 (*Kāiguó Jìniàn Bì* ["Founding Commemorative Coin"]). There are ornate five-petaled rosettes with stems, one per side. Denticles surround along the rim.

Reverse. In the center, within a solid circle and outer ring of beads, are the Chinese characters 壹圓 (*Yī Yuán* ["One Dollar"]). The denomination is cradled by a wreath of grain, tied with a ribbon in a bow at the bottom. Clockwise around the top half, the English inscription: THE REPUBLIC OF CHINA in serif font. Counterclockwise along bottom, the denomination in English: ONE DOLLAR. Two five-pointed stars, with a single dot or bead in each center, separate the two inscriptions, one on each side. The stars are low on the reverse. Denticles surround along the rim.

Composition	Weight	Diameter	Alignment	Edge
Gold		39.5 mm	Medal	Reeded
Mintage	**Mint**		**Collecting Difficulty**	**References**
Unknown	Tientsin Mint		Virtually impossible	K-1550; KM-Pn9; L&M-1086

Sun Yat-sen with members of the Singapore branch of Tongmenghui.

Bronze statue of Sun Yat-Sen in the Memorial Hall in Taipei, Taiwan.

SOUTH AFRICA 1902 VELD POND

A crude but necessary siege coin.

Obverse. In the center are ornate but crudely executed initials and the date. Above is the inscription ZAR (Zuid-Afrikaansche Republic) And below is 1902. The rim is crude.

Reverse. In the center, the denomination is ornate but crudely executed, written as EEN POND (one pound). The rim is crude.

Composition	Weight	Diameter	Alignment	Edge
Gold	8.12 grams	22.8 mm	Coin	Reeded
Mintage	**Mint**		**Collecting Difficulty**	**References**
986 (U.S. sources); 530 (South African sources)	Pilgrim's Rest Mint		Extremely difficult	KM-11; Hern-Z54

One of South Africa's most famous coins, the 1902 veld pond (from the Dutch: "field pound") is a siege coin struck on the very gold that was the source of a three-decade struggle for territorial control, pitting the descendants of the region's first European settlers, the Dutch, against a much more powerful British army.

On paper, the Boers had little to no chance to prevail against the expansionist wishes of the British Empire. The Boer population consisted mostly of farmers and frontiersmen, who had escaped the rule of the Dutch East India Company by trekking out into the South African frontier. There, they established two independent states: the Orange Free State and the South African Republic.

Trade and governance were hard for these landlocked territories, and the Boers were faced with bankruptcy until the discovery of diamonds and gold in the 1870s. The Boers' sudden change in fortunes did not go unnoticed. Eventually, the British wanted in on the action and the Boers, intimidated by Zulu uprisings, were forced to accept annexation.

In the closing months of the struggle, with the Boers aware they were on the losing side, the need for money to buy provisions was an acute problem. Cut off from the rest of the world, trade was only possible with agreeable tribes. The problem, of course, was age-old: money.

South Africa's oldest gold mines were under the control of General Benjamin Viljoen at Pilgrim's Rest. Dormant though still operational, the mines sprang back to life in 1901. Viljoen would not preside over the production of the coinage, as he was captured on January 25, 1902, but his replacement, General Christiaan Hendrick Muller, sought and received permission to mint a coinage from the modest amount of gold recovered from the mines (approximately US$73,200 worth in today's dollars).

The resulting coins were crudely struck and bear only the most necessary of inscriptions: ZAR 1902 on the obverse and EEN POND on the reverse. Nevertheless, it is remarkable for the fact that despite using crude tools and alluvial gold, the coins had a higher gold value than the British sovereign.

The total mintage of this issue is somewhat in dispute. In American catalogs, the number 986 is widely agreed upon; however, sources that we have read, including scholarly ones from South Africa, put the actual mintage at 530 pieces. That number is just a starting point, as the total number of survivors is a small fraction of that.

In the numismatic marketplace, the appearance of the veld pond occurs with some regularity, with major auction houses enjoying the opportunity to offer one or two a year. Typically, these examples are impaired in some way. Some have been removed from jewelry, others are damaged due to improper care. Those that are worthy of a numerical grade will often appear in lightly circulated condition. These pieces sell for about US$13,000 to $15,000 each, depending on eye appeal. Choice to Gem Uncirculated examples are extremely scarce and command much higher prices. In 2017, Heritage Auctions sold a Gem example graded MS-65 by NGC for $39,950. The finest example to appear at auction (NGC MS-66) sold in 2008 for $92,000.

Black, Chinese, and white laborers in a gold mine in South Africa (late 1800s or early 1900s)

For the people of Ireland, independence was hard fought and a long time coming.

From 1919 until 1921, the Irish Republican Army fought a guerrilla war against the British. The cessation of violence in this period only occurred after the signing of the controversial Anglo-Irish Treaty, which established the Irish Free State *(Saorstát Éireann)* as a self-governing dominion of the British Empire. The treaty also called for the withdrawal of British troops and allowed Northern Ireland to opt out of the newly established state within one month of ratification, which it did.

The treaty may have promised the Irish a degree of autonomy, but not all who fought for the cause approved of the agreement. One of the notable dissenters was President of the Republic Éamon de Valera (1882–1975), who was incensed that Irish negotiator Michael Collins did not confer with him or the Irish Parliament (the *Dáil Éireann*) before signing the treaty. While the Irish Parliament narrowly approved the measure by a vote of 64 to 57, de Valera resigned from his post and began a campaign of recruitment and instigation.

Joined by a cadre of Irish Republican Army officers who also opposed the treaty, the group took up arms against their fellow Irish, many of whom had fought beside them just a few years before in the effort to gain independence.

The Irish Civil War turned out to be more brutal and personal than the war for independence. Even after the end of hostilities, personal animosity between factions was entrenched in Irish politics for generations.

The coins of the Irish Free State were authorized by the Coinage Act of 1926. The act called for the production of silver, nickel, and bronze coins in specific denominations and sizes, but it left the issue of design to Finance Minister Ernest Blythe. Blythe opened the selection process of the new coins to a select committee of leading Irish academics, as well as world-renowned poet-turned-senator William Butler Yeats.

Eamon de Valera, between 1918 and 1921.

IRELAND 1938 PENNY PATTERN

Everyday animals immortalized on coinage.

Obverse. A Celtic harp in the center. The inscription ÉIRE ("Ireland") is on the left and the date 1938 on the right. Denticles or beading surround along the rim.

Reverse. A stylized hen, facing left, stands on a thick line with its right foot off the ground. Five chicks follow it. In exergue is the denomination PINGIN ("Penny") in Gaelic lettering. At the top is the denomination 1^d. Denticles or beading surround along the rim.

Composition	Weight	Diameter	Alignment	Edge
Bronze (.955 copper, .030 tin, .015 zinc)	9.45 grams	30.9 mm	Medal	Reeded

Mintage	Mint	Collecting Difficulty	References
2 (estimated)	Royal Mint (London)	Virtually impossible	KM-Pn1

National Army troops lined up for a roll call during the Irish Civil War, circa 1922.

Yeats sought designs that could be appreciated by the free Irish, designs that represented Ireland and could inspire artists and children. He proposed a series based on Irish animals, from the working horse to the salmon, a fish steeped in Irish lore. After an international competition, the committee chose the designs of English artist Percy Metcalfe—a decision that was not without considerable controversy, as the idea of coins featuring barnyard animals designed by an Englishman and struck in England was a bit much for critics of the Irish Free State government.

Some even argued that the coins were pagan in nature, although it has been said that each of the animals is mentioned in relevant Biblical verses. The horse, the pig, the rabbit, and the fish are all symbols from Christian tradition. So, too, is the Irish harp, which traces its origins to the harp of David.

Despite these objections, the coins of the Free Irish State went into production and remained so until a new constitution, establishing the Irish Republic, was drafted in 1937.

In terms of coinage released into circulation, 1938 was a dormant year. Behind the scenes, designer Percy Metcalfe worked on improving the designs so they would strike up better. The change in government led to a change in the legend of Irish coins. Saorstát Éireann, which identified the coins as being struck by the Irish Free State, was changed to Éire. Metcalfe

A group of Irish-American women tearing up a British flag, as they protest against United States support of the English against the Irish Independence. Washington, D.C., June 3, 1920.

also moved the location of the date to the right side of the coin. To that end, some test strikes were produced; to our knowledge, only three coins survive.

All three of the test-strike coins or patterns—an Irish half-crown and two Irish pennies—bore the new legend and the date 1938. Documentation exists tracing possession of the half-crown and one of the pennies to Metcalfe. These coins were surrendered to the Department of Finance in November 1938, where they remained until they were transferred to the National Museum of Ireland in 2000. The second 1938 penny somehow made it into the wild and remains the only 1938-dated Irish coin in private hands.

With just one example of the issue available to collectors, the 1938 Irish penny is the rarest collectible Irish coin of the modern period. The coin circumnavigated the globe before ending up in the collection of its current owner. Previously, it was owned by an Australian collector. Then in 2010, it was offered by a Spink of London sale, where the piece (then in a PCGS MS-65 BN holder) brought £22,000 (US$34,100).

In 2012, the Numismatic Guaranty Corporation (NGC) announced that the coin had been submitted to its location for grading. In a company press release, NGC's experts noted that great care had been taken in its production due to the high-quality nature of the strike. They considered the coin a Specimen strike and awarded it the grade SP-66 BN.

Due to the simplicity and beauty of their designs, modern Irish coins are collected abroad as well as in their homeland. Many of Metcalfe's designs remained in use up until 2002, when Ireland issued its first euro coins. As our countdown of the "Greatest Modern World Coins" continues, you will see that the 1938 penny is not the only Irish coin that captures our undivided attention.

Anglo-Irish treaty.

METCALFE IRISH PENNY

The Metcalfe Irish penny was struck from 1928 to 1968. The coin was demonetized on February 18, 1971, as Ireland transitioned to decimal coinage. The new, smaller penny featured a Celtic bird motif designed by Gabriel Hayes. Hayes' design remained in circulation until Ireland adopted the euro in 2002.

This is yet another example of a Chinese silver coin design struck in gold as a presentation piece.

As the tides changed in China during the late nineteenth and early twentieth centuries, Yuan Shikai (袁世凱, *Yuán Shìkǎi*) changed with them. After serving in an advisory role to the Korean government and in the military during the First Sino-Japanese War (1894–1895), Yuan was appointed commander of the first New Army, tasked with modernizing Chinese military forces.

After aligning with Empress Dowager Cixi and conservative elements within the Qing dynasty, Yuan was made governor of Shandong and brutally suppressed the Boxer Rebellion (1899–1901) within his province.

His star continued to rise in China's government until the death of the Empress Dowager and the Guangxu Emperor in 1908, after which Yuan was effectively exiled. With the support of much of the Chinese army still behind him, however, Yuan was a highly desirable asset both for the Qing government and for revolutionaries when rebellion broke out in Wuchang (武昌, *Wǔchāng*) in 1911.

After delaying to secure higher titles and more power, Yuan fought a military campaign for the Qing dynasty that allowed him to negotiate for peace with the revolutionaries at his leisure. This led to the abdication of the four-year-old Xuantong Emperor (宣統帝, *Xuāntǒng Dì*) Pu Yi (溥儀, *Pǔyí*). With this, Yuan Shikai became the president of the Republic of China on February 14, 1912, replacing Sun Yat-sen (孫逸仙, *Sūn Yìxiān*), who was serving as provisional president.

In the early months of the new republic, Yuan and his allies strongly opposed efforts to create an independent and powerful parliamentary system. As a result of Yuan's thirst for power, Sun Yat-sen agitated for a second revolution, seeking help from Japan. Yuan's forces quelled the rebellion and dissolved Parliament in January 1914.

Now in charge of the entire government, Yuan began to institute measures that strengthened his power, one of which created a national coinage, led by the release of the Yuan Shikai silver dollar.

Eventually, Yuan became the Hongxian Emperor (洪憲皇帝, *Hóngxiàn Dì*), a goal he achieved despite much resistance on December 12, 1915, but held barely more than three months.

The image on the obverse of the 1914 gold dollar is strikingly similar to a 1915-dated photograph by French photojournalist Charles Chusseau-Flaviens (1866–1928), though the coin features Yuan Shikai from the bust up while the photo is a full-body seated portrait. The design was created by Italian engraver Luigi Giorgi at the Tientsin Mint in the city of Tientsin (天津, *Tiānjīn*).

On the reverse, the denomination is rendered as 壹圓 (*Yī Yuán* ["One Dollar"]). The numeral 壹 is used in financial and official records for the number one (*yī*) to avoid possible confusion with other Chinese numerals, and 圓 is an alternative form of the now-more-common symbol for yuan, 元.

The seventh edition of Lin Gwo Ming and Ma Tak Wo's (L&M) *Illustrated Catalog of Chinese Gold & Silver Coins* (2012) gives a value of US$32,000 for an UNC specimen and $90,000 for one in BU. An example from the Ultima Collection, graded MS-64 by NGC, sold for $91,062.50 (including a 17.5 percent buyer's premium) at the Heritage ANA World & Ancient Coin Platinum Night Auction on August 8, 2014. Another specimen, graded MS-62 by NGC and pedigreed to the W&B Capital Collection, sold for $54,000 (including a 20 percent buyer's premium) at the Heritage Hong Kong International Numismatic Fair (HKINF) in June 2018.

Chinese army commander, later emperor, Yuan Shikai.

Obverse. Yuan Shikai, wearing a plumed shako or visored cylindrical hat, in a full general's uniform facing the viewer. Military decorations (epaulettes, orders, medals, and ornately embroidered collars) are visible. A ring of denticles surrounds the top portion of the side, running clockwise from the lower left side to the lower right side (no denticles are along the portion of the rim touching Yuan Shikai). Otherwise, the field is empty, which—aside from the detailed portraiture—greatly adds to the eye appeal of the design.

Reverse. At the very center is the vertical inscription 壹圓 (*Yī Yuán* ["One Dollar"]). Surrounding the denomination is an open vegetal (cereal) wreath, with a ribbon tying two sprigs together at the bottom. A tightly packed ring of small beads or dots surrounds the central motif. Counterclockwise beneath is the English denomination ONE DOLLAR. Counterclockwise along the top half is the Chinese inscription 中華民國共和紀念幣 (*Zhōnghuá Mínguó Gònghé Jìniànbì* ["Republic of China Commemorative Coin"]). Between each end of the Chinese inscription and the English denomination is a roseate element (two in total), consisting of a vaguely floral pattern hemmed in by four concave sides with four relatively large dots resting against each one. A ring of small dots or beads, with a minuscule dart between each one, encircles the entire side next to the rim.

Composition	Weight	Diameter	Alignment	Edge
Gold		39 mm	Medal	Reeded
Mintage	**Mint**		**Collecting Difficulty**	**References**
Unknown (at least 6)	Tientsin Mint		Extremely difficult	L&M-108; K-1558

DANISH WEST INDIES 1904-H GOLD 10 DALERS

One-year colonial type honors the "father-in-law of Europe."

Obverse. A highly detailed effigy of an older King Christian IX, facing left. Clockwise from bottom left is the inscription CHRISTIAN IX * 1904. A small P (the mint master's initial) is after the date. A heart-shaped mintmark begins the clockwise inscription DANSK * VESTINDIEN ("Danish * West Indies"). The rim is decorated with a horizontal bead and dart pattern.

Reverse. The personification of the Americas sits on the side of a boat or canoe, wearing an animal tooth necklace, large earrings, and a headband. There is a bangle on her upper left arm and a paddle in her right hand. A bundle tied crosswise in the canoe is to her right, behind a stylized prow. On the ground to her left is the top of a palm tree with large fronds and coconuts. The moneyer's initials G.I. are to the right of DALER. The rim is decorated with a horizontal bead and dart pattern.

Composition	Weight	Diameter	Alignment	Edge
.900 gold	16.1290 grams	28 mm	Medal	Reeded

Mintage	Mint	Collecting Difficulty	References
2,005 (per NGC)	Copenhagen†	Difficult	Fr-1; Hede-29; KM-73; Schl-93; Schön-9; Schou-5; Sieg-32

† Mintmark: H, or heart

Workers in Danish West Indies with sugar canes, circa 1910s.

The Danish West Indies consisted of three islands in the Caribbean: St. Croix, St. Thomas, and St. Jan, which readers in the United States may recognize as the U.S. Virgin Islands. The Danish West India–Guinea Company assembled the colony over the course of six decades from the late seventeenth to mid—eighteenth centuries. Like other colonies in the Caribbean, the Danish West Indies existed to profit from the transatlantic slave trade. When the company went bankrupt in 1755, the Danish crown assumed direct control over the island territories.

Within a hundred years, slavery had been abolished and the crown was looking to dispose of its American possessions. Denmark finally sold the islands to the United States in 1917 due to their proximity to the Panama Canal (see number 78) and strategic value during World War I.

For most of the time the colony was on the market, the Kingdom of Denmark had been ruled by King Christian IX (1818–1906; reigned 1863–1906). Initially an unpopular king, his 42-year reign and moral character managed to sway public opinion, so by the time this coin was minted (two years before his death), Christian had become something of a beloved institution.

Since Denmark posed little threat to the powers-that-be at the time, the king's six children were unusually successful with their royal marriages. His grandchildren would include King George V of England, Czar Nicholas II of Russia, and Constantine I of Greece (see number 52), among other future rulers. Many of these lines continue down to the present day, with Queen Elizabeth II as perhaps the most prominent of his descendants. Because of this, Christian IX became known as the "Father-in-Law of Europe."

Even though the king's portrait on the 1904 10-daler gold coin looks like a monarch in his declining years, the truth is Christian IX was always rendered old, numismatically speaking (he was, after all, almost 50 when he ascended to the throne). There is a refreshing lack of vanity to this effigy; it is so detailed that you can see the bags and crow's feet under and around his eyes, and you can even spot an eyebrow peeking out from behind the right side of his face. The slight jowls covered in bushy sideburns and the receding hairline are true-to-life details that nevertheless do not detract from the strength and authority of the portrait. It's an overall naturalistic approach (reminiscent of Roman republican bronzes) that can also be found on the coinage of other contemporary European nations, such as Prussia.

St. Thomas, Virgin Islands, circa 1922.

While the portraiture and design work on the obverse is of the highest artistic quality, it is to the reverse that the glory belongs.

An exotic-looking, topless female—the personification of the Americas—appears to sit on the side of a boat or canoe. She is rendered in a Greco-Roman style, as exemplified by the physicality of her body and the "weight" and folds of the drapery covering her legs. The positioning of her limbs, too, is classical, albeit stiffer than is found on the best ancient examples. Still, the relief of the coin is such that (for example) her left forearm appears to project forward in space ahead of the rest of her arm and shoulder.

To symbolize the "savage" nature of the Americas, she wears an animal tooth necklace. She also wears earrings that extend past the lobe, a headband, and a bangle on the upper part of her left arm. In her right arm, she holds a long, stylized paddle, much as Lady Liberty might hold a Liberty pole.

A bundle tied crosswise sits in the canoe to her right, behind a stylized prow. On the ground to her left rests the top of a palm tree, replete with large fronds and coconuts.

The design shares many affinities with the early-twentieth-century coinage of other imperial colonies, such as that struck for German East Africa (see number 99). It also appears on the Danish East Indies 20-franc / four-daler gold coin (KM-72; Schön-8).

The 1904 10-daler coin was struck under the authority of Copenhagen Mint Master Vilhelm Burchard Poulsen, who served in that capacity from 1893 through 1918. Poulsen's full initials, V.B.P., are found on other coins, but here we see a small P after the date on the obverse. The initials G.I. of moneyer Knud Gunnar Jensen (moneyer from 1901 to 1933) are found on the reverse. The gold and silver coinage of the Danish West Indies was struck according to the standards of the Latin Monetary Union starting in this year, though Denmark was never a member state.

Krause gives the following values: US$2,250 for VF-20, $4,600 for XF-40, and $7,500 for MS-60. An NGC MS-61 example sold at a January 2015 Heritage NYINC World Coin Signature Auction for $6,168.75 (including a 17.5 percent buyer's premium). In April 2015, an NGC MS-64 PL (the only prooflike example) sold at a Heritage Chicago International Coin Fair (CICF) World Coin Signature Auction for $28,200 (plus buyer's premium). And finally, an NGC MS-64 sold for $16,801.20 (includes buyer's premium) at an August 15, 2019, ANA Heritage Platinum Night Auction.

King Christian IX.

CANADA 1916-C GOLD SOVEREIGN

A scarce coin with an unknown fate.

Obverse. A bareheaded King George V, facing left. Clockwise from left, the inscription: GEORGIVS V D. G. BRITT: OMN: REX F. D. IND: IMP: (abbreviated Latin for *GEORGIUS V DEI GRATIA BRITANNIARUM OMNIUM REX FIDEI DEFENSOR INDIAE IMPERATOR* ["George V, by the Grace of God, King of all the Britons, Defender of the Faith, Emperor of India"]). The designer's initials B.M. are in the neck truncation. Denticles surround along the rim.

Reverse. A muscular rendering of St. George, clad in a crested Roman helmet, soldier's cloak, and leather boots, atop a horse, which rears up to trample a European-style dragon. St. George pulls back the reins with his left hand and brandishes a short Roman sword *(gladius)* in his right. His left foot is barely visible under the horse. The point of the spear is broken off in the dragon's side; the spear shaft is on the ground behind the horse. The date 1916 is beneath the tableau. Above and to the right of the date are the designer's initials, B.P. The mintmark C is above the date in the ground.

Composition	Weight	Diameter	Alignment	Edge
.9167 gold	7.9881 grams	22.05 mm	Medal	Reeded

Mintage	Mint	Collecting Difficulty	References
20–50 (estimated)	Royal Canadian Mint (Ottawa)	Extremely difficult	KM-20; Marsh-224

The 1916-C gold sovereign was but one of a series of gold sovereigns struck at Canada's Ottawa Mint from 1908 through 1919. The period overlaps the reigns of King Edward VII, who appears on the 1908–1910 issues, and King George V, whose portrait is seen on sovereigns minted from 1911 through 1919. Mintages for circulation-strike sovereigns range from 3,715 for the 1913-C issue to 256,946 in the case of the 1911-C.

Of these, the 1916-C Canada gold sovereign is regarded as the scarcest, even though its original mintage of 6,111 was (though small) not the lowest among the series. It is unknown how many pieces survive today. According to *A Guide Book of Canadian Coins and Tokens* by numismatic researcher Dr. James A. Haxby, there are 20 to 25 survivors[1]. The *Standard Catalogue of Canadian Coins* by W. K. Cross, published annually by Charlton Press, gives an estimate of twice as many[2]. Meanwhile, Heritage Auctions reports the existing number is "less than 50 pieces."

The greater question, however, is what happened to the rest of them?

Without a doubt, the British sovereign is one of the world's most widely recognized coins, having been struck since 1817. All sovereigns ever since have featured the same design on the reverse: a neoclassical depiction of *St. George and the Dragon* by nineteenth-century Royal Mint Chief Engraver Benedetto Pistrucci (1783–1855).

But while the British-derived coin had been popular among collectors for its artistic and numismatic merits, the 1916-C issue saw little demand in circulation. Nevertheless, Ottawa strikes truly became essential in the late 1910s to make British payments to the United States for war supplies during World War I without the risk of interception by German U-boats in open waters. It's possible that most of the mintage wound up at the United States Treasury, with much of the remainder melted. Similarly, Cross asserts that "most of the small mintage may have been melted, accounting for the rarity, though this is by no means an established fact."

While the numismatic community has yet to learn for certain what happened to the 6,000-plus 1916-C gold sovereigns, the coins remain an alluring object of curiosity for collectors and an incredible rarity. One example, certified as MS-65 by PCGS, sold at a Heritage sale in 2010 for US$86,250 (including 15 percent buyer's premium).

Canadians return from World War I.

(Left) World War I poster for Canadian wartime fundraising depicts three French women pulling a plow.

The "gunboat diplomacy" of the United States that forced Japan to open its ports to international trade in the 1850s (in reality, to deregulate its foreign trade on Western terms) was the culmination of centuries of Western attempts to break into the tightly controlled Japanese market. In turn, the capitulation to American demands resulted in open rebellion against the shogun, which was itself the culmination of centuries of political discontent. An important point in the overthrow of the shogunate was the desire to reinstate the Japanese emperor as the de facto head of the Japanese state—a point that Emperor Kōmei (孝明天皇, *Kōmei-tennō*; ruled 1846–1867) embraced.

With the death of Kōmei in 1867, his young son Mutsuhito (1852–1912) adopted the era name Meiji (明治; "Enlightened Reign") and became the emperor (明治天皇, *Meiji-tennō*; ruled 1867–1912). His reign would become known as the Meiji Restoration (beginning in 1868), and the emperor himself would become known as Meiji the Great (明治大帝, *Meiji-taitei*).

Acutely aware of the imperialistic motives of the West, the Japanese government saw the Meiji Restoration as a proactive attempt to modernize many aspects of Japanese society for the country to become an imperial power in its own right, in order to preserve the nation's independence and sovereignty. Envoys were sent abroad to study and observe modern techniques of education, economics, and statecraft. Military reforms based on the Prussian model were enacted. The army was equipped with modern weaponry, and a powerful modern navy was built.

The country rapidly industrialized, seeking to become independent of other nations' exports. Political reforms approached a kind of democracy, creating a system of prefectures, eliminating caste distinctions, encouraging entrepreneurship and upward mobility, and revoking the privileges of the samurai class. These changes, in actuality, primarily served to erase the

JAPAN 1901 SILVER YEN PATTERN

"Enrich the nation, strengthen the armies."

Obverse. The center is a rising sun (a circle of incuse vertical lines surrounded by rays like a sunburst, which alternate relief and incuse in sets of three). This is encircled by two solid rings with a gap between them. Clockwise from left (with the coin's outer rim as a baseline) are the legends 大日本 (*Dai Nihon* ["Great Japan"]) and 明治三十四年 (*Meiji San Jū Shi Nen* ["Meiji Year 34"]). Counterclockwise at the bottom, in English, is 1 Yen. Three florettes with five petals separate all three inscriptions from each other. Denticles surround the design along the rim.

Reverse. In the center from top to bottom is the denomination 一圓 ("1 Yen"), surrounded by an open wreath, tied at the base with ribbon. Above the denomination at the top of the coin, between open ends of the wreath, is a stylized chrysanthemum flower with 16 petals. Denticles surround the design along the rim.

Composition	Weight	Diameter	Alignment	Edge
.900 silver	26.96 grams	38.1 mm	Coin	Reeded
Mintage	**Mint**		**Collecting Difficulty**	**References**
2	Japan Mint (Osaka)		Extremely difficult	J&V-Q51; KM-Pn32

Japanese dragon, color engraving on wood.

Japanese print showing Commodore Matthew Perry during his expedition to Japan, 1852-1854, which led to the opening of trade.

traditional support system that had propped up the shogunate and to centralize power in the person of the emperor.

Due to these radical changes, this period is regarded as the founding of modern Japan.

The Meiji period also brought change to Japan's coinage, starting with the adoption of Western-style round coins in 1870. And in 1871, the emperor sought to centralize the nation's currency with the creation of a new monetary unit known as the yen. Replacing a locally produced system of paper money (as well as the coins of the shogunate), the new currency was based on European decimal coinage. One yen (圓) was divisible into 100 sen (錢), and one sen was divisible into 10 rin (厘). The word sen is the Japanese equivalent of the Korean chon, and both are derived from the Chinese word qián, which means "money." The name "yen," of course, comes from the Chinese word "yuan" (also 圓, but later 元), which meant "round" or "circle" and referred to the shape of the Spanish silver piece of eight (the peso).

The yuan also became known as the won in Korea; see number 5 in our list, the 1909 Korean gold three-coin set.

Originally valued at about 0.78 troy ounces of silver, the Coinage Act of 1897 (Meiji 30) devalued the yen by half, to approximately 50 US cents. The devaluation put the yen in line with gold and silver values throughout the rest of the world. The size of the 1901 silver pattern may have been determined by this decision.

Another consideration behind the creation of this pattern, struck in the 34th year of the Meiji era, may have been a feeling that the original design of the yen, featuring a dragon curled around a cintamani (or *yeouiju* in Korea; a jewel or pearl that grants omnipotence to the one who wields it), was too Chinese. A "Rising Sun" motif, seen earlier on the yen of 1870 (which also featured the dragon design on one side), was selected to take its place. Yet while the Rising Sun appeared on other denominations from 1901, the design did not take hold on the yen, which continued to bear the dragon until the last silver yen was issued in 1914.

The yen did, however, continuously feature the chrysanthemum flower on the reverse as a symbol of the emperor and the imperial throne of Japan.

This pattern, among other key Japanese coins, was brought to the attention of an English-speaking numismatic audience in Drs. Norman Jacobs and Cornelius C. Vermeule III's book *Japanese Coinage: A Monetary History of Japan*. One specimen was sold by Heritage as part of the Vermeule collection in 2004. The other example—an NGC MS-62 from the Jacobs collection of Japanese and Korean coins—sold for US$80,500 (including a buyer's premium) at a September 2011 Heritage sale.

Japanese chrysanthemum in Osaka

Brazil bid adieu to precious metal circulating coinage in the years immediately preceding World War II. For silver coinage, the last circulating coin series was the silver 5,000 reis, a debased (.600) silver coin honoring aviation pioneer Alberto Santos-Dumont (1873–1932). That coin was issued from 1936 to 1938. For gold denominations, the final two-coin series were the "Republic" 10,000 and 20,000 reis issues struck between 1889 and 1922.

In a typical year, neither issue was struck in considerable quantity. Mintages of a few hundred to a few thousand were typical of both issues, with the exception of the 1908 strike of the 20,000 reis, which had a staggering mintage of over six million. That issue today can be acquired for a slight premium over prevailing bullion price. The lower mintage issues, however, are generally more difficult to acquire, especially in collectible grades.

The 10,000 reis from 1922, however, is rare in an absolute sense with a reported mintage of just six pieces.

Of the six pieces reportedly struck, only two that we have found have been offered for sale over the course of the past 20 years. In March 1997, Spink America offered the Norweb specimen, which it noted was in Uncirculated condition and had a prooflike appearance. That example brought US$22,000 against a $15,000 to $25,000 pre-sale estimate[1].

More recently, an example graded MS-64 by NGC advanced the price considerably, realizing $105,750 at a January 2014 Heritage auction. That coin was one of many highlights of an impressive collection of Brazilian coins and medals built over many years by Dr. Roberto Monteiro[2].

In January 2014, Heritage Auctions offered an example from the RLM Collection that also had a prooflike appearance but was not denoted as such when graded MS-64 by NGC. That example brought $105,750.

PCGS accounts for an additional specimen, this example graded MS-63.

BRAZIL 1922 GOLD 10,000 REIS

The last of Brazil's gold coins.

Obverse. Inside a circle is a left-facing Liberty head wearing a Phrygian cap. Outside the circle is the Portuguese inscription REPUBLICA DOS ESTADOS UNIDOS DO BRAZIL ("Republic of the United States of Brazil"). On the bottom, bordered by two five-pointed stars, is the date 1922. The designer's initials, F.C., are located below the bust truncation.

Reverse. The coat of arms of Brazil: A round shield with the five stars of the Southern Cross encircled by an outer ring of 27 stars. The shield is placed atop a five-pointed star, and these two motifs are placed on a sword in pale. A wreath of coffee and tobacco surrounds the design and a glory of sun rays fan out in the background. Below, a ribbon reads ESTADO UNIDOS DO BRAZIL 15 DE NOVEMBRO DE 1889 ("The Republican Federation of Brazil 15 November 1889"). The motto wraps around the design at the top and reads ORDEM E PROGRESSO ("Order and Progress"). Wrapping around the bottom of the design is the denomination 10,000 REIS.

Composition	Weight	Diameter	Alignment	Edge
.9167 gold	8.9645 grams		Coin	Reeded

Mintage	Mint	Collecting Difficulty	References
6	Brazil Mint (Rio de Janeiro)	Virtually impossible	Fr-125; KM-496; Russo-710

Statue of Epitacio Pessoa, president of Brazil from July 1919 to November 1922.

Rio de Janeiro, Brazil, circa 1910.

WÜRTTEMBERG 1913-F GOLD 20 MARKS, PROOF

The German Empire unifies kingdoms.

Obverse. A young effigy of King Wilhelm II with a beard, facing right. Clockwise from left is the inscription WILHELM II KOENIG VON WUERTTEMBERG ("Wilhelm II, King of Württemberg") around the effigy. The mintmark F is beneath the neck truncation. Small denticles are around the entire rim.

Reverse. The German imperial single-headed (Prussian) eagle displayed (spread out) and langued (tongue protruding). A crown is above the head and a shield with the imperial eagle and coat of arms covers the breast. The collar chain of the Württemberg Order of the Crown surrounds the shield. Clockwise from left along the top is the inscription DEUTSCHES REICH 1913. Counterclockwise at the bottom is the denomination 20 MARK, with a small, fat five-pointed star on each side. Small denticles are around the entire rim.

Composition	Weight	Diameter	Alignment	Edge
.900 gold	7.965 grams	22.5 mm	Medal	Lettered†

Mintage	Mint	Collecting Difficulty	References
Unknown surviving	Freudenstadt Mint (Stuttgart)	Extremely difficult	J-296; KM-634

† GOTT MIT UNS ("God With Us") ‡ Mintmark: F

King Wilhelm II, the fourth and last king of Württemberg.

The German Empire was officially founded in 1871 with the unification of most of the German states into one federation and the declaration of Prussian King Wilhelm as emperor (or kaiser). Individual kingdoms, duchies, and free cities retained their own sovereignty but acknowledged the supremacy of the kaiser in Berlin—much like the states of the United States of America, except ruled by noble houses. Imperial Coinage Acts of 1871 and 1873 refused to establish a central mint, instead allowing any state capable of doing so to continue minting its own coinage.

The Kingdom of Württemberg was one such state.

Now part of the federal state of Baden-Württemberg in the southern part of Germany, the kingdom was founded in 1806 when Elector of the Holy Roman Empire Frederick II made himself king. Wilhelm II (1848–1921), Frederick's great-grandson, became king in 1891 and reigned until he abdicated the throne after Germany's defeat in World War I in 1918. A popular king who was not afraid to mingle unguarded among the people, his rule saw further progress in the democratization of the state. The German Revolution of 1918–1919 resulted in the establishment of the Weimar Republic and the transformation of the kingdom into the Free People's State of Württemberg. Wilhelm died in 1921, leaving no potential heirs.

One interesting characteristic of the coin's design is the coat of arms on the reverse. The German imperial eagle features a shield on its breast that also portrays the eagle and the imperial coat of arms. This, in turn, bears a shield on its breast, which also features the imperial eagle and coat of arms, ad infinitum. Such recursive, self-referential designs occur with some frequency in heraldry and coin designs based on coats of arms and other symbols.

The F mintmark stands for the Freudenstadt Mint based in Stuttgart, the largest city in Württemberg and the kingdom's capital. The town of Freudenstadt is located in the Black Forest (the famous *Schwarzwald*) and is close to important mines that were the presumable source for metal for the region's coins.

Fairly common in circulation strike (42,897 were minted), the gold coin's rarity comes from the fact that most of the 1913 issues were melted down (along with the next year's output). An unspecified number of Proofs were produced. NGC says the 1913-F Proof 20 mark is worth $95,000. Among all issues of the type, only high-quality circulation strike specimens of the 1913-F come close to this value.

A Girl of the Black Forest, circa 1890–1900.

Much like the Meiji Restoration in Japan, the Gwangmu Reform (1897–1907) was intended to modernize Korean society. The period was named for Gojong (高宗; 1852–1919), the 26th king of the Joseon dynasty (ruled 1863–1897), who then became the first emperor of the short-lived Korean Empire (ruled 1897–1910) Also like the earlier Meiji movement, there were political reforms that established a greater social equality, military reforms that recreated fighting forces along Western lines (with a core unit trained by Russian advisors), industrial and infrastructure modernization, and educational reform.

But unlike the Japanese restoration, Korea's modernization came decades later. This meant that despite everything, Korea was still under threat of the imperial ambitions of its neighbors. Two especially—Russia and Japan—contended for influence in the empire before and during the time of the reforms. After the defeat of Russia by Japan in the Russo-Japanese War (1904–1905), Korea was forced to sign the Protectorate Treaty of 1905, losing its independence to imperial Japan. Guangmu was forced to abdicate, and his son Sunjong became the Emperor Yunghui (隆熙帝, *Yunghuije*; ruled 1907–1910—see number 5).

This coin, however, was struck as a one-year type by the Russo-Korean Bank—as were 5-chon and half-chon denominations—during a period of predominant Russian influence from before that country's loss in the war. The Russian imperial eagle on the obverse is given an exotic, stylized appearance; instead of coats of arms and military decorations, we see the *taegeuk*, a traditional symbol of Korea with links to Taoism (the Chinese *taiji* or yin-yang is a related symbol) and trigrams, representing (clockwise from top): water, thunder, mountain, valley, fire, earth, wind, and heaven (though the trigrams have other meanings as well).

On the reverse, the character for *chon*, 錢, is the same as that used for the Japanese denomination *sen*. Both are related to the Chinese word *qián*, which means "money." The plum flower of the imperial seal is displayed at the top of the side.

Krause gives a mintage of over three million for this issue, which drastically belies its immense rarity. The *Standard Catalog of World Coins* gives estimated values of US$4,500 for an example in F-12, $9,000 in VF-20, $16,000 in XF-40, $27,500 in MS-60, and $130,000 in MS-63. Heritage Auctions has offered only two over the last 20 years: a piece from the Piedmont Collection in June 2000 and an NGC MS-65 Brown specimen from the Dr. Norman Jacobs Collection of Japanese and Korean coins in September 2011. The Jacobs piece sold for $149,500 (including a buyer's premium).

KOREA 1902 CHON, RUSSIAN DENOMINATION

Modernization under imperialistic influences.

Obverse. Within a ring of beads or dots, the stylized imperial eagle of Russia, crowned, displayed (spread out), and langued (tongue protruding). There are ribbons to either side of the crown. In the center of the breast is a taegeuk, surrounded by eight trigrams representing (clockwise from top) water, thunder, mountain, valley, fire, earth, wind, and heaven. Four additional taegeuks are arranged vertically on each wing, for a total of eight. There is a ceremonial sword in the right talon and a globe in the left talon, with latitude and longitude lines extending from a visible pole. Clockwise from left around the central ring are inscriptions 大韓 • 光武六年 • 일전 • 1 CHON (*Daehan Gwangmu Yuk Nyeon Il Jyeon* ["Great Korea, Kuang Mu Year Six, One Jeon"]). Denticles surround along the rim.

Reverse. In the center from top to bottom is the denomination 一錢 (*Il Jyeon* ["One Chon"]). A wreath is tied at the bottom with a ribbon and a large plum flower is at the top, between the open ends of the wreath. Denticles surround along the rim.

Composition	Weight	Diameter	Alignment	Edge
Bronze (.955 copper, .030 tin, .015 zinc)	6.8 grams		Coin	Smooth

Mintage	Mint	Collecting Difficulty	References
3,001,000 (unknown surviving)	Chonhwankuk (Seoul)	Extremely difficult	KM-1121

Japanese infantry marching through Seoul during the Russo-Japanese War.

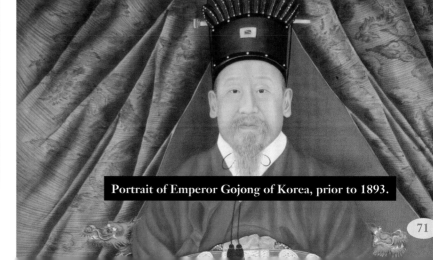

Portrait of Emperor Gojong of Korea, prior to 1893.

SWITZERLAND 1910-1911 GOLD 10 FRANCS, ESSAI

The forerunner of monetary cooperation in Europe.

Obverse. The head of Helvetia, the personification of Switzerland, with braided hair in back, facing left. There are edelweiss flowers on her left shoulder and the Swiss Alps in the far background. HELVETIA, the Latin name for Switzerland, is inscribed clockwise at the top. The designer's signature, F. LANDRY, is found counterclockwise on the left side near the bottom. A ring of dots along the rim surrounds the design.

Reverse. At the center top is the radiant Swiss cross, and the denomination below is 10 FR. The date, centered, is below the denomination 1910 (or 1911). A floral arrangement wraps around the bottom, and at the center bottom is the mintmark B (Bern). ESSAI is on the left near the rim. A ring of dots along the rim surrounds the design.

Composition	Weight	Diameter	Alignment	Edge
.900 gold	3.225805 grams	19 mm	Coin	Smooth

Mintage	Mint	Collecting Difficulty	References
56	Banque Nationale Suisse (Bern)†	Extremely difficult	KM-E4
	† Mintmark: B		

A statue depicting Helvetia in Bern, Switzerland.

By the time the head of Helvetia, the female personification of Switzerland, appeared on the 1910-B 10-franc gold essai, engraver Fritz Ulisse Landry's "Vreneli" design had been in use since 1897 on Swiss 10- and 20-franc gold coins. These gold coins were produced according to the standards and rules of the Latin Monetary Union (LMU), which was formed in 1865 and ended in 1927. Switzerland was one of the original signatories to the establishing treaty, along with France, Italy, and Belgium.

The parties of the LMU agreed to produced gold coinage according to the standards of the French franc and silver coinage at a 15.5:1 bimetallic ratio, both of which could now be easily interchangeable among the member nations. While ultimately unsuccessful, the idea inspired other countries to adapt their coinages to the Union's specifications and, a century later, it informed the Eurozone project (see number 100).

Only 56 total examples of the pattern were struck dated 1910 and 1911. Krause gives an estimated value of US$50,000 for a Mint State example of one of these rare essais of the popular gold coin denomination.

The Alps in Troistorrents, Switzerland.

In 1949, the people of New Zealand were anticipating the arrival of King George VI. The king's visit—which also included a tour of Australia—would have been the first time in history that a ruling monarch stepped foot in the "Kiwi Nation," which was first settled by the Māori over 1,000 years ago and had been part of the British Empire since 1840. It was not to be.

Only in his early 50s but a heavy smoker, the king was stricken with an arterial blockage in his right leg and underwent surgery in March 1949. His overseas journey was cancelled.

The change came too late for mint officials in New Zealand, however, who had already begun to strike 1949 silver crowns honoring the royal visit.

The 1949 silver crown depicts a portrait of King George VI by English medalist Thomas Humphrey Paget, OBE (1893–1974), on the obverse and a silver fern (*Cyathea dealbata*) on the reverse. Also known as "ponga" or "punga," the silver fern is an endemic plant species in New Zealand and was critical to early Māori hunters, whose paths were illuminated at night when the silver undersides of the fronds shimmered in the moonlight. The fern is positioned within the stars of the constellation Crux Australis—the "Southern Cross"—which also appears of the flag of New Zealand. Local artist Reginald George James Berry (1906–1979) created the reverse.

The fern has served as a quasi-national symbol since the 1800s, appearing in various emblems—including some of the country's professional sports teams. There have also been several official propositions to incorporate the silver fern into New Zealand's national flag, nearly making it onto the country's banner following referendums in 2015 and 2016.

Some 200,000 circulation-strike examples of the 1949 crown were produced, and these patriotically designed coins remain popular with coin collectors today. In addition to the circulation strikes, a tiny mintage of Proofs was also produced.

The 1949 Proof silver crown has since become known as one of the rarest of New Zealand's coins. It is also the only coin New Zealand ever struck bearing a portrait of King George VI, gaining a special place in the hearts of the nation's collectors for both reasons.

An exact production figure for the 1949 silver Proof is unconfirmed, though Krause's *Standard Catalog of World Coins* proffers an estimate of three survivors. Also touting this minuscule population figure is Heritage Auctions, which in January 2015 sold the finest example (PCGS PR-66) of the coin for US$21,150 (including a 17.5 percent buyer's premium). It was the fourth public offering of the elusive issue in a decade, a circumstance serving as an anecdotal reminder of the coin's extraordinary rarity.

King George VI lived three years after the production of the 1949 crowns that were to herald his proposed visit to New Zealand. Though poor health impeded the planned 1949 tour of the island nation, the king rescheduled the trip for May 1952. Unfortunately, deteriorating health sidelined the ailing George yet again, who by late 1951 had his left lung removed following the discovery of a malignant tumor.

The king then asked his eldest daughter, Princess Elizabeth, to visit the nation in his place. This tour was also cancelled. On February 6, 1952, upon her arrival in Kenya en route to New Zealand, Elizabeth learned that her father had passed away. She returned immediately home. Following her coronation on June 2, 1953, the newly crowned Queen Elizabeth II and her husband Prince Philip arrived in New Zealand for a summer tour in December 1953.

Māori Battalion survivors of wartime military action in Greece performing a haka in Helwan, Egypt, for the king of Greece in 1941. In the foreground, left to right, are John Manuel, Maaka (Bill) White, Te Kooti (Scotty) Reihana, and Rangi Henderson.

NEW ZEALAND 1949 SILVER CROWN, PROOF

Celebrating a tour that would never happen.

Obverse. An effigy of King George VI facing left, without crown. Clockwise from lower left, the inscription: KING GEORGE THE SIXTH. The designer's initials H.P. are in the neck truncation. Denticles surround along the rim.
Reverse. A silver fern leaf inside the Southern Cross. Clockwise from the lower left, the denomination: NEW ZEALAND CROWN. Counterclockwise at the bottom is the date 1949. There is a dot between 1949 and CROWN. Denticles surround along the rim.

Composition	Weight	Diameter	Alignment	Edge
.500 silver	28.28 grams	38.61 mm	Medal	Reeded
Mintage	**Mint**		**Collecting Difficulty**	**References**
3 (estimated)	Royal Mint (London)		Difficult	KM-22

RUSSIA 1912 CZAR ALEXANDER III MEMORIAL SILVER RUBLE

An autocrat whose rule would lead to revolution.

Obverse. In the center is a left-facing portrait of Czar Alexander III. The initials of engraver Abraham Griliches (АГ) are in the bust truncation. Wrapping around the inside of the rim is the inscription АЛЕКСАНДРЪ III ИМПЕРАТОРЪ И САМОДЕРЖЕЦЪ ВСЕРОССІЙСКІЙ ("Alexander III Emperor and Autocrat of All Russians"). Wrapping around the inscription in smaller letters, bracketing the bust, are the birth and death dates of the monarch, written as (left) РОДИЛСЯ 26 ФЕВРАЛЯ 1845 ГОДА ("Born 26 February 1845") and (right) ВЪ БОЗЪ ПОЧИЛЪ 20 ОКТ. 1894 ГОДА ("Died on 20 Oct. 1894"). Beaded denticles surround the design.

Reverse. The center is a monument to Czar Alexander III. A small star is located above the head. The denomination РУБЛЬ ("Ruble") is in the exergue. Bracketing the left and right sides and wrapping around the inside of the rim: (left) СООРУЖЕНЪ ЛЮБОВЬЮ НАРОДА ВЪ МОСКВЪ ("Constructed by the Love of the People of Moscow") and (right) ИМПЕРАТОРОМЪ НИКОЛАЕМЪ II ОТКРЫТЪ ВЪ 1912 Г ("Emperor Nicholas II Opened [the monument] in the year 1812"). At the base of the podium, in incuse letters, are the Cyrillic initials AP for Alexander Redko of St. Petersburg Mint. Beaded denticles surround along the rim.

Composition	Weight	Diameter	Alignment	Edge
.900 silver	20 grams	33.65 mm	Medal	Lettered†

Mintage	Mint		Collecting Difficulty	References
2,100 (plus unreported Proofs)	St. Petersburg Mint		Extremely difficult	Bitkin-330; KM-Y69; Uzd-4199

† ЧИСТАГО СЕРЕБРА 4 ЗОЛОТНИКА 21 ДОЛѦ (Э • Б)
("Pure Silver of 4 zolotniks and 21 dolyas (EB)")

Coins often outlast the memories of the events they were struck to memorialize, but few present on May 30, 1912, at the unveiling of the Alexander III monument, which faced the flowing waters of the Moscow River on the hallowed grounds of the Cathedral of Christ the Savior, could have guessed that within six short years, the newly installed communist government would order the statue's destruction. A photograph of a gaggle of peasant children standing next to the statue's oversized and decapitated head likely sent shivers up the spines of western Europe's elite aristocracy.

Struck to honor the dedication of this grandiose public monument—said to have cost more than two million rubles at a time when 80 percent of the population of the Russian empire were peasants—this silver ruble coin was not struck as a national collectible, but as a memento for the small minority of Russians who could afford to collect them (such as Alexander's cousin, Grand Duke George Mikhailovich, whose reconstituted coin collection now sits in permanent residence at the Smithsonian Institution's National Numismatic Collection and in other international museums and private collections).

The coin's obverse features a left-facing portrait of Alexander III, a brutish autocrat who sought to undo many of the social reforms enacted by his father, Alexander II (the latter's assassination at the hands of a gang of revolutionaries bore no small influence in this decision). Alexander III's reign lasted only 13 years and ended rather unexpectedly due to kidney disease, with his son Nicholas II thrust into power without warning or preparation.

The coin's design was one of the final works of Abraham Avenirovich Griliches, the younger of a father-son team of engravers employed by the Imperial Mint at St. Petersburg. Abraham's father, Avenir, joined the Mint as a self-taught medalist in 1871 and was joined by his son, who trained at the St. Petersburg Academy of Fine Arts, in 1876[1]. The two worked hand-in-hand on numerous commissions, coins, and medal designs for the

Czar Alexander III in Danish Royal Life Guards uniform.

The former Cathedral of Christ the Savior in Moscow, circa 1883–1918.

duration of their service at the Mint. The elder Griliches died after a long illness in 1905, still drawing a salary despite his inability to work full time for several years. His son died a month after the Mint marked his 35th year of service and a month before the unveiling of the Alexander III monument.

In all conditions, the Alexander III Centenary ruble has proven to be elusive. Many, one presumes, were surrendered or destroyed over the course of 70 years of communist rule. Those that survive appear in various states of preservation, with many known examples not qualifying for numerical grades by the two leading American grading services. Only 2,100 pieces, plus an unreported number of Proof strikings, were issued.

In September 2008, Heritage Auctions sold a Gem example from the cabinet of noted American collector Dr. Robert Hesselgesser for US$80,550[3]. The coin was lightly toned and one of five examples to earn the grade of MS-65 from NGC. PCGS reports a population of one coin at this level. Combined, the two services have certified 62 examples. While the Hesselgesser piece's price realized may be a little high based on current market levels, the scarcity of this issue, especially in Choice to Gem grades, make it one of the most important twentieth-century numismatic coins issued by imperial Russia.

Monument to Alexander III of Russia in front of the Marble Palace in St. Petersburg.

MONTENEGRO 1910 GOLD 100 PERPERA, PROOF

Beautiful craftsmanship in a brief coinage.

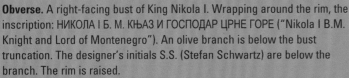

Obverse. A right-facing bust of King Nikola I. Wrapping around the rim, the inscription: НИКОЛА I Б. М. КЊАЗ И ГОСПОДАР ЦРНЕ ГОРЕ ("Nikola I B.M. Knight and Lord of Montenegro"). An olive branch is below the bust truncation. The designer's initials S.S. (Stefan Schwartz) are below the branch. The rim is raised.

Reverse. In the center of the design, enveloped by a crown and ermine-draped mantle, is the coat of arms of Montenegro: a double-headed eagle with an inescutcheon of a lion passant. In the eagle's (facing) left talon is a scepter; in the right talon is a globus cruciger. A wreath of oak and olive wraps around the device. Wrapping around the rim, above, the inscription: КЊАЖЕВИНА ЦРНА ГОРА ("The Kingdom of Montenegro"). The denomination is located at the base of the emblem, written as "100 ПЕРПЕРА," with the date 1910 below. The rim is raised.

Composition	Weight	Diameter	Alignment	Edge
.900 gold	33.8753 grams	34.5 mm	Medal	Smooth

Mintage	Mint	Collecting Difficulty	References
301 (plus 25 Proofs)	Austrian Mint (Vienna)	Extremely difficult	Fr-1; KM-12; Y-10

King Nikola I of Montenegro.

M ontenegro, a small central European state located on the eastern coast of the Adriatic Sea and bordering Serbia, Albania, and Bosnia-Herzegovina, saw limited production of national coinage throughout much of its history.

In the past two centuries, standard catalogs note just two periods of production: an occupation coinage struck as an emergency issue during the Napoleonic Wars, and a short-lived run of national coinage struck between 1906 and 1914. This latter coinage, which ended with the outbreak of World War I, saw coins produced with denominations of 1 *para* to 100 *perpera*. They were struck under the authority of the autocratic Crown Prince Nikola I, who declared himself king on August 28, 1910. His reign ended with deposition; Montenegro soon thereafter was folded into the Kingdom of Serbia and then, within months, into the Kingdom of Yugoslavia.

The coinage of Nikola I consisted of copper and nickel para coinage in denominations of 1, 2, 10, and 20; silver perpera (100 para equals one perper) in denominations of 1, 2, and 5 perpera; and a one-year emission of standard gold and commemorative gold coins struck in 1910 in the denominations of 10, 20, and 100 perpera.

Sculptor Stefan Schwartz (1851–1924) designed the 100-perpera gold coin. He was a professor of sculpture and medal engraving at the Vienna School of Arts from 1884 through the first decades of the twentieth century.

For standard issues, the perpera design is mostly uniform across all denominations. It features a right-facing portrait of Nikola I on the obverse, with an ornate mantled coat of arms on the reverse. The commemorative gold issues reuse the reverse but use a left-facing portrait of the king with modified inscriptions.

All perpera type coins carry significant numismatic premiums, especially in Mint State as attrition has taken its toll and quality pieces are far fewer than each issue's vintage and mintage might otherwise suggest. The large format 100 perpera, however, is rare, especially in Proof.

Of the two 100 perpera types, the regular issue in Proof qualifies as one of the century's 100 Greatest. Its commemorative counterpart is no slouch and with a mintage of 501 pieces, including Proofs, it is quite scarce. Mint State examples routinely sell for US$17,500 to $20,000, or more.

The regular issue is much scarcer having a published mintage of 301 pieces and 25 Proofs. Whether in Mint State or Proof, the coin is seldom encountered at auction, and those that do come to market typically have problems such as hairlines, spotting, or some other evidence of mishandling. Most business strikes that have come to market in recent years would grade Choice (MS-63) or below. A typical price for this issue at the lower Mint State grade level is between $20,000 and $25,000.

Where this issue really shines is in its Proof striking. The 100 perpera was struck at the Vienna Mint and the quality of the craftsmanship is quite evident in the intricacy of the design, especially the reverse, and the completeness of the strike.

Both grading services note that Proofs come with varying intensities of cameo contrast. While not an exhaustive accounting of all specimens existing, NGC has certified a total of seven Proofs (none finer than Proof 63 Ultra Cameo), while PCGS has certified three. One is a phenomenal Proof 65 Deep Cameo, by far the finest we have ever seen, and a coin that may very well be the finest existent[1].

Given that Heritage Auctions sold the finest example certified by NGC in 2017 for $49,350[2], it is not out of the question that the only certified Gem would bring upwards of $100,000 or more if offered for sale in today's market. A bargain price for a large-format, historic gold coin with a mintage of just 25!

King Nikola I of Montenegro.

Constantine I was the first Greek-born member of the ruling Glücksburg dynasty. He ruled for a total of six years spread over the course of two reigns—both of which began due to and ended in disaster.

On the matter of his first reign, Constantine ascended to the throne after the assassination of his father George I at the hands of anarchist gunman Alexandros Schinas in March 1913. Already in preparation to take over for his father, who had put plans in motion to abdicate that October after a Jubilee celebration, Constantine was no neophyte to either Greek or international politics, although his resume was mixed.

In 1896, he saw the triumphant rebirth of the Olympic movement by hosting the first modern games in Athens. A year later, those good feelings were wiped out by his role as army commander in the country's defeat in the first Greco-Turkish War, also called the Thirty Days' War, where his army of 36,000 men was roundly defeated at Farsala and Domokos. He made up for the military loss as king by defeating the Bulgarian army at Kilkis-Lahanas and Kresna Gorge when the Second Balkan War broke out in June 1913, just months into his reign.

Further complicating matters, a schism developed between the German-leaning king, who wished for Greece to remain neutral after the outbreak of World War I, and his prime minister, Eleftherios Venizelos, who lobbied unsuccessfully for the country to enter war in support of the entente powers of France, Russia, and Great Britain.

Constantine faced the threat of civil war at home after carrying out a series of unpopular anti-democratic acts, sacking the prime minister and installing allies, coupled with his inability to protect Greek territory seized by the Central Powers. Venizelos and his supporters drew upon that public outrage and forced the king into exile, beginning the reign of his second-born son, Alexander, who served as a puppet king while Venizelos exerted his control over the government.

Alexander's reign was unremarkable save for the curious case of his untimely demise. While walking his dogs along the grounds of the King's Forest at the Tatoi estate, he was bitten by a barbary macaque. Alexander's wounds on the leg and torso quickly became infected and he died days later.

The next month, after a deeply partisan and closely decided election, Venizelos was rebuffed in a referendum by Greek voters, 99 percent of whom called for the return of Constantine I. At first popular upon his return, Constantine's standing rapidly declined following a series of losses at the hands of the Turks, which set the stage for a humiliating defeat for Greece in the second Greco-Turkish War (1919–1922). Constantine abdicated once again, his second-born son George II oversaw the continued decline of Greek civil society, and the man who was twice king lived the remainder of his days in exile in the Sicilian capital, Palermo.

FIVE KINGS

There is one opportunity for collectors on a budget to acquire a legal tender coin bearing the likeness of Constantine I, although it was created decades after his rule.

In 1963, Greece issued a commemorative 30-drachmai silver coin marking the centennial of the rule of the House of Glücksburg. This .835 fine silver coin weighs 18 grams and features five coin-like portraits, bearing the likenesses of the each of the Glücksburg kings. The coin was designed by V. Falireas. Three million examples were struck.

A certified example of this coin in Gem sells for about $60.

GREECE 1915 SILVER 2 DRACHMAI PATTERN

The king who ruled twice.

Obverse. A left-facing bust portrait of King Constantine I. A laurel wreath is in the hair, and a bow and ribbon extend behind the neck. The designer's name is below the bust truncation: Κ. ΔΗΜΗΤΡΙΑΔΗΣ (K. Dimitriades). The inscription ΚΩΝΣΤΑΝΤΙΝΟΣ ΒΑΣΙΛΕΥΣ ΤΩΝ ΕΛΗΝΩΝ ("Constantine, King of the Hellenic People") wraps around the rim. The date is below the bust truncation. ESSAI is in small text to the right of the date. Beaded denticles around the rim.

Reverse. In the center of the design, enveloped by a crown and an ermine-draped mantle, is a simplified version of the Greek coat of arms: a shield with horizontal lines (azure tincture) and a cross represents the blue and white shield of Greece. Below is a small crown and a badge of the Order of the Redeemer, which hangs from a ribbon, on which is written: ΙΣΧΥΣ ΜΟΥ Η ΑΓΑΠΗ. ΤΟΥ ΛΑΟΥ ("My Power, the Love of the People"). Wrapping around the top of the design is the legend: ΒΑΣΙΛΕΙΟΝ ΤΗΣ ΕΛΛΑΔΟΣ ("Kingdom of Greece"). Wrapping around the bottom of the design is the denomination ΔΙΔΡΑΧΜΟΝ (2 drachmai). ESSAI appears in small text to the right of the denomination. Beaded denticles are around the rim.

Composition	Weight	Diameter	Alignment	Edge
.8350 silver	10 grams	27 mm	Coin	Reeded
Mintage	**Mint**		**Collecting Difficulty**	**References**
Unknown (very rare)	Paris Mint, Monnaie de Paris		Extremely difficult	Divo-P98; KM-E35

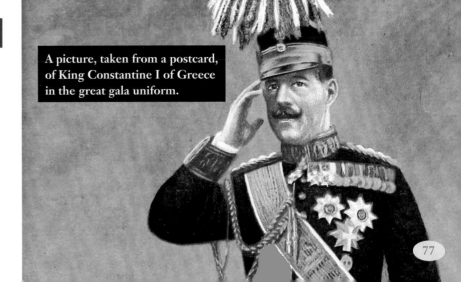

A picture, taken from a postcard, of King Constantine I of Greece in the great gala uniform.

Given the on-again, off-again nature of Constantine's rule, the Greek government did not introduce a circulating coinage bearing the monarch's likeness during either of his reigns.

Leptas and drachmas were struck on and off at the Paris Mint during the reign of his father, George I. Two of these coin types, the drachma and 2 drachmai, bore the ruler's effigy.

In 1915, the Paris Mint did undertake some effort in designing new drachma and 2-drachmai coins bearing the likeness of Constantine I; however, these concepts never made it past the pattern stage.

Examples that are known were struck in various compositions, including silver and gold, and feature a completely redesigned obverse and reverse. The Constantine patterns show a distinctive bust portrait of the monarch wearing an olive crown, with the minor Greek coat of arms on the reverse.

Each of these patterns is very rare and seldom offered at auction.

The most significant one, the 1915 2 drachmai (KM-E35) in silver, brought US$57,500 when it was offered in April 2012 by Heritage Auctions[1]. This example, graded PF-64 by NGC, is the finer of two silver examples certified by the service. None have been certified by PCGS. A 2-drachmai pattern struck in gold, also rare, brought $18,000 at a 2008 Numismatica Genevensis SA auction. It would likely bring much more if offered today.

The drachma patterns of Constantine also bring significant prices at auction. In August 2014, Heritage sold a 1915 drachma pattern struck in an alloy of copper, silver, nickel, and zinc for $19,975[2], while a copper-nickel example brought $15,275 in January 2017[3].

Street scene, Patras, Greece, circa 1910.

Statue of King Constantine I in the Square of Democracy.

While struck in Bombay, Calcutta, and London, the British trade dollar was actually struck to facilitate trade in British-controlled territories along the coast of China. Struck from 1895 to 1935, the series was issued during the reigns of Queen Victoria, Edward VII, and George V and marked the continuation of Britain's expansionist policies in Asia.

The British footprint in the territory was greatly broadened after its victory in the Opium Wars (1839–1842 and 1856–1860) gave it tremendous leverage over the Qing dynasty, which had until that point been reluctant to open up trade within its territories to British exports.

Prior to these wars, Britain's thirst for Chinese tea, porcelain, and silk was insatiable, but Chinese import controls were so strict under the Canton System that foreign merchants were often frustrated when trying to exchange their western goods for Chinese ones. To counter this, Britain became the world's largest dealer in illicit drugs, dumping millions of pounds of opium into the ports along the Chinese coast. When Viceroy Lin Zexu (林則徐, *Lín Zéxú*) seized 20,000 chests of the illicit drug without offering compensation, the British forces had the justification they needed to launch a large-scale military act to seize control of Chinese ports and the island of Hong Kong.

Over the next several decades, European and American trade into China expanded. This weakened the Qing dynasty and ultimately helped seal its fate. Opening up ports to western goods eventually led to the opening of the Chinese mainland, creating a valuable market for Great Britain while fomenting populist resentment in China that ultimately led to a civil war and the establishment of the Chinese communist government.

The motif of the British trade dollar denotes power and dominion over Chinese territory—European colonialist imagery at its best. Greek key scrollwork dominates both obverse and reverse, while a fully armed Britannia carries a trident aloft in one hand while holding onto a shield adorned with the cross-striped pattern of the Union Jack in the other. She stands in the foreground, a British trade ship at full sail in the background. It's a not-too-subtle warning: our trade ships are coming and the full force of our empire stands ready to protect them. The tiny B mintmark for Bombay is hidden in the center prong of Britannia's trident.

Centered on the reverse is the Chinese symbol for longevity. Surrounding it is an arabesque quatrefoil with the denomination inscribed in both Chinese and in Malay. Also on the reverse is an older form of the denomination. 壹圓 means "one yuan" or "one dollar;" the numeral 壹 is used in financial and official records for the number one (*yī*) to avoid possible confusion with other Chinese numerals, and 圓 is an alternative form of the now-more-common symbol for yuan, 元.

Before this period, all manner of international silver coinage poured into the region. This lack of a standard and an earned distrust for forgeries and counterfeits are why so many silver coins of the period bear counterstamps from Chinese merchants and assayers.

The British trade dollar was struck intermittently through the first two decades of the twentieth century. In years when the coins were produced, mintages would easily eclipse a million coins or more annually; 1911, for instance, saw a prodigious output of over 37 million pieces struck at the Bombay Mint. Production of new coins was put on hiatus after 1.5 million coins were struck in 1913. The striking of the 1921-B, the coin we presently discuss, marked the resumption of production of this silver trade coin.

In total, 50,211 examples were struck but the coin was never released into circulation. Krause reports a "mintage" of five pieces in their *Standard Catalog* of twentieth-century world coins. Other reports put the survivors at six.

Commissioner Lin and the destruction of opium in 1839.

GREAT BRITAIN 1921-B SILVER TRADE DOLLAR

The sun never sets on British international trade.

Obverse. Britannia stands on land looking out to the ocean, with a British trade ship behind. A trident is in her right hand, a shield with the Union Jack is in her left hand. The scene is bordered by a round band with denticles and a meander or key pattern. The denomination • ONE [Britannia's Head] DOLLAR • wraps around the perimeter. The date is in small numerals in the exergue.

Reverse. In the center is a Chinese symbol for longevity and an arabesque design featuring a large quatrefoil. There is a round band of denticles and a key pattern as on the obverse. The denomination is inscribed in Chinese characters and Jawi script: 壹圓 (*Yī Yuán* ["One Dollar"]) and ساتو رڠڬيت.

Composition	Weight	Diameter	Alignment	Edge
.900 silver	25.9568 grams	39 mm	Medal	Reeded
Mintage	**Mint**		**Collecting Difficulty**	**References**
50,211 (5 known surviving)	Royal Mint (Bombay)†		Extremely difficult	KM-T5

† Mintmark: B

Also rare is the 1935-B issue, of which 6,811,995 were struck. Nearly all were melted after the Currency Ordinance of 1935 rendered the issue irrelevant. To date, there is some dispute as to which of the two emissions, the 1921-B or the 1935-B, is rarer.

In 1937, the British trade dollar was demonetized.

Speaking to the rarity of the issue—especially as it comes to examples entering into the U.S. market—PCGS has graded over 5,000 British trade dollars struck from 1895 through 1935; only two of those were the 1921-B and none are the 1935-B.

One piece, currently the plate coin of PCGS Coinfacts, is a golden russet-toned example graded MS-63+. This coin was last offered publicly at the March 2014 St. James's auction number 26, where it brought £36,000 (US$45,000). At the time, the coin was encapsulated in an NGC MS-63 holder.

The second recorded PCGS coin was sold by Heritage Auctions in 2005 at the HWCA New York Signature Sale, where it brought $48,300 (lot 22416). That coin was in Brilliant Choice Uncirculated condition, grading MS-63.

NGC's census accounts for four grading events. The abovementioned MS-63 remains on the books, as do examples in MS-62, AU-55, and a details-grade specimen. Spink restrikes of the 1921-B trade dollar in Proof were manufactured in 1960 and are rare.

A Chinese tea set.

The clipper *Cutty Sark* in full sails (before 1916), a ship similar to those used in British opium trade.

The Long Whisker silver dollar pattern is one of the most ornate numismatic treasures of modern Chinese coinage. Struck in 1911, one year before the Xuantong Emperor (宣統帝, *Xuāntǒng Dì;* era name meaning "declaration of unity") Pu Yi (溥儀, *Pǔyí*), the last emperor of the Qing dynasty, abdicated the throne, the coin marks one of the last imperial efforts to reform Chinese currency and produce a universal coinage to supersede the provincial issues circulating at the time.

While China had a number of mints striking coins, the goal was to centralize production of the national coinage at the mint in Tientsin. For this coin, the mint turned to the West, enlisting the work of talented Italian engravers to design the patterns and cut the new dies.

The design of the 1911 Long Whisker Dragon silver dollar was ornate and beautiful but never adopted. A small number of coins were struck in silver and at least one example, probably a presentation piece, was struck in gold.

An NGC MS-61 specimen sold for US$76,375 (including buyer's premium) in Heritage's April 2014 sale, while an example one point better (NGC MS-62) pedigreed to the W&B Capital Collection exceeded presale estimates and brought $131,450 at the August 2016 Stack's Bowers' Hong Kong sale.

Gathering even more interest was a PCGS SP-64 (secure holder) specimen that sold for $200,000 at a Stack's Bowers May 2015 rarities auction (also of the rounded petals variety).

The gold striking tracks an impressive pedigree, once belonging to King Farouk of Egypt and later to Austrian banker and numismatist Eduard Kann; the coin now resides in the collection of Chen Gi Mao.

CHINA 1911 LONG WHISKER SILVER DOLLAR PATTERN

China's last effort at imperial coinage.

Obverse. In the center, large Chinese characters 大清 (top to bottom: *Dà Qīng* ["Great Qing"]) and 銀幣 (right to left: *Yínbì* ["Silver Coin"]), encircled by a thin beaded border. Wrapping around the design are Manchu characters at the top and Chinese characters (right to left) 宣統三年 (*Xuāntǒng Sān Nián* ["Xuantong Year Three"]) at the bottom, both of which refer to the third year of the reign of the Xuantong Emperor. A floral motif separates the two inscriptions on the left and right sides of the coin. Beaded denticles around the rim.

Reverse. In the center, 壹圓 (1 Yuan), surrounded by a dragon with long whiskers. An auspicious orb is situated in the center, below the Chinese characters and above the English translation of the denomination ONE DOLLAR. Small floral motifs embellish the design, wrapping around the rim. Beaded denticles.

Composition	Weight	Diameter	Alignment	Edge
Silver	26.9 grams	39.25 mm	Medal	Reeded
Mintage	**Mint**		**Collecting Difficulty**	**References**
Unknown	Tientsin Mint		Extremely difficult	K-223; KM-Pn304; L&M-28

(Above) A 2012 stamp issued with a historic picture of the Xuantong Emperor.

(Right) A fan showing the Qing dynasty's map of "all under heaven," circa 1890.

AUSTRALIA 1919–1921 SQUARE KOOKABURRA PATTERNS

A distinctive bird, a failed coin.

Obverse. In the center is the left-facing portrait of King George V. The initials B.M. in the truncation. Wrapping around the bust is the inscription •GEORGIVS V D. G. BRITT: OMN: REX• (abbreviated Latin for *GEORGIUS V DEI GRATIA BRITANNIARUM OMNIUM REX* ["George V, by the Grace of God, King of all the Britons"]). The date is centered below the bust truncation, and the rim is raised. Type 9 and Type 10 issues of 1920 feature obverse inscriptions that wrap around the inside of the squared rim. Type 10 issue features the crowned portrait of George V.

Reverse. In the center is a right-facing kookaburra on a branch. Above its head, slightly arched, is the legend AUSTRALIA. On some examples, the denomination appears below the bird. On others, the denomination is stacked, appearing to the bottom right of the bird. The rim is raised.

Composition	Weight	Diameter	Alignment	Edge
Various, including copper-nickel	Various	Various, including 18 mm for penny (KM-Pn22, Type 13)	Medal	Smooth

Mintage	Mint	Collecting Difficulty	References
200 (estimated)	Royal Mint (Melbourne and London)	Extremely difficult	Various

A failed experiment, Australia's unusual rounded square kookaburra pattern coins, which were struck between 1919 and 1921, represent an effort by the government to implement much needed cost-cutting monetary reforms.

The proposals for change came from Treasurer William Watt shortly after the conclusion of World War I. After the war, the Australian government found itself deeply in debt and as part of a government-wide austerity program, Watt proposed that the treasury shift away from the bimetallic standard to a fiat system. He called for the reduction of silver content for the nation's coins and the adoption of smaller, cheaper coins to replace the cumbersome and expensive copper penny and half penny.

While Watt's kookaburra patterns did just that, they also marked a radical shift in not only the cosmetic character of Australian coinage (which up to that time had been serious, regal, and ornate), but the proposed metal composition of copper-nickel was a dramatic departure from the traditional bronze composition. Two hundred or so examples were struck and distributed to government officials for review but for various reasons, including pushback from the vending industry, the kookaburra initiative was never implemented.

For numismatists, *fascination almost always follows failure.* The kookaburra patterns never saw circulation but were instead struck as official proposals of what could have been, providing a captivating "what if" to the study of Australian numismatic history.

Couple this with the character of the design, both in the coin's shape and the endearing quality of the engraving, and you have something truly special.

The coin's obverse features a portrait of King George V and Sir Edgar Bertram Mackennal's simple engraving of the small bird on the reverse. The kookaburra, a carnivorous bird native to Australia and the surrounding islands, was already seen as something of a national symbol before its depiction on the proposed coinage. Just five years before, in 1914, the bird adorned Australia's sixpence postage stamp.

The portrait of George V caused considerable concern on the part of the Royal Mint, as it was standard practice to show the king with a crown. Nevertheless, after lengthy discussions among mint officials at Melbourne and London, the king signed off on the design and allowed the crownless effigy to be used. In time, many Commonwealth coins would be struck with crownless bust portraiture.

In total, there are 23 known subtypes: 21 penny and two half penny types. 20 are struck in copper-nickel. Most of the cosmetic differences between the patterns deal with the size of the bird, the length of the branch, and the location and orientation of the denomination. A 1920 type features a crowned George V.

As a collectible, kookaburra patterns appear on the market with sufficient frequency and in sufficient variants to establish a viable collector market for them for the advanced collector.

Silver versions of three types of 1919 pennies were struck under the order of Melbourne Mint Deputy Mint Master A.H. Le Souef. These are valued at about US$400,000 each.

The 1920 half penny is exceptionally rare with only three known examples, one of which is in the permanent collection of the Museums Victoria. Estimated value of the two remaining pieces is about $400,000. More affordable and available is the half penny issue of 1921; in 2016, a choice example sold for AU$95,000.

Kookaburra in Kensington Park, Sydney, Australia.

In the U.S., examples certified by either PCGS or NGC have brought considerable interest. A 1919 penny (Type 6) graded SP-63 by PCGS brought US$86,250 at a January 2012 Heritage auction[2]. A PCGS SP-65 1921 issue (Type 11) brought $23,500 at a 2017 Stack's Bowers auction. The last time a kookaburra half penny was offered at a U.S. auction was in 2014, when an NGC MS-65 (Type 2) from the John L. Ahbe and Osborne Collection failed to meet its reserve.

Scarcity by Type

The following table, produced by the leading Australian numismatic firm CoinWorks, details the scarcity of the kookaburra patterns by type[1]:

Penny		
Date:	Type	Mintage
1919	3	15
1919	4	4
1919	5	8
1919	6	8
1920	7	12
1920	8	4
1920	9	7
1920	10	7
1920	13	1
1921	11	20
1921	12	40

Half Penny		
Date:	Type	Mintage
1920	1	3
1921	2	9

KOOKABURRAS FOR THE REST OF US

While $100,000 pattern coins may be a little too upmarket for most collectors, Australian silver bullion coins bearing the kookaburra have been issued on an annual basis since 1990. Several emissions in the series have mintages well below the maximum number authorized, and since each year's release comes with a new kookaburra design, collectors may enjoy building a set of these popular Perth Mint issues.

Terraced houses on Macquarie Street, Sydney, circa 1915.

World War I recruitment poster in Australia.

RUSSIA 1921 SOVIET FEDERATIVE SOCIALIST REPUBLIC SILVER RUBLE

A time of political and social upheaval.

Obverse. In the center, the coat of arms of the RSFSR inlaid within a beaded circle. The coat of arms depicts an ornate shield, on which a design shows a hammer and sickle aloft with the rising sun in the background. A wreath of wheat surrounds it on the left and right. Below the coat of arms, in an ornate ribbon, is the Cyrillic legend РСФСР ("RSFSR"). Wrapping around the design, outside the beaded circle and inside the raised rim, is the inscription ПРОЛЕТАРИИ ВСЕХ СТРАН, СОЕДИНЯЙТЕСЬ! ("Workers of the World Unite!")

Reverse. Within a beaded circle is a five-pointed star with a circle at the center. The numeral 1 is within the center circle on the star. The date is below the star. Outside of the beads, wrapping around the design, is a wreath of olive and oak branches. The word РУБЛЬ ("ruble") above. The rim is raised.

Composition	Weight	Diameter	Alignment	Edge
.900 silver	19.996 grams	33.5 mm	Medal	Lettered†

Mintage	Mint	Collecting Difficulty	References
1,000,000	Leningrad Mint (St. Petersburg)	Easy	Y-84

† "ЧИСТОГО СЕРЕБРА 4 ЗОЛОТНИКА 21 ДОЛЯ" ("Pure Silver 4 Zolotniks 21 Parts"), with mint master's initials (А·Г, for A.F. Hartman, 1921)

Vladimir Lenin, circa 1920.

Economic and social calamity were the immediate result of the Revolution of October 1917. With more than a little help from Germany, which hoped that its support would lead to a withdrawal of Russian forces from the Eastern Front, Vladimir Lenin and his Bolsheviks sought to redraw the political map not only in Russia, but throughout the world.

After unseating Russia's nascent post-czarist democratic government, which made the fatal mistake of continuing Russia's involvement in the unpopular war, the Bolsheviks carried out a reign of terror, which historians refer to as War Communism.

During this period, the country saw unprecedented declines in GDP; its industrial production dropped by 85 percent, its national monetary system was abandoned, and as many as ten million Russians died of hunger as a result. It was a catastrophic time for the Russian people, who saw their standard of living fall to levels unseen since before the Industrial Revolution[1].

Eventually, economic reality set in and the Lenin government, fully entrenched in power by 1920, set in motion a plan to re-stabilize the Russian monetary system. It did so, ironically, by adopting a bimetallic system based on gold *chervonetz* (10-ruble coins) and silver rubles.

The first of the new rubles was struck in 1921. Often referred to as the "Star Ruble" due to the prominent five-pointed star on the coin's reverse (a symbol for the global communist movement), the silver coin saw production one million circulation strikes plus a small number of Proofs in 1921. The Leningrad Mint would double production of the ruble in 1922 and add emissions of 10-, 15-, and 20-kopek coins to the country's circulating coinage in 1923.

The circulating life of this ruble was as short-lived as its production life. The Russian Soviet Federative Socialist Republic soon gave way to the Union of Soviet Socialist Republics. As communist revolutionaries became entrenched government leaders, new rivalries and agendas formed. Ultimately, the Russian proletariat would be no better off.

The coat of arms of the Soviet Federative Socialist Republic.

Hungry Russian women kneel before American Relief Administration officials, circa 1922.

Nevertheless, these issues represent the beginning of something new for the world: the money of communist regimes. Far from the ideal of fairness and rationing for all or a society free from capital, coins like the RSFSR ruble and the gold chervonetz prove that money, in all of its forms, is durable and necessary.

The RSFSR ruble coin was struck for only two years: in 1921 and 1922. As a collectible coin, the ruble issues of the RSFSR are important for their place in history more so than for their rarity. Nevertheless, these issues represent an important beginning for a revolutionary economic system that would play a central role in shaping global social and economic politics for more than 70 years.

In Mint State, circulation-strike ruble coins from 1921 and 1922 (both the Hartman and Latishev issues) can be acquired for under $500 per piece up to the certified grade of MS-63, with finer pieces bringing considerably more depending on factors such as eye appeal and conditional rarity. To date, NGC has certified 588 examples of the 1921 issue, with just five in the grade of MS-66. While PCGS has certified 122 examples, three tied for finest at MS-65.

Proof strikings are scarce and bring $15,000 or more for upper-end pieces. Certified populations reflect a paucity of examples available to American collectors, with fewer than 20 grading events reported at both services combined. Two examples in PF-67 are reported by NGC; one of the two, a nicely toned piece, brought $17,250 at a September 2007 Heritage Auction[2]. More recently, the other PF-67 piece, this one pedigreed to the Dr. Moore Collection, brought $16,450 when it was sold in January 2017[3].

Vladimir Lenin delivers a speech to troops in the Soviet-Polish War, May 5, 1920.

Soviet Russia famine victims, circa March 1922.

A mounted police officer on a Russian street.

SOUTH AFRICA 1967 GOLD KRUGERRAND

The spark of international bullion investment.

Obverse. A left-facing bust of Paul Kruger. Wrapping around the top of the design is the legend, written in Afrikaans and English: SUID-AFRIKA ♦ SOUTH AFRICA. Beaded denticles around the design.

Reverse. In the center is a right-facing springbok, walking on the top of a rounded cut-out of an earthen field. The date is divided to the left and right at the center line. Wrapping around the top of the design, inside of the rim, the inscription KRUGERRAND. Wrapping around the bottom of design is the metal content, written as FYNGOUD 1 OZ FINE GOLD. The designer's initials C.L.S. (Coert Laurens Steynberg) are written in small text above the word GOLD. Beaded denticles around the rim.

Composition	Weight	Diameter	Alignment	Edge
.9167 gold	33.93 grams	32.7 mm	Medal	Reeded

Mintage	Mint	Collecting Difficulty	References
40,000 (plus 10,000 Proofs)	South African Mint (Pretoria)	Easy	Hern-K1-58, Hern-GRCO1-7; KM-73

Paul Kruger, circa 1880.

South Africa had become one of the world's leading producers of gold by the 1960s, as the Bretton Woods Agreement, a formal system of stabilizing exchange rates among major powers by pegging gold to the U.S. dollar, began to fray. Officially, the gold standard that had dominated the global economic system up until the early-twentieth century had fallen, leaving in its wake heightened tensions amongst the world's major powers. Fearing that economic warfare might trigger a third world war—coupled with a real fear among the Western liberal powers that economic pain felt by European and Asian countries rebuilding after the war might incentivize them to fall into the Soviet economic model—America took on the mantle of the primary global economic power.

This dominance would set in place a period of prolonged and sustained economic vitality in the American economy and help propel global rebuilding and modernization. Eventually, America's competitive edge was ceded to resurgent modern foreign economies. Pressure on the dollar ultimately drove President Richard Nixon's administration to withdraw from Bretton Woods and investors, seeing danger and inflation in fiat currencies, turned to hard money as a hedge.

It was this sentiment that led the South African Mint to introduce a legal tender bullion coin to the market. That coin, the 22-karat Krugerrand, was first struck in 1967 and would go on to change the face of the minting industry. Fifty years later, in a market crowded by legal tender bullion issues, it remains a well-known and respected bullion product.

The Krugerrand name is an amalgamation of the last name of South African Republic leader Paul Kruger, and the rand, the monetary unit of South Africa. It is Kruger's familiar bearded profile on the obverse. On the reverse is a springbok, a type of antelope native to South Africa and a national symbol. Both sides used designs from historic South African coins, representing the prestige and authority of the South African government: the obverse was designed by Otto Schultz of the Imperial German Mint for the issue of South African Republic (ZAR) rands from 1892; the springbok motif was borrowed from the South African 5 shilling's reverse, designed by South African sculptor Coert Steynberg.

The metal of the Krugerrand is comprised of a copper-gold alloy known as crown gold, which is the same alloy used for the production of the United Kingdom's gold sovereigns. The alloy not only increases the coin's durability but also gives it that famous rose-orange sheen. This, coupled with its classic design, added greatly to the Krugerrand's eye appeal.

The coin, which weighs slightly more than one troy ounce (1.0909 ounces, or 33.93 grams), features no face value or denomination on either side—its value instead is based solely on the spot price of gold.

A springbok in Etosha National Park, Namibia.

The Chamber of Mines Building, Johannesburg.

An anti-apartheid poster from around 1975.

APARTHEID'S CONTRABAND COIN

Apartheid was the official government policy of South Africa from 1948 to 1991. It was a policy of brutal, systematic racial discrimination and segregation aimed at preserving minority white control over the majority black African population. As the extent of this oppression became too much for the international community to ignore (it's important to note that racist policies of Western countries proved to be a recurring target in Soviet and communist propaganda), various countries began to take action on the economic stage. In 1986, the United States passed the Comprehensive Anti-Apartheid Act, which imposed sanctions on the country that could not be lifted without certain conditions being met—which would also mean the unraveling of South Africa's white supremacist regime and apparatus.

One impact of Apartheid in the bullion coin market was that the Krugerrand was now contraband. American buyers, who had flocked to the coin once private bullion ownership was made legal, fled to other sources. The success of the Krugerrand as an investment instrument during the 1970s spurred many imitators and provided the world's mints a roadmap to a new kind of profitable business. In 1979, Canada issued the Gold Maple Leaf. In 1986, the United States inaugurated the Gold and Silver Eagle program. Other countries followed suit and today the Krugerrand is just one of a number of state-backed bullion coins in an increasingly crowded marketplace.

Production of the Krugerrand was a joint venture between the South African Mint and the Rand Refinery. Located in Germiston, South Africa, the Rand Refinery was the sole producer of Krugerrand planchets and was established in 1920 by the South African Chamber of Mines.

About 50,000 gold bullion Krugerrand coins were struck in its debut year of 1967. An additional 10,000 Proofs were also minted. This was just a modest start to a coin series that would see more than 60 million ounces of gold pass through the South African Mint's coin presses.

In the United States, the biggest drawback to ownership of a gold Krugerrand was the fact that private ownership of gold was illegal. It wasn't until 1974 that Americans could legally purchase gold bullion coins. By the 1980s, however, international attitudes about South Africa's social policy of Apartheid tainted all of South Africa's exports, including the Krugerrand.

MEXICO 1916 OAXACA GOLD 60 PESOS

Revolutionary heroes enter Mexican legend.

Obverse. The left-facing head of Benito Juárez, offset slightly high of the center. Beneath, a vegetal wreath is tied together at the center by a ribbon. An inscription wraps around the central device and reads ESTADO L. Y S. DE OAXACA-60 PESOS ORO ("Free and Sovereign State of Oaxaca—60 Gold Pesos"). A vegetal ornament borders the rim.
Reverse. LIBERTAD is inscribed on the cap before a glory of rays. Beneath are a balance scale, sword, and scroll, which reads LEY. The inscription wraps around the motif and reads REPUBLICA MEXICANA 902.7 * T.M. * 1916. T.M. are the initials of Mint Director Teofilo Monroy[1].

Composition	Weight	Diameter	Alignment	Edge
Gold	49.994 grams	39 mm	Coin	Reeded

Mintage	Mint	Collecting Difficulty	References
Unknown	Oaxaca	Extremely difficult	Fr-174; G-OAX 79; HW-178; U-OAX-30b; Vogt & Bruce 755

Benito Juárez, circa 1850–1872.

The Mexican Revolution (1910–1920) stands as one of the most consequential domestic upheavals of the twentieth century. It began as an attempt to wrest control away from corrupt elites, eliminate international interference in domestic politics (of which the American government and businesses played a large role), and remove perennial president General Porfirio Díaz from office via the ballot box. But it devolved into a decade-long bloody and chaotic conflict that cost more than 1.2 million Mexicans their lives and displaced hundreds of thousands of people—many of them forming the first major wave of Mexican immigrants to the United States.

It was a period of brave heroes and ruthless villains, of roaming posses and military chieftains, and of cultural re-awakening. The major players remain firmly enshrined in Mexican folklore.

There was Emiliano Zapata, a poor tenant farmer from the South-Central Mexican state of Morelos who rose up against the federal armies, took Mexico City three times, and fought to return lands to the indigenous population. He was betrayed and killed in 1919.

Then there was social reformer and failed President Francisco Madero, a revolutionary leader who overthrew the Diaz regime in 1911 but ultimately failed to stabilize the country or enact needed reforms. He was assassinated in 1913.

From the northern state of Chihuahua was José Doroteo Arango Arámbula, better known as Francisco "Pancho" Villa. Villa was a firebrand of a revolutionary leader whose exploits, both real and imagined, captured the imaginations of people on both sides of the U.S.–Mexico border. His love for his fellow countrymen and pursuit of social reforms made him a hero; his brutality and ruthlessness made him a target for his political adversaries—as well as General John J. Pershing and the United States Army. Almost executed by firing squad in 1912 after slapping revolutionary general and eventual dictator Victoriano Huerta in the face, Villa met his end in 1923, when gunmen ambushed his Dodge touring car on the streets of Parral.

From this period of political upheaval, vying factions, and larger-than-life revolutionaries survives an incomprehensibly complex tranche of coins and banknotes. Some are well-documented, while others remain enigmatic and mysterious.

Francisco "Pancho" Villa (1877–1923), Mexican revolutionary general, wearing bandoliers in front of an insurgent camp, circa 1910–1915.

Of the hundreds of state and regional issues (many of which are scarce or rare today), perhaps the most coveted are the revolutionary coinage of the Mexican state of Oaxaca (pronounced "wuh HA ca").

This southern state is far removed from the U.S.–Mexico border. Its geography comprises dense forests and rugged mountains, and its shores open up to the Pacific Ocean by way of the Gulf of Tehuantepec. Its population largely consists of the indigenous tribes of the Zapotec and Mixtec. Its largest city, Oaxaca, had a population of roughly 50,000 people at the time of the revolution. This was hardly an area out of which one would expect one the twentieth century's greatest coins.

After seceding from Mexico on June 3, 1915, Governor José Inéz Dávila ordered the reopening of the old Oaxaca Mint so the newly formed republic could begin to strike its own coinage. An American engraver residing in Oaxaca named John DeCoe was hired to cut the dies. The resulting coins, produced in limited numbers and mostly destroyed, featured the likeness of Benito Pablo Juárez, the nineteenth-century revolutionary who overthrew the Mexican Empire of Austrian-born Maximilian I. Juárez was a native son of Oaxaca.

The coins, issued in denominations ranging from 1 centavo to 60 pesos, were struck in copper, silver, and a limited number of pieces in gold. The rarest of them was the 60 pesos, a large gold coin weighing nearly 50 grams.

American collectors first caught notice of the coinage in the years immediately following their manufacture. In 1916, coin promoter and past ANA President Farran Zerbe exhibited some 50 examples of the coinage to those in attendance at Baltimore's Peabody Institute for the 17th convention of the American Numismatic Association. In 1920, collector M.

Sorenson wrote of the coinage in great detail in the April issue of *The Numismatist*. Of the 60 pesos, Sorenson noted the mintage was but a paltry 21 pieces. He claimed that two were in the hands of consuls from France and England, one belonged to a German merchant, and two arrived in New York in April 1917 by way of Oaxaca resident Gustave Bellon. One of these is impounded in the collection of the American Numismatic Society, and Sorenson claimed possession of the other. The ANS also has in its collection the original dies, which were donated on January 27, 1941, by collector E. H. Windau[3]. Sorenson also claimed a total of 14 were allegedly buried by wealthy Oaxaca natives. What became of the two outstanding pieces not listed in Sorenson's account is unclear.

What is known is that the 60 pesos is seldom seen at auction. NGC reports seven grading events for the issue, with the finest one being a dazzling example with full luster that grades MS-66. An example, formerly part of the Josiah K. Lily collection, was donated to the Smithsonian Institution by the Lily estate and is currently on display at the National Museum of American History's "Value of Money" exhibition. In 2003, Heritage Auctions offered a curious example, one that was struck over a "Hand on Book" 8 escudos. It is unclear whether this possibly unique piece was struck contemporaneously with the regular issue or made later using original dies.

When numismatic writer Richard Giedroyc compiled his list of "Top 100 World and Ancient Coins of the Millennium" for PCGS, he ranked the ersatz Oaxaca 60 pesos overstrike number 72. Although we are inclined to gently disagree with that assessment, there's no denying that the "original" 21 certainly rank among the "greatest" world coins of the twentieth century.

Downtown Oaxaca City.

CHINA 1928 KWEICHOW SILVER AUTO DOLLAR

One of China's most famous modern coins.

Obverse. Encircling the top half of the coin from right to left are the Chinese characters 中華民國十七年 (*Zhōnghuá Mínguó Shíqī Nián* ["Republic of China Year 17"]), with four-petal rosettes on either side. Right to left along the bottom are the characters 壹圓, which represent the denomination of one yuan. In the center, divided from the other inscriptions by a circle of small beads, the characters 貴州銀幣 are arranged in a crosswise pattern. 貴州 (*Guizhōu* ["Kweichow"], modern Guizhou province) runs from the top to the bottom; 銀幣 (*Yínbì* ["silver coin"]) reads from right to left. At the very center is a stylized poppy flower, which serves as the mintmark for the Kweichow Mint.

Reverse. The inscription along the top (right to left): 貴州省政府造 (*Guizhōu Shěng Zhèngfǔ Zào* ["Made by the Provincial Government of Kweichow"]). Four-petal rosettes divide the top from the bottom, where the denomination 七錢二分 (*Qī Qián Èr Fēn* ["Seven Mace Two Candareens"]) is found. A circle of small beads divides the inscribed outer area from the central design. Inside is an American-made automobile from the same era as the coin—possibly a Packard touring car, manufactured by the Packard Motor Car Company in Canton, Ohio. Beneath the car is a semi-circle of unusually articulated grass, which, if you rotate the coin 90 degrees, is said to contain the name of Kweichow Governor Zhou Xicheng.

Composition	Weight	Diameter	Alignment	Edge
Silver	26.8 grams	39 mm	Medal	Reeded

Mintage	Mint	Collecting Difficulty	References
648,000	Kweichow	Moderately difficult	K-757; L&M-609; Y-428

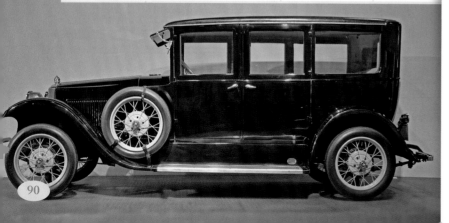

A 1924 Packard Single Six Touring Model 233.

Compared to many of the Chinese coins in this list, the 1928 Kweichow auto dollar is probably the one most familiar to American collectors of world coins. A quick look at the design and you will see why—on the coin's reverse is depicted an American automobile, contemporary to the period.

Why would such an unusual (and modern) motif be deemed suitable on the coinage of one of the most impoverished and inaccessible Chinese provinces?

The answer lies with the warlord of Kweichow province, Zhou Xicheng (周西成, *Zhōu Xīchéng*), who ordered the coins struck to commemorate the completion of the Kweichow Provincial Highway, the first modern road in the province. According to cataloger Bruce Smith, the road was built with the direct help of American missionaries as part of the International Famine Relief Commission. It did not, apparently, connect to any other road, but it did serve to facilitate travel within the province.

The car depicted on the coin is said to be the one owned by Zhou. Although the design is clearly not a direct match, it is believed that the coin shows a Packard touring car. The warlord's automobile was purchased from the United States, transported to China by ship, disassembled, carried to Kweichow, and then reassembled. It's likely that it would have been the only car on the road at the time.

It was while driving his car on the road he had built that Zhou met his violent end a year later. While driving ahead of his troops (something he was warned not to do), he was ambushed by assailants. Ditching his car by the side of the road, Zhou attempted to escape on foot but was ultimately caught and assassinated.

Legend has it that when he was proposing the design of the coin, Zhou wanted it to depict him and the car. His advisors warned against placing his own image on the design and that doing so would invite bad luck. Zhou relented and opted for the car motif. But unbeknownst to his advisors, Zhou had the engraver hide the warlord's name among the blades of grass. If you rotate the coin face 90 degrees, you can (kind of) make out the characters.

On the reverse, viewers can spot the numeral 壹, used in financial and official records for the number one (*yī*) to avoid confusion with other numerals. The numeral 圓 is an alternative form of the yuan symbol, 元, which is now more common. The denomination "seven mace two candareens" (7.2 mace), corresponds to one *tael* or yuan.

There were 648,000 pieces of the issue reportedly struck, but most are lost to time. A details-grade example in a low circulated grade can bring about a thousand dollars, while better-grade examples, especially ones of the scarcer varieties, can bring prices of more than US$100,000.

An AU-58 example, graded by PCGS, brought US$74,750 at an April 2011 sale. In 2016, Champion Auctions sold the finest known example, which traced its pedigree to the important collection of Asian coins assembled by H.K. Bowker (NGC MS-63) for a record price of US$115,000.

The "24 Bends" Mountain Road in Guizhou Province, circa 1944-1945.

The numismatic history of Cuba is both rich and exciting. It is a history linked in many ways to the bilateral relationship the island country has had with the United States. For years before the Cuban Revolution, the Cuban government sourced its coinage from the U.S. Mint, which, with its extra production capacity, produced coins for smaller countries that fell under the umbrella of America's sphere of influence.

In the pre-revolutionary period of 1898–1962, the bulk of Cuban coinage bore a striking resemblance in graphical composition and typography to its American counterparts. In the first two decades of the twentieth century, Cuban coins featured the designs of U.S. Chief Engraver Charles Barber. In many ways, one can see similarities between Barber's American and Cuban designs.

After the revolution, the Cuban-American relationship famously changed. The Cuban ruling class, many of whom had connections to business and political interests in the United States, saw their livelihoods upended by the Castro government's sweeping takeover of the national

Statue of José Marti in Central Park, Havana, Cuba.

economy. With these new social reforms came repression and diaspora. Hundreds of thousands fled to America, where many made new lives for themselves in South Florida.

Tensions between the formerly friendly neighbors is well-documented. One of many ill-fated American plots to overthrow the Castro regime ended in disaster in the Bay of Pigs. In retaliation, the Cubans sought nuclear armaments from the Soviet Union to be deployed on the island. The specter of a nuclear-armed Cuba set in motion a 13-day confrontation between the United States and the Soviet Union that nearly led to the outbreak of World War III.

CUBA 1916 SIX-COIN GOLD PROOF SET

A relic of the Cuban-American relationship.

CONFLICTING SYMBOLS, A LASTING LEGACY

The Cuban flag and coat of arms have been sources of pride for the Cuban people for more than 150 years. Symbols of national strength and independence, their origin is traced back to a husband and wife living in exile in New York in the 1850s.

Cuban playwright Miguel Teurbe Tolón (1820–1857) designed the coat of arms, and his wife, Emilia, sewed and designed the flag. The Tolóns' calls for Cuban independence led to charges of sedition by the Spanish crown, but it was during their time in New York City that the revolutionary couple befriended fellow agitator Narciso López, whose filibustering adventures in Cuba were carried out with the purpose of freeing Cuba from Spain to join the United States as a slave state.

The United States would eventually seize control of Cuba in the aftermath of the Spanish-American War in 1898. Cuba was one of three major territories ceded by Spain for a sum of $20 million (the other two being Puerto Rico and Guam). In 1902, Cuba was granted a limited form of independence, with the United States allowed to intervene in Cuba's domestic, financial, and international affairs. Another part of the deal gave America an indefinite lease on a naval base at Guantánamo Bay.

Despite or possibly because of the connection to America and the revolutionary spirit of the 1850s, the Cuban government adopted the Tolón flag and coat of arms as its national symbols in 1906. They continue to serve in that role today.

Common Obverse. In the center, the right-facing head of José Martí. The inscription reads • PATRIA Y LIBERTAD • ("Father of Liberty"). At the bottom, wrapping around rim, is written the coin's weight • date • 900 M. Square denticles are around the rim.

Common Reverse. In the center, the coat of arms is surrounded by a wreath made of sprays of oak and laurel. Wrapping around the inside of the rim at the top is the inscription • REPUBLICA DE CUBA •; at the bottom is the denomination UN PESO. The other coins in the series have the same design, except for the denominations: DOS PESOS (2 pesos), CINCO PESOS (5 pesos), DIEZ PESOS (10 pesos), and VEINTE PESOS (20 pesos).

Peso				
Composition	Weight	Diameter	Alignment	Edge
.900 gold	1.6718 grams	15 mm	Coin	Reeded
Mintage	Mint		Collecting Difficulty	References
100	United States Mint (Philadelphia)		Extremely difficult	Fr-7, KM-16
2 Pesos				
Composition	Weight	Diameter	Alignment	Edge
.900 gold	3.3436 grams	16 mm	Coin	Reeded
Mintage	Mint		Collecting Difficulty	References
8	United States Mint (Philadelphia)		Extremely difficult	KM-17
4 Pesos				
Composition	Weight	Diameter	Alignment	Edge
.900 gold	6.6872 grams	19 mm	Coin	Reeded
Mintage	Mint		Collecting Difficulty	References
90	United States Mint (Philadelphia)		Extremely difficult	KM-18
5 Pesos				
Composition	Weight	Diameter	Alignment	Edge
.900 gold	8.3592 grams	21 mm	Coin	Reeded
Mintage	Mint		Collecting Difficulty	References
Unknown	United States Mint (Philadelphia)		Extremely difficult	KM-19
10 Pesos				
Composition	Weight	Diameter	Alignment	Edge
.900 gold	16.7185 grams	27 mm	Coin	Reeded
Mintage	Mint		Collecting Difficulty	References
Unknown	United States Mint (Philadelphia)		Extremely difficult	KM-20
20 Pesos				
Composition	Weight	Diameter	Alignment	Edge
.900 gold	33.437 grams	33 mm	Coin	Reeded
Mintage	Mint		Collecting Difficulty	References
10	United States Mint (Philadelphia)		Extremely difficult	KM-21

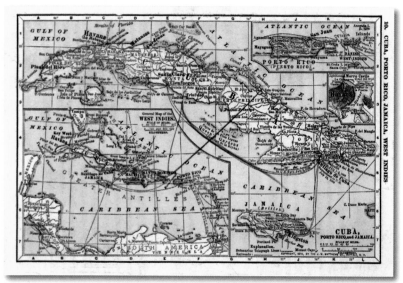

A circa 1916 map of Cuba, Jamaica, and Puerto Rico.

A postcard showing a U.S. Navy baseball game at Guantánamo Bay, Cuba, circa 1912.

Havana, Cuba, circa 1916–1917.

For Cubans in the United States and for U.S. collectors of coins of the Americas, pre-revolutionary coinage harkens back to a better time. The issues of the First Republic were struck in copper-nickel, silver, and gold. While some are scarce, most issues in the series are collectible.

The rarest and most important of the period are the Proof issues of 1915 and 1916. In terms of rarity, the 1916 is the scarcer of the two. While minor denominations were struck in Proof, the gold issues (struck in denominations of 1, 2, 4, 5, 10, and 20 pesos) stand out as truly great.

The Cuban coat of arms adorns the common obverse. This important symbol remains in use to this day. On the reverse is an effigy of modernist writer and Cuban political hero José Martí (1853–1895). It's a clean and simple design, and one that illustrates how underrated Charles Barber is as an engraver. This is a work that has weight and is not bogged down by unnecessary detail.

The gold Proofs are rare, but some are quite a bit rarer than others. Essentially a one-year issue, Cuba's 20-peso gold coin was struck for circulation in 1915, with 56,700 pieces struck at the Philadelphia Mint. Ten Proof presentation pieces were struck in 1915 and then again in 1916. After this, the issue ceased production.

One hundred examples of the gold peso were struck. NGC has certified 21 examples to date, with the finest example being a Proof 68 Ultra Cameo. PCGS has certified 15 examples, with two earning PCGS' finest grade PR-67 DCAM.

Eight examples of the 2-peso denomination were struck. PCGS and NGC combine for just three grading events of this issue. The finest known (PCGS PR-65) sold at a January 2013 Heritage auction for US$51,750. PCGS has graded one example of the 4-peso Proof; that coin graded Proof 63. NGC has graded four of the type. The finest is a Proof 66 Cameo.

Continuing the theme of rarity, some denominations have only been certified by NGC. In the 5-peso Proof, NGC has certified four, with the finest being a Proof 65. The service also notes four grading events of the 10-peso Proof, with the finest graded Proof 65. For the 20-peso, only two grading events are reported: one in Proof 63 and the other a Proof 63 Cameo.

These are fantastic rarities that seldom come to auction. But when they do, record interest is sure to follow.

Also worthy of mention is the 1915 Cuba gold Proof set. It is also quite rare, with just 24 sets reported.

KOREA 1909 YUNGHUI COPPER-NICKEL 5 CHON

A new empire modernizes.

Obverse. A left-facing flying imperial eagle is surrounded by jets of wind within a beaded circle. The inscription wraps around top of the design and reads 大韓 • 隆熙三年 • 오젼 ("Greater Korean Empire • 3rd Year of Yunghui • 5 Chon"). Denticles wrap around the raised rim.

Reverse. In the center, in large hanja script, the denomination is written as 五錢. Surrounding this is a large wreath surmounted by a plum flower, the imperial seal of Korea.

Composition	Weight	Diameter	Alignment	Edge
Copper-nickel	4.5 grams	21 mm	Coin	Smooth
Mintage	**Mint**		**Collecting Difficulty**	**References**
Unknown	Japan Mint (Osaka)		Extremely difficult	KM-1138

Emperor Sunjong of the Korean Empire, circa 1910 or earlier.

Korea had only just begun to open its borders to trade and modern reforms as the nineteenth century wound down. Leery of the rapidly modernizing Japanese Empire to the east, reliant on the declining Qing dynasty of China for protection, and facing bankruptcy and popular uprisings among members of its peasant class, the Korean government finally began to modernize its monetary system in 1882 after centuries of using cast money.

This first experiment in producing Western-style struck coins yielded denominations of 1, 2, and 3 chon (錢), the word "chon" signifying a tenth of an ounce.

While this effort to modernize the Korean monetary system yielded little in the way of material success (the higher quality coins were expensive to produce and struck in insufficient numbers to have a material impact on the economy), the improvements compelled the government to invest in expensive minting machinery imported from Germany and to continue its efforts to create a modern coinage. A year later, a second series of coins was produced, also struck in limited numbers, that included coin denominations struck in brass, copper, and silver. Thematically, the coins were similar to contemporary issues struck in Japan.

Further coinage reforms continued even as the political situation in Korea deteriorated. In 1894, a peasant rebellion ignited a proxy war between Japan and China. The forces of the Qing dynasty were outclassed by the modern army and navy of Japan.

As a result of Japan's victory, Korea declared itself the Korean Empire and undertook a series of radical modernist reforms. It also fell under the influence of the Empire of Japan, which had a free hand in shaping the contours of these reforms in its favor.

The decade saw the Korean monetary system revised to make the *yang* (兩) the primary unit, with coin denominations of 1, 2 and 5 *fun* and the quarter yang. This series of coinage also yielded great rarities like the 1893 *whan*, with its mintage of 77 pieces.

To date, NGC has certified a total of seven examples of the Year Three 1909 5 chon.

Only two of these examples earned numerical grades from the service and only one appears to be in Mint State.

Of that total, five were circulated details-grade pieces that did not qualify for a numerical grade, one was certified Very Fine, and one piece, an extraordinary example from the Dr. Norman Jacobs Collection, earned the grade MS-66.

Korean Empire Army training on a machine gun with a non-Korean trainer.

The story of European involvement in Vietnam mirrored, in many ways, the story of most other Asian countries whose borders were easily accessible via naval shipping lanes. Vietnam's earliest engagement with Europeans began in the early 1600s, when Jesuit Catholic missionaries from France arrived. This effort established an ongoing trade relationship, and over time French religious authorities became involved in the region's politics. By the middle of the nineteenth century, many in Vietnam had come to resent this involvement.

Facing a threat to imperial control from Vietnamese nationalists, France took military action to rule directly over more territory. With a victorious war against China came control over the north, and by 1885 France controlled the entirety of Vietnam. With the addition of the neighboring country of Cambodia—already a French protectorate—in 1887, the colony of French Indochina was created.

The next 50 years saw intermittent conflict with other nations in the region as France sought to gain more territory, recapture territory it had lost in previous wars, and suppress multiple rebellions that popped up throughout the colony.

During World War II, France was unable to maintain control of much of its global empire. The Japanese invasion of French Indochina lasted just four days. It is important to note that France was effectively occupied by Germany at the time.

After the war, France wanted to reclaim its former colonies; to do so in Asia, it fought a two-front war against the Chinese and the Viet Minh to recapture Indochina. In carrying out this campaign, France asked for the United States' help, which it received in 1954.

With the United States engaged in the region, France saw an exit plan. The goal of returning France's empire to its pre–World War II form was never fully realized. Over the course of the next two decades, France would further cede ground in this ambition in other parts of the world.

French Indochina formally ceased to be with the drafting of the Geneva Agreements on July 20, 1954. The document called for the cessation of hostilities and foreign involvement in the country, divided Vietnam into northern and southern zones, and ultimately called for a national election. The southern delegation, backed by the United States, rejected the accord, citing the lack of free elections under the communist system in the north.

It would take more than 20 years of violence and bloodshed to resolve this issue.

The French Indochinese piastre (piastre de commerce) was first issued in 1885 to affect price stability in the area. It remained in use until the Vietnamese đồng and other regional currencies replaced the piastre following World War II.

The coin was produced at the Paris Mint, and special trial or pattern versions of the coin are marked with the term "essai." Essais of the piastre were struck in various compositions, including silver and aluminum. A thicker silver piefort was also struck. The coin's design is iconic and is the work of French engraver Edmond-Émile Lindauer (1869–1942).

Unlike many of the issues in this book, 1931 piastre essai pieces are collectible.

A cut canceled PCGS SP-58 silver example (lot 29304) sold for US$5,019 at a December 2015 Heritage auction. A perforated canceled PCGS SP-45 silver example (lot 37469) sold for the same price almost a year later at another Heritage sale. Another cut canceled silver example (lot 37468), this one graded PCGS SP-50, sold for $3,585 at the same 2016 auction.

Geneva Conference, July 21, 1954. The last plenary session on Indochina in the Palais des Nations.

FRENCH INDOCHINA 1931 PIASTRE ESSAI SET

Imperialist ambitions in southeast Asia.

KM-EA26 (aluminum)

Obverse. The head of Liberty, facing left, wears a pileus cap and crown. The designer's name, EM.LINDAUER, appears below the bust truncation. The legend REPUBLIQUE FRANÇAISE wraps around the design and is bookended by two florettes. Ornate filigree encircles the design and wraps around the inside of the rim.

Reverse. An ornate quatrefoil shape dominates the center of the design. In the center, the denomination is written 1 PIASTRE. The date 1931 is below. The legend INDOCHINE FRANÇAISE wraps around the design. On some versions the word ESSAI appears above the date, while in other versions it appears below the quatrefoil. Ornate filigree encircles the design and wraps around the inside of the rim.

Composition	Weight	Diameter	Alignment	Edge
Silver; aluminum	20 grams (silver); 15 grams (aluminum)	35 mm	Coin	Reeded

Mintage	Mint	Collecting Difficulty	References
Unknown	Paris Mint, Monnaie de Paris	Difficult	KM-E24, E25, EA26, E26

No. 63

USSR 1991/1992 GOVERNMENT BANK EIGHT-COIN SET

A global superpower crumbles from within.

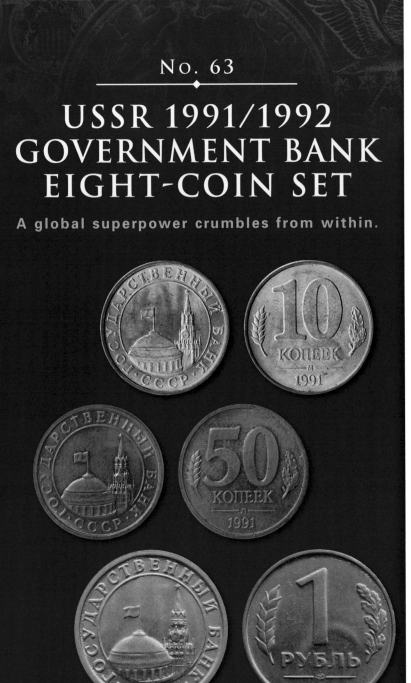

mericans of a certain age remember how it felt.

By the 1980s, the United States had lived with the fear of mutually assured nuclear Armageddon for more than 30 years. While the threat was arguably not as intense as, say, during the Cuban Missile Crisis of 1962, the Cold War between the United States and the Union of Soviet Socialist Republics (USSR) could still turn hot at the slightest provocation or radar malfunction. American news and popular media were saturated with an existential dread (*The Day After*, anyone?) that individuals born in the '80s and beyond may have a hard time comprehending.

This is why, for the West, the fall of the Berlin Wall in 1989 came as such a relief.

There were hopeful signs before then, of course. Soviets and Americans cooperated in space and worked to curtail the nuclear arms race. Mikhail Gorbachev's policies of *glasnost* ("openness") and *perestroika* ("restructuring") put forward a public face of reform and friendliness. Behind the scenes, the Soviet empire was crumbling from within.

Gorbachev's reforms had already angered hard-line communists, but the overthrow of communist governments in Eastern Europe and separatist movements in several Soviet republics pushed the hard-liners over the edge.

A coup was staged in August 1991, but it failed due to resistance from the people of Moscow. They had become emboldened and seized upon the opportunity to define their own future. Many sought integration with the West. They hungered for freedom.

Ukrainian President Leonid Kravchuk (second from left, seated), Chairman of the Supreme Council of the Republic of Belarus Stanislav Shushkevich (third from left, seated), and Russian President Boris Yeltsin (second from right, seated) during the signing ceremony to eliminate the USSR and establish the Commonwealth of Independent States.

Television footage of tanks invading Moscow, and of resistance leader and soon-to-be Russian President Boris Yeltsin delivering a speech atop one of them, provided an iconic coda to the Cold War. For Gorbachev, however, it was the end; he resigned on December 25, 1991, handing power over to Yeltsin. The next day, the Soviet Union was no more. In the eyes of American observers, it was, as American political philosopher Francis Fukuyama suggested, "the end of history."

The new Russian state, still disorganized but building towards something new, faced the immediate need of introducing post-Soviet money and stabilizing the economy. As a result, new currency and new coins were introduced.

On the coinage front, the 1991 (and sole 1992 date) Government Bank issues were the first government-authorized coins struck. It was a temporary solution. The 1991 issue includes the denominations of 10-, 5- and 1-ruble coins, plus 50 and 10 kopeks (a kopek being a hundredth of a ruble). Several coins (the 50 kopeks and all the rubles) were struck at the mint in Leningrad and feature a ЛМД or Л mintmark (with the exception of the 1992 10 rubles and the 1991 ruble, which have no marks). A few of the coins (10 kopeks, 5 and 10 rubles) were struck in Moscow and bear a ММД or M mintmark. Together, this makes for eight different dates and issues. The coins were demonetized the next year and replaced by a new series.

Six of the coins are common and should not be hard to locate. The relative rarities are the bimetallic 1991-M and 1992 10-ruble coins. Far from difficult to collect, expect to pay around $300 to $400 for a mediocre example. Copper-nickel and brass trials are known to exist for the 10 kopeks.

The common obverse design features the dome of the Kremlin Senate and the clock face of Spasskaya ("Savior") Tower. Both landmarks are located at the northern corner of the Kremlin in Moscow.

For Russia, many possible paths toward the future existed when these coins were struck. Practical realities, however, tempered the enthusiasm of the democratic movement. Today's Russia no more resembles the Russia of 1991 than it did in the final years of the Soviet Union. Much of the international order created around the dynamic of the U.S./USSR rivalry continues to exist, but the character of the problems that order faces concerning Russia's place in the world has shifted and is unquestionably darker.

But in that moment, these coins may have served as a symbol—for better and for worse—of those possibilities.

Spasskaya Tower, Moscow.

Common Obverse. The Spasskaya tower with the Kremlin Clock is in the background, right; the dome of the Kremlin Senate is in the foreground, left. A flag is flying atop the dome. The inscription ГОСУДАРСТВЕННЫЙ БАНК ("Government Bank") is clockwise along the top (on the outer ring of 10 rubles). At bottom is the inscription • СССР • ("• SSSR •").

Common Reverse (5 Rubles, 1 Ruble, 50 Kopeks, 10 Kopeks). The denomination—5 РУБЛЕЙ ("5 Rubles"), 1 РУБЛЬ ("1 Ruble"), 50 КОПЕЕК ("50 Kopeks"), 10 КОПЕЕК ("10 Kopeks")— is in the center, with the large numeral extending to the top edge. The mintmark is in the small oval below (ЛМД or ММД) with darts to either side, pointing in their respective directions. A sprig of wheat is on the left and a sprig of oak leaves is on the right. The date 1991 is at the bottom.

10 Rubles Reverse. The inner disc has the denomination 10 РУБЛЕЙ ("10 Rubles") in the center. A mintmark is in the small oval below (ЛМД or ММД). The outer ring has a sprig of wheat on the left and a sprig of oak leaves on the right. The date 1991 or 1992 is at the bottom, and a solid five-pointed star is at the top.

10 Kopeks				
Composition	Weight	Diameter	Alignment	Edge
Copper-plated steel	2 grams	17.9 mm	Medal	Smooth
Mintage	**Mint**		**Collecting Difficulty**	**References**
	Moscow†		Easy	KM-296; Schön-148

† Mintmark: M

50 Kopeks				
Composition	Weight	Diameter	Alignment	Edge
Copper-nickel	2.2 grams	18 mm	Medal	Reeded
Mintage	**Mint**		**Collecting Difficulty**	**References**
	Leningrad†		Easy	KM-292; Schön-249

† Mintmark: Л

Ruble				
Composition	Weight	Diameter	Alignment	Edge
Copper-nickel	3.7 grams	21.2 mm	Medal	Reeded
Mintage	**Mint**		**Collecting Difficulty**	**References**
	Leningrad		Easy	KM-293; Schön-250

5 Rubles				
Composition	Weight	Diameter	Alignment	Edge
Copper-nickel	5.25 grams	24 mm	Medal	Alternating reeded/smooth (15 sections each)
Mintage	**Mint**		**Collecting Difficulty**	**References**
	Leningrad; Moscow†		Easy	KM-294; Schön-251

† Mintmark: ЛМД (Leningrad); ММД (Moscow)

10 Rubles				
Composition	Weight	Diameter	Alignment	Edge
Bimetallic: copper-nickel (ring), aluminum-bronze (disc)	6.1 grams	25 mm	Medal	Alternating reeded/smooth (12 sections each)
Mintage	**Mint**		**Collecting Difficulty**	**References**
60,000 (1992, according to Schön)	Leningrad; Moscow†		Easy	KM-295; Schön-252

† Mintmark: ЛМД (Leningrad, 1991); ММД (Moscow, 1991); no mintmarks 1992

GRAND DUCHY OF FINLAND 1912-L GOLD 20 MARKKAA

Minted under Russian imperial control.

Obverse. The Russian imperial double eagle, crowned, is holding a scepter and a globe with cross. The L mintmark (the mint's master mark) is beneath the tail. FINLAND SUOMI is inscribed counterclockwise along the bottom, with a rosette between the two words.

Reverse. The denomination 20 MARKKAA (20 Marks) and date 1912 are in the center, surrounded by a ring of dots or beads. Around the rim is the inscription 0,645..GRM. KUPARIA * 5,806..GRM. KULTAA ("0.645 grams copper, 5.806 grams gold").

Composition	Weight	Diameter	Alignment	Edge
.900 gold	6.4516 grams	21.3 mm	Medal	Reeded

Mintage	Mint	Collecting Difficulty	References
881,000	Mint of Finland (Helsinki)†	Extremely difficult	KM-9.2; Schön-9

† Mintmark: L

Helsinki, Finland, in 1907.

The Autonomous Grand Duchy of Finland was founded in 1809 when the Russian Empire invaded Finland after signing a peace treaty with Napoleonic France. The treaty made allies of the two countries in the fight against France's two main enemies, Great Britain and Sweden, so the conquest of Finland was justified as a maneuver against neighboring Sweden. Native resistance was strong, however, and so Russia offered the Finnish people self-governance and religious freedom in exchange for loyalty to the Russian Empire and help against Sweden.

With the ascension of Czar Alexander III (see number 51) to the Russian throne in 1881, the empire took a more aggressive stance toward assimilating the duchy into the empire. Then, the ascension of Czar Nicholas II in 1894 and the harsh governance of his generals eventually inspired a Finnish independence movement, which achieved its goal in 1917 as the Russian Revolution raged on.

Minted under Russian Czar Nicholas II in Helsinki, the L on the obverse is the initial/mark of engineer and mint master Johan Konrad Lihr, who served in that capacity from 1885 through 1912. Other than his work with the Mint of Finland, Lihr is most famous for leading the expedition that discovered gold in the northernmost region of the country in 1868 (when he was an assistant manager at the Mint), setting off the Lapland Gold Rush. Since 1912 was the last year of Lihr's service, this is a very rare date/mint master combo. It is also of the wide eagle variety (the narrow eagle variety [KM9.1] was issued in 1878-S).

Dominant on the obverse is the double eagle, a symbol of the Russian Empire. The crowned eagle holds a royal scepter and globe with cross (*globus crucifer*). The L mint master's mark is beneath the tail. FINLAND SUOMI is written counterclockwise along the bottom, a rosette between the two words. On the reverse around the rim is the inscription 0,645.. GRM. KUPARIA * 5,806..GRM. KULTAA., which details the fineness of the coin, "kuparia" being copper and "kultaa" meaning "of gold (kulta)."

PCGS has graded only one example of this coin, an MS-62. NGC has graded a total of seven: one in MS-62, one in MS-63, one in MS-64, two in MS-65, and two in MS-66. The NGC MS-63 specimen was lot 24488 in the Heritage Auctions September 25–October 1, 2013, Long Beach sale; it sold for US$25,850, including a buyer's premium.

Gold-washing in Lapland.

Collectors and investors around the world love the gold Panda. Upon the success of the South African Krugerrand (first issued in 1967; see number 58 on our list) and the Canadian Gold Maple Leaf (1979; see number 66 below), the Chinese government followed suit and issued the first gold Panda coins in 1982. The coins, designed by Shanghai artist Chen Jian, were struck in denominations of 1 ounce, half an ounce, a quarter of an ounce, and a tenth of an ounce. The issue's humble beginnings are a stark contrast to the series' current release mintages, which often surpass one million coins struck per year. In 1987, the gold Panda was joined by a silver version.

The obverse features the Hall of Prayer for Good Harvests (祈年殿, *Qínián Diàn*), the largest of the buildings that make up the Temple of Heaven (天壇; *Tiāntán*) in the eastern district of Beijing (北京, *Běijīng*). The building is round, with three roofs or gables, and sits atop three marble plinths with a main stairway in the center and two side stairways leading to the hall. It was the site of annual royal ceremonies to ensure a good harvest for the people. Originally begun during the reign of the Yongle Emperor (永樂帝, *Yǒnglè Dì*), the third ruler of the Ming dynasty in the early fifteenth century, the Temple of Heaven complex was designated a UNESCO World Heritage Site in 1998.

A giant panda.

The reverse of the panda changes every year, but the design always features the giant panda (*Ailuropoda melanoleuca;* in Chinese: 大熊猫, *Dà Xióng Māo* ["Great Bear Cat"]) in a variety of styles, poses, ages, and activities. Pandas are found wild exclusively in China, their habitat limited to a small number of mountain ranges in a few central provinces. Once listed as "endangered" by the International Union for the Conservation of Nature, efforts to preserve panda habitats and encourage population growth have increased its numbers enough to now be listed as "vulnerable," instead. The large creature is known as a gentle giant, with a diet primarily consisting of bamboo stalks and leaves, but it is an opportunistic eater when necessary (including meat) and dangerous when provoked. Pandas are found in captivity at select institutions around the world, loaned out infrequently by the People's Republic in what is known as "panda diplomacy." The effort is so popular abroad that pandas have become almost as iconic a symbol of the nation as the Chinese dragon. Indeed, the symbolism is so popular that the Chinese themselves have adopted it domestically—hence the Chinese panda coins.

CHINA 1982 PANDA FOUR-PIECE GOLD SET

Lovable panda creates popular collector set.

According to panda coin expert Peter Anthony, the circulation strike quarter ounce is easier to find in MS-69 than the half and 1-ounce denominations. Unfortunately, all the coins issued in 1982 came in small, sealed plastic pouches made of polyvinyl chloride (PVC), which means unopened sets are at extreme risk of PVC damage. Collectors pay significant premiums over spot for certified examples. A conditionally rare example of the set graded MS-69 by Numismatic Guaranty Corporation (NGC) sold for $29,218 in a 2016 Heritage Auction. The four-piece set, in uncertified but unimpaired condition, has a current market price of about $5,500 (with coins in the expected grade range of MS-66 to MS-67).

Common Obverse. In the center, a detailed frontal view of the Hall of Prayer for Good Harvests in Temple of Heaven complex in Beijing. Clockwise along the top, the inscription: 中华人民共和国 (*Zhōnghuá Rénmín Gònghéguó* ["People's Republic of China"]). On the bottom, in exergue, is the date 1982. The rim is relatively thick.

Common Reverse. A stylized panda, seated, eating a bamboo stalk with leaves at both ends. The face and main body have a textured finish, while that of the inner ears, eyes, nose, arms, and legs are the same as the empty field. Three nails or claws extend slightly from the paws and feet. To the right of the panda are the inscriptions 成色99.9% (*Chéngsè 99.9%* ["Quality 99.9%", or "99.9% fine"]) and the weight: 含纯金 1 盎可 (*Hán Chún Jīn 1 Àng Kě* ["Containing one ounce pure gold"]), 含纯金 ½ 盎可 (*Hán Chún Jīn 1/2 Àng Kě* ["Containing one half ounce pure gold"]), 含纯金 ¼ 盎可 (*Hán Chún Jīn 1/4 Àng Kě* ["Containing one quarter ounce pure gold"]), or 含纯金 ⅒ 盎可 (*Hán Chún Jīn 1/10 Àng Kě* ["Containing one tenth ounce pure gold"]). The rim is relatively thick.

Tenth Ounce (10 Yuan)

Composition	Weight	Diameter	Alignment	Edge
.999 gold	1/10 ounce (3.393 grams)	18 mm	Medal	Reeded

Mintage	Mint	Collecting Difficulty	References
75,432	Shanghai Mint	Easy	Fr-B7; KMX-MB8; PAN-5a

Quarter Ounce (25 Yuan)

Composition	Weight	Diameter	Alignment	Edge
.999 gold	1/4 ounce (8.483 grams)	22 mm	Medal	Reeded

Mintage	Mint	Collecting Difficulty	References
42,243	Shanghai Mint	Easy	Fr-B6; KMX-MB9; PAN-4a

Half Ounce (50 Yuan)

Composition	Weight	Diameter	Alignment	Edge
.999 gold	1/2 ounce (16.966 grams)	27 mm	Medal	Reeded

Mintage	Mint	Collecting Difficulty	References
13,339	Shanghai Mint	Easy	Fr-B5; KMX-MB10; PAN-3a

1 Ounce (100 Yuan)

Composition	Weight	Diameter	Alignment	Edge
.999 gold	1 ounce (33.931 grams)	32.05 mm	Medal	Reeded

Mintage	Mint	Collecting Difficulty	References
15,971	Shanghai Mint	Easy	Fr-B4; KMX-MB11; PAN-2a

The Hall of Prayer for Good Harvest at the Temple of Heaven in Beijing.

The South African Krugerrand gold bullion coin captured the world's interest when it debuted in 1967. That coin became a global phenomenon and allowed a generation of gold investors to add the metal to their portfolios. Within years, the International Monetary Fund (IMF), the United States, and the Soviet Union all became net sellers of gold, dumping millions of ounces into the market. Still, the price of gold rose from an average price of US$38.90 in 1970 to $183.77 in 1974.

In Canada, gold producers lobbied Parliament to introduce a gold coin to compete with the Krugerrand. This coin would use Canadian-produced gold and be more palatable to investors uneasy about buying coins from South Africa's Apartheid government. They saw the potential in a Canadian-made coin to service not only Canadian investors, but also investors in the United States (gold bullion became legal to own in the United States in 1974). In 1976, the Canadian Parliament approved a plan to strike the "Maple Leaf," a .999 fine 1-ounce gold coin, for three years on a trial basis.

By any definition the trial succeeded, and in 1981 the authorization to continue the program was extended indefinitely. Seven years later, the silver Maple Leaf was added to Canada's bullion coin program.

CANADA 1979 GOLD MAPLE LEAF

A response to bullion investment interest.

Obverse. A bust of Queen Elizabeth II, facing right. ELIZABETH II is inscribed clockwise at top. The denomination 50 DOLLARS and date 1979 are counterclockwise at bottom.

Reverse. A large realistic maple leaf. Fineness 999 is inscribed on both sides of the leaf. CANADA is written clockwise at the top, and FINE GOLD 1 OZ OR PUR is counterclockwise along the bottom.

Composition	Weight	Diameter	Alignment	Edge
.999 gold	31.15 grams	30 mm	Medal	Reeded

Mintage	Mint	Collecting Difficulty	References
1,000,000	Royal Canadian Mint (Ottawa)	Easy	KM-125.1

Arnold Machin works on his portrait of Queen Elizabeth II, which is featured on the Canadian Maple Leaf gold coin.

(Right) Queen Elizabeth II visits Winnipeg, Canada, in 1970 to attend a celebration for the 100th anniversary of the province's entry into Confederation.

PALESTINE 1927 SEVEN-COIN PROOF SET

Palestine's complicated social and political tensions.

The creation of coins for the British Mandate of Palestine proved to be controversial, offending Orthodox Jews as well as Palestinians. At issue was the Hebrew inscription, which read פלשתינה(א"י) ("Palestine").

The history of the land that makes up modern-day Israel and its surrounding countries is long, complicated, and rife with disagreement, even among learned historians. In that way, history reflects the tense reality of culture and politics in conflict.

Perhaps much of that conflict could have been avoided had it not been for the Western powers and the failure of the League of Nations to adequately represent the rights and aspirations of the peoples and countries of the Middle East—an area that grew in importance to the West after the discovery of oil at the start of the century. The increasing significance of that extracted resource in geopolitical terms had become clearly evident by the end of World War I.

During the war, the Levant was a site of fierce fighting between Western allies and the Turks. After the war, Palestine would be split up, with the land on the eastern bank of the Jordan river forming the Emirate of Transjordan and the western bank territory becoming Palestine. Overseeing all of this was Great Britain, whose governance of Palestine was granted by the League of Nations following the Central Powers' (led by the German and Ottoman Empire) defeat.

Before, the region had been under Ottoman control since the defeat of the Mamluk Sultanate in 1516.

The redrawing of political boundaries in the region under the League of Nations mandate system was capricious and determined solely on the basis of geographical lines, not the realpolitik of cultural realities. The result of this was generations of protracted conflict and human suffering.

While the British took control of Palestine in 1922, it took five years before a new coinage system could be implemented for the region. What resulted were seven-coin denominations in values of 1 mil to 100 mils, which complemented paper currency valued from 500 mils to 100 pounds. All but the 50- and 100-mil coins were struck in base metal. The two higher denomination coins were struck in an alloy of 0.720 silver. A 1,000-mil coin in gold was proposed, but never struck.

The coin designs bear a simple design of olive sprigs and wreaths. Architect Austen St. Barbe Harrison (1893–1976) is credited with the design[1].

To denote the beginning of this new coinage, the Royal Mint struck a limited number of Proofs and issued them in sets of two configurations. The first was an eight-coin set with one example of each coin housed in a red leather presentation case. The coins were mounted on soft cloth with a ribbon tab underneath each. The single-coin set case featured the Royal Mint seal on the inside of the case.

The second was a 16-coin set of two examples of each coin—with the obverse and reverse of each coin facing up. Again, the coins were housed in a soft cloth-lined red leather presentation case. On the outside of the red case was an embossed gilt inscription: "Palestine Currency Board 1927." Thirty-three of these sets were produced.

According to Howard Berlin, a noted expert in the series, two of the 16-coin sets were distributed to the Royal Mint Museum and the British Museum in London, while a 34th set was presented to King George V in a deluxe case[2].

Of the 31 remaining sets, today, fewer than 20 are believed to have survived. Dealer William Rosenblum estimates ten sets in the hands of collectors and the Numismatic Antiquarian Service Corporation of America (NASCA) estimates six in museum collections and one in the archives of the Hebrew University in Jerusalem[2].

Mil				
Composition	**Weight**	**Diameter**	**Alignment**	**Edge**
Bronze	3.2 grams	21 mm	Medal	Smooth
Mintage	**Mint**		**Collecting Difficulty**	**References**
68	British Royal Mint (London)		Moderate	KM-1

2 Mils				
Composition	**Weight**	**Diameter**	**Alignment**	**Edge**
Bronze	7.8 grams	28 mm	Medal	Smooth
Mintage	**Mint**		**Collecting Difficulty**	**References**
68	British Royal Mint (London)		Moderate	KM-2

5 Mils				
Composition	**Weight**	**Diameter**	**Alignment**	**Edge**
Copper-nickel	2.9 grams	20 mm	Medal	Smooth
Mintage	**Mint**		**Collecting Difficulty**	**References**
68	British Royal Mint (London)		Moderate	KM-3

10 Mils				
Composition	**Weight**	**Diameter**	**Alignment**	**Edge**
Copper-nickel	6.5 grams	27 mm	Medal	Smooth
Mintage	**Mint**		**Collecting Difficulty**	**References**
68	British Royal Mint (London)		Moderate	KM-4

20 Mils				
Composition	**Weight**	**Diameter**	**Alignment**	**Edge**
Copper-nickel	11.3 grams	30.5 mm	Medal	Smooth
Mintage	**Mint**		**Collecting Difficulty**	**References**
68	British Royal Mint (London)		Moderate	KM-5

50 Mils				
Composition	**Weight**	**Diameter**	**Alignment**	**Edge**
Copper-nickel	5.8319 grams	23.5 mm	Medal	Reeded
Mintage	**Mint**		**Collecting Difficulty**	**References**
68	British Royal Mint (London)		Moderate	KM-6

100 Mils				
Composition	**Weight**	**Diameter**	**Alignment**	**Edge**
Copper-nickel	11.6638 grams	29 mm	Medal	Reeded
Mintage	**Mint**		**Collecting Difficulty**	**References**
68	British Royal Mint (London)		Moderate	KM-7

In his excellent book on the subject, *The Coins and Banknotes of Palestine Under the British Mandate, 1927–1947* (2005), Berlin tracked only a handful of public sales for the sets from 1974 to 1981:

Silvia Hafner Sale (1974): $8,000
Alexander Goldstein Sale (1976): $10,000
Sidney L. Olson Sale (1978): $10,000
The Shield Collection (1981): $12,500
The Los Angeles Sale (1981): $10,000

Coin dealer William Rosenblum last handled a set in 2014. This set, which was part of a collection that includes another of our 100 Greatest Modern World Coins, the 1931 Palestine Mandate 100 mils (number 67), sold for $38,000.

Single sets were scarcer; Berlin knew of one in the package—offered in a 1976 Goldstein sale for $4,600. Another in 1979 sold without a case for $3,500 in a Paramount sale. In 2004, a single set offered by Heritage Auctions realized just $2,875, a significant retreat from previous prices. However, 11 years later, in 2015, a single coin from the set, a 50-mil coin graded PF-65 by NGC, brought $3,760[3].

Common Obverse (Mil, 2 Mils). In the center, justified, the legend is written in Arabic, English, and Hebrew, one stacked upon the other: فلسطين, PALESTINE, פלשתינה(וא), followed by the date written in Western and Eastern Arabic numerals. Beaded denticles surround the rim.

Common Reverse (Mil, 2 Mils). In the center is an olive tree with seven leaves and six olives. The denomination, written in Western and Eastern Arabic numerals, bookends the trunk of the tree. Wrapping around the rim, the denomination is written in Hebrew, English, and Arabic, separated by dots. Beaded denticles surround the rim.

5 Mils Obverse. An annular (holed) coin type. A wreath of olive surrounds the inner hole. Wrapping around the rim is the legend, written in Hebrew, Arabic, and English: פלשתינה(וא), PALESTINE, فلسطين, with dots separating each. Below, the date is written in Western and Eastern Arabic numerals. Beaded denticles surround the rim.

5 Mils Reverse. The denomination is written in English (top), Hebrew (bottom left), and Arabic (bottom right). Beaded denticles surround the rim.

10 Mils Obverse. An annular (holed) coin type. Wrapping around the rim is the legend, written in Hebrew, Arabic, and English: פלשתינה(וא), PALESTINE, فلسطين, with dots separating each. Immediately above and below the hole, the date is written in Western and Eastern Arabic numerals. Beaded denticles surround the rim.

10 Mils Reverse. The denomination is written in English (top), Hebrew (bottom left), and Arabic (bottom right). An olive wreath wraps around the inner hole. Beaded denticles surround the rim.

20 Mils Obverse. An annular (holed) coin type. A wreath of olive surrounds the inner hole. Wrapping around the rim is the legend, written in Hebrew, Arabic, and English: פלשתינה(וא), PALESTINE, فلسطين, with dots separating each. Below, the date is written in Western and Eastern Arabic numerals. Beaded denticles surround the rim.

20 Mils Reverse. The denomination is written in English (top), Hebrew (bottom left), and Arabic (bottom right). Beaded denticles surround the rim.

50 Mils Obverse. Centered inside the inner circle is an olive tree with leaves, four olives, and a trunk that bisects the coin from north to south and extends to the border of the circle. The dual date is written in Western and Eastern Arabic bookending the base of the tree. Wrapping around the rim, the legend is written in Hebrew, English, and Arabic: פלשתינה(וא) (aleph and yod letters in parenthesis are acronyms for *Eretz Yisra'el* ["land of Israel"]) • PALESTINE • فلسطين. Beaded denticles surround the rim.

50 Mils Reverse. In the center, justified, the denomination is written in Arabic, English, and Hebrew, one stacked upon the other. This is bordered on the top and bottom by the number 50 written in Eastern and Western Arabic numerals. Beaded denticles surround the rim.

100 Mils Obverse. Wrapping around the rim, the legend is written in Hebrew, English, and Arabic: פלשתינה(וא) (aleph and yod letters in parenthesis are acronyms for *Eretz Yisra'el* ["land of Israel"]) • PALESTINE • فلسطين. In the center, an olive tree with seven branches and six berries grows out of a wavy ground, which forms the exergue. The date, written in Western and Eastern Arabic numerals, bookends the trunk of the tree. Beaded denticles surround the rim.

100 Mils Reverse. Inside the circle, in the center, 100 is written in large font below ١٠٠. Outside of the circle, wrapping around and separated by dots, the denomination is written in English, Hebrew, and Arabic: ONE HUNDRED MILS (top), מאה מיל (bottom left), and مائة مل (bottom right). Beaded denticles surround the rim.

Beyond the 1927 single and double sets, the area of Palestine Mandate Proof coinage presents quite a challenge for collectors. The Royal Mint struck limited numbers of coins in various denominations off and on through 1946. The 1927 emission, however, remains the only attempt at the Royal Mint to produce a complete Proof set.

SPAIN 1949 SILVER 5 PESETAS (52)

Franco's mixed legacy.

1949 (51) 5 pesetas.

Obverse. A right-facing portrait of Francisco Franco. Wrapping around the bust, the inscription: FRANCISCO FRANCO CAUDILLO DE ESPAÑA POR LA G. DE DIOS • 1949 ("Francisco Franco the Leader of Spain for the Glory of God • 1949").

Reverse. The Francoist coat of arms. The coat of arms features the shielded Eagle of St. John between the two Pillars of Hercules. Ribbons adorn the pillars with the words PLUS ULTRA ("further beyond"). Behind the eagle's head is a sun and a ribbon. The ribbon reads UNA GRANDE LIBRE ("one great liberty"). Beneath the eagle's wings are a yoke and arrows representing the country's Catholic monarchs. The coin's denomination, CINCO PESETAS, is split on either side of the coat of arms. Stars bookmark the two sides of the word CINCO. In the first star is the incuse 19, and in the second is the incuse 52. This, not the date on the obverse of the coin, represents the year of production.

Composition	Weight	Diameter	Alignment	Edge
Silver	15 grams	32 mm	Coin	Reeded

Mintage	Mint	Collecting Difficulty	References
21,963,000 (estimated)	Spanish Royal Mint, Fabrica Nacional de Moneda y Timbre (Madrid)	Extremely difficult	KM-778

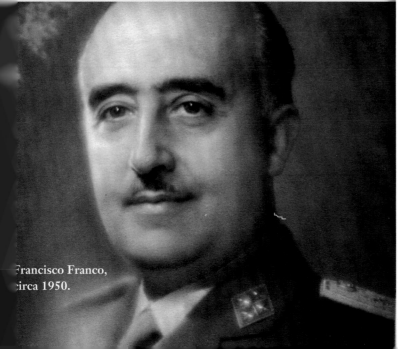

Francisco Franco, circa 1950.

Spain endured its own unique hell throughout much of the twentieth century. It was a century filled with domestic strife and civil war, all dominated by one figure: General Francisco Franco. Franco was many things: a fascist, a monarchist, a brutal strongman, and a fervent Catholic. His vision for Spain was of a return to feudalism with him and his allies in full control of the strings of government. To achieve this goal, he carried out pogroms against his political enemies, filling the Spanish countryside with victims' bodies by the hundreds of thousands. Mass rapes and atrocities against children were carried out in the open with the intent to traumatize and terrorize. The symbol of the yoke and arrow found on the reverse of this coin, part of the Spanish coat of arms under Franco, was sometimes branded on the breasts of their victims.

Yet even today, Franco remains a revered figure in some parts of Spanish society. Those willing to overlook decades of atrocities carried out against their fellow citizens give the despot credit for keeping Spain out of the second World War. They believe Franco's economic policies spurred low unemployment (a hard argument to support given the sheer number of working age adults that the regime "disappeared"). Others point to the fact that Franco kept the country from becoming communist as justification for his policies. It's hard to be sympathetic to such a view.

As it pertains to numismatics, Franco's effigy dominated Spanish coin design from 1949 until his death in 1975, after which time King Juan Carlos I took his place. Spanish coins of this period were denominated using a decimalized system, with 100 centimos being the equivalent of one peseta. It was a limited coinage, at first. In 1949, the Spanish mint issued just three denominations: the 50 centimos (two types), the peseta, and the 5 pesetas. After a robust mintage of 21 million pieces in 1950, the mint struck 151,000 in 1951 (including 6,000 pieces struck for the Second National Numismatic Exposition) and 20,000 in 1952. Nearly the entire mintage of both years is believed lost.

Differentiating the coins of this type by year requires astute observation. The obverse of all issues of this type bears the date 1949. On the reverse, however, the date of production is stamped in small incuse numerals on the inside of the two stars that bookend the word CINCO. The leftmost star carries a small 19 in it (with the exception of the Numismatic Exposition coinage—these carry the letter E). The star on the right carries the final two digits of the date. The 5-peseta coin with the date 50 in the star is common. Five pesetas with the date 51 or 52 are rare, with the latter being extremely rare.

Records of public sales of the 52 or even the 51 proved extremely difficult to track down. There's little doubt any example, if found and authenticated, would sell for many multiples of the US$2,760 that a PCGS-certified MS-63 example brought at a 2010 Heritage auction.

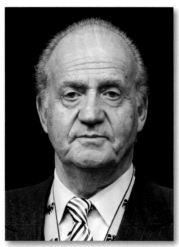

King Juan Carlos I, 2007.

Close-up of the stars on the reverse of a 1949 (51) coin.

Defiant, provocative, and untamed. These three words are but a few of the powerful adjectives that could be used to describe Mexico's Caballito peso, a coin that marries French Beaux Arts with motifs drawn from Mexican culture and history.

The coin's release in 1910 coincided with the 100th anniversary of the Mexican War of Independence, a war that concluded with Mexico coming out from under the yoke of Spanish rule. The central motif of an unshod horse galloping with the free-flowing garb of the Goddess of Liberty, torch held aloft and head facing backwards as if to rally the troops, could not have come at a better time. The Mexico of the Caballito peso was a country in the grip of revolution.

Many had risen up to fight against the perpetual corruption of the Mexican government—the very government that issued this coin. Dictators and tyrants throughout history have often called upon the state gods and goddesses to back their claims of power. Our subversive reading of the coin has us seeing the wild and full-throttle Liberty as a warning to tyrants.

The Caballito peso design was designed by French medalist Charles Pillet (1869–1960). It was Pillet's second project for the Mexican government; his first project was of a medal commemorating the inauguration of the Canal Porfirio Díaz, named for the president of the time, Porfirio Díaz (1830–1915).

President Díaz so liked the sculptor's work that he had the Mint extend a commission for the redesign of Mexico's silver coinage. The fruit of Pillet's work is apparent in 1907, when his concept for a 50-centavo coin was produced at the Paris Mint. However, the emission of this pattern proved to be just the beginning of a multi-year process.

The Mexican Mint ultimately decided to limit the adoption of Pillet's design to the larger peso coin. Pillet retooled the design and shipped a number of pattern variants dated 1909 across the Atlantic. Like the 50 centavos, these were also struck at the Paris Mint.

According to Caballito peso expert collector and author Allan Schein, the patterns were likely double struck to bring out the crisp detail of the design. He also notes the 1909 patterns differ slightly from the production coin. Minor edits to the relief were undertaken, and Pillet's name was removed from the coin's reverse.

The sharp detail of the patterns shows Pillet's work at its fullest, making the coin a perennial favorite for collectors of the series. The 1909 Caballito peso patterns are scarce, with but 30 to 40 known in all varieties and finishes. Schein notes the example in his collection (our plate coin) came with the original presentation box and is graded SP-66 by PCGS.

Previously, it resided in the Keech and Searle collections. The current finest known was discovered in October 2016 as part of a large collection of world coins. It was submitted to NGC and bettered Schein's coin by two points.

MEXICO 1909 CABALLITO PESO PATTERN

A design representing revolution.

Obverse. In the center, an eagle, clutching a rattlesnake in its beak and right talon, stands atop a cactus on a mound surrounded by water. The legend ESTADOS UNIDOS MEXICANOS ("United States of Mexico") wraps around the rim at the top of the design. The denomination UN PESO bookends the left and right side of the base of the cactus. A wreath wraps around the rim at the bottom of the design. An ornamental border encircles the design at the rim.

Reverse. Liberty rides side-saddle on a horse. In Liberty's right hand is an oak and laurel branch, and in her left is a torch. Fourteen sun rays are in the background, with the sun behind an earthen mound. The date is between the two dots in exergue. An ornamental border encircles the design at the rim.

Composition	Weight	Diameter	Alignment	Edge
.903 silver	27.55 grams	39 mm	Coin	Lettered†
Mintage	**Mint**		**Collecting Difficulty**	**References**
Unknown across all variants	Paris Mint, Monnaie de Paris		Difficult	Numerous, including Pn177–Pn182

† ESTADOS UNIDOS MEXICANOS UN PESO

THE CABALLITO TODAY

While the Caballito's production run lasted just five years, the coin's timeless motif endured through the years as the subject of contemporary commemoration. The design appeared on the 1986 $250 World Cup gold coin, on the 2010 5-peso silver coin, and most recently on the 2011 100-peso bimetallic coin.

Porfirio Diaz.

IRAN 1963 GOLD 5 PAHLAVI

The last shah before religious revolution.

Obverse. In the center of the coin is the left-facing bust of the Iranian Shah. Above his head is the inscription محمدرضا شاه پهلوی شاهنشاه ایران ("Shah Mohammad Reza Pahlavi Shah of Iran"). Below the bust is the date, written in Eastern Arabic numerals. Beaded denticles wrap around the rim.

Reverse. Situated slightly above center mass, the left-facing lion and sun emblem is surmounted by the royal crown Pahlavi. Below the ground is the denomination پنج پهلوی, ("Five Pahlavi"). The bottom and sides of the design are surrounded by a wreath of olive and oak. Beaded denticles wrap around the rim.

Composition	Weight	Diameter	Alignment	Edge
.900 gold	40.6799 grams	40.2 mm	Medal	Reeded

Mintage	Mint	Collecting Difficulty	References
20	Markazi Mint (Tehran)	Difficult	KM-1164

Due in large part to the discovery of oil in 1901, the twentieth century for Iran was a period of struggle, upheaval, and rebirth. It was a time marked by social unrest, both internal and stirred by foreign influence. It was a time of territorial occupation, coups, revolution, and terror.

The current Iranian regime, dominated by anti-Western theocrats, came to power after a violent revolution in 1979. The revolution upended the country's social order and overthrew the Shah Mohammad Reza Pahlavi (reigned 1941–1979), a playboy poltroon and the last shah of Iran.

Pahlavi's ouster led to a diaspora of millions of Iranians who felt they no longer had a place in a society dominated by the strict, sermonizing mullahs, who exercised total control over the country and demanded total allegiance under the penalty of death.

Hardening American attitudes toward the new regime, one of the Islamic Republic's first international acts was to lay siege to the American embassy in Tehran and to take captive 52 American diplomats. The 444-day ordeal did incalculable damage to U.S.-Iran bilateral relations. Despite this fact, the United States has accepted hundreds of thousands of Iranian immigrants, including many ethnic minorities and those with ties to the former government.

During the reign of Shah Mohammad Reza Pahlavi, Iranian coins were struck in base metal, silver, and gold. Base metal coins were denominated in dinars and rials and served as the country's circulating coinage. Silver issues were denominated in rials and were struck for commemorative purposes. Gold issues were sometimes struck as rials but more typically were struck as Pahlavi—named, of course, after the ruling family.

The coins came with face values of quarter, half, 1, 2-1/2, 5, and later 10 Pahlavis.

The 5 Pahlavi is a large .900 fine gold coin that measures 40.2 mm in diameter and contains a little more than 1.29 ounces of actual gold weight. The denomination was struck in two types from 1960 to 1979. The first type was struck from 1960 to 1974 and the second type, with a slightly revised obverse inscription, was struck from 1975 to 1979.

In an absolute sense, the denomination was never struck in quantity. The first type is scarcer than the second, with a highest reported mintage of 2,500 pieces. The key of the series, and all of twentieth-century Iranian coinage, is the 1963 issue. The total mintage: A paltry 20 pieces, of which only a handful of examples have appeared at auction over the last two decades.

To date, only three examples of this rare issue have been certified by any of the leading American grading services, with all three having been graded by NGC.

The typical example survives in the lower tier of Mint State grades and shows weakness at points of high relief. On the obverse, the hair detail above the ear is usually muted, with porosity evident. On the reverse, the lion's face, mane, and chest are flatly struck, with the nose and mouth details virtually unstruck.

The single finest example, graded MS-64, was offered for sale in April 2017 by Heritage Auctions, where it brought what seems like a bargain price of US$7,050 (lot 30958).

Shah Mohammad Reza Pahlavi of Iran, circa 1962.

Struck when large circulating silver coins (often referred to as "crowns") were standard in monetary systems worldwide, the 1901 5-lire coin stands among Italy's most popular rarities. During the first decades of the twentieth century, Italy produced several 5-lire coins bearing an obverse image of King Victor Emmanuel III, who reigned from 1900 through 1946. The 5 lire from 1901 represents two tantalizing narratives: Italy's sociopolitical scene during the first half of the twentieth century and the European monetary reforms that preceded the development of the European Union.

Similar in size and weight to other crown-size silver coins, the Italian 5 lire circulated throughout much of the nineteenth century. In 1878, the Latin Monetary Union (LMU), to which Italy was a party, restricted the minting of crown-size silver coinage following significant decreases in bullion values during the recession of the late 1870s. The LMU was founded in 1865 by France, Italy, Switzerland, and Belgium in order to unify the currencies of those nations nearly 130 years before the European Union was officially established in 1993.

The concept originated in France, which at the time had a bimetallic monetary system based on silver and gold coinage. As France was already an economic juggernaut, its coinage circulated widely throughout the neighboring countries of Italy, Switzerland, and Belgium. For France, the formation of the LMU allowed the nation to become a bigger player in the broader European economic picture. Meanwhile, government officials in Italy, Belgium, and Switzerland hoped joining the LMU would create more trade opportunities and provide greater capital access through an economic alliance with France. The LMU permitted each member nation to issue its own coins on the provision that they follow certain uniform coinage standards based on the French franc.

By 1868, Greece and Bulgaria had also joined the LMU. Other European nations that were not official member states but considered entry, such as Spain and Romania, nonetheless adapted their coins to the Union's standards.

Ultimately, however, certain policy flaws led to the alliance's undoing. One such policy was fixed silver pricing, designed to stabilize the economy at a time when silver prices were falling. Not surprisingly, this scenario led to the purchase of LMU gold coins with the use of overvalued silver. Gold coins all but disappeared from circulation in the LMU as they flowed into non-Union nations.

Other such policies included those implemented by LMU nations that favored their own interests, undermining the integrity of the alliance. These and a variety of other issues, not to mention World War I, brought about the demise of the LMU by 1926.

Economic issues aside, Italy faced major problems on the social front, including the nation's colonization of Eritrea and Somalia in Africa, the occupation of Sicily and Naples, the spread of socialism, and violations of civil liberties. These helped fuel public hostilities against the crown, which boiled over on July 29, 1900, when anarchist Gaetano Bresci assassinated King Umberto I. The king's son, Victor Emmanuel III, ascended to the throne and remained there until his abdication following World War II and political reform brought an end to the Italian monarchy.

The Kingdom of Italy is recalled on classic Italian coinage of the late nineteenth and early twentieth centuries. At the nexus of the two centuries is the 1901 5-lire coin. Though categorized as a pattern due to its violation of LMU coining standards, that year's 5 lire was struck to numismatically honor the new King Victor Emmanuel III, an enthusiastic coin collector. It became the first coin to bear the effigy of the newly crowned king as ruler.

King Umberto I of Italy in the late 1890s with his wife, Queen Margherita of Italy.

ITALY 1901-R SILVER 5 LIRE

The first coin of a numismatic king.

Obverse. An uncrowned effigy of King Victor Emmanuel III, facing right. The inscription VITTORIO EMANUELE III wraps clockwise around the rim from the left. The designer's signature SPERANZE is beneath the neck truncation. Denticles surround along the rim.

Reverse. The Savoy eagle is displayed (spread out) and langued (tongue protruding), facing left. The Savoy shield covers the breast and the crown of Savoy, with ribbons to either side, is above the head. Clockwise from the left along the top half is the inscription REGNO D'ITALIA ("Kingdom of Italy"). The denomination L* 5, mintmark R, and date 1901 wrap counterclockwise along the bottom, separated by two five-pointed stars to either side of the R. Savoy knots divide the top inscriptions from the bottom on each side. Denticles surround along the rim.

Composition	Weight	Diameter	Alignment	Edge
.900 silver	25 grams	37 mm	Coin	Lettered†
Mintage	**Mint**		**Collecting Difficulty**	**References**
114 (unknown surviving)	Istituto Polografica e Zecca dello Stato (Rome)‡		Extremely difficult	KM-34

† FERT FERT FERT between knots and rosettes ‡ Mintmark: R

The 5 lire was produced with a prooflike finish at the Polygraphic Institute and State Mint in Rome, which is represented by an R mintmark located on the reverse, directly under the crowned eagle. The piece was designed by Italian medalist Filippo Speranza (1939–1903); his signature is found directly beneath the neck truncation on the obverse.

The edge of the 5 lire from 1901 features the inscription FERT FERT FERT. The "word" FERT is an acronym, used as the motto of the Royal House of Savoy beginning with Vittorio Amedeo II (ruled 1666–1732). The exact meaning is unknown, but some possible meanings include: *Foedere et Religione Tenemur* ("By Alliance and Religion Are We Bound")*; Fortitudo Eius Rhodum Tenuit* ("His Strength Held Rhodes," referring to Amadeus V's victory against the Saracens in 1315)*; Fortitudo Eius Rempublicam Tenet* ("His Strength Maintains the State"); or *Fides Est Regni Tutela* ("Faith is the Protector of the Kingdom"). It may also simply be the Latin word *fert* ("he suffers"), which most likely would refer to Jesus.

The House of Savoy, founded in 1003, was one of the oldest continuous houses in Europe. A cadet branch, the House of Savoy-Carignano, ruled the Kingdom of Italy from its beginnings in 1861 through its dissolution in 1946.

An original mintage of 114 was struck but many were melted, leaving behind an unknown quantity for collectors today. The 1901 issue is the scarcest of a trio of early-twentieth-century 5-lire types, which also includes 1911 and 1914 5-lire coins. The 1911 issue has a mintage of 60,000 and commemorates the 50th anniversary of the Italian kingdom, while the 1914 coin, with a mintage of 273,000 pieces, symbolizes Italy as a warrior riding aboard a mighty chariot.

Counterfeits of these early-twentieth-century 5-lire coins abound, with many turning up on Internet auction sites such as eBay, as well as flea markets, antique stores, and garage sales. Of the silver 5-lire coins, a genuine example of the 1901 issue is certainly the least likely to turn up in a typical estate sale or general online auction site, so buyers must beware.

When real specimens do cross the auction block, these rare relics of the Italian monarchy command kingly sums. One of the finest specimens, an example graded prooflike "fleur-de-coin," was sold by A.H. Baldwin and Sons in May 2014 for £38,000 (about US$50,255, including a 20 percent buyer's premium).

The monetary system of British East Africa underwent a number of changes in the years immediately following World War I. An influx of Indian railroad workers in the African colony meant the Indian rupee had become a de facto coinage. To get a handle on the situation, the East Africa Currency Board was established so a new coinage system could be introduced.

The first attempt established a decimal system with the East African florin, a coin loosely based on the rupee it replaced, being the main unit of account. Under this standard, six coin denominations were introduced. The 1-cent, 5-cent, and 10-cent denominations were annular coins struck in copper-nickel, and the 25-cent, 50-cent, and florin denominations were struck in a 50 percent silver alloy.

These East African issues were produced by three mints, with the bulk of the coinage handled by the Heaton Mint in Birmingham. The Royal Mint augmented Heaton's mintage of 9,669,000 florins by striking 1,479,000 coins of its own. Additional overflow was handled by private contractor Ackroyd and Best.

Ackroyd and Best was based in Morley, West Yorkshire, in England and is best known as a manufacturer of miner's and workman's lamps, but they also produced lamp checks and tokens. The company struck coins for the colony for many years after procuring a contract to do so. Their coinage carries the A mintmark.

Effectively a one-year issue, this coinage system was replaced in May 1921 by a new system that replaced the florin with a schilling. The schilling coin was smaller and struck on planchets made of silver billon alloy.

In the months before the change in policy, two denominations of the 1920 standard were struck by the Royal Mint in London: a sizable mintage of 920,000 cent coins and an emission of 2-florin coins. Neither issue was released for circulation and a lion's share of the cent coin's mintage was melted down. Today, both issues are major rarities, with the florin being one of the rarest coins struck during the reign of George V.

Regimental Sergeant Major LIanyier Dagarti of the Gold Coast Regiment, Royal West African Frontier Force, was the first Gold Coast soldier to receive the M.B.E. (Member of the Order of the British Empire) in World War II for his continuous gallantry and devotion to duty while under fire in the East African campaign.

EAST AFRICA 1921 KING GEORGE V FLORIN

Standardizing currency in the British colonies.

Obverse. A crowned portrait of King George V, facing left. The inscription starts at the lower left and runs clockwise: GEORGIUS V REX ET IND: IMP: ("George V King and Emperor of India"). The initials of the designer B.M. are found in the truncation on the right. A ring of beading or denticles surrounds the design along the rim; these extend further into the field than the "Old Effigy" type.

Reverse. Wrapping around the top of the design is the legend EAST AFRICA, bordered by two diamonds. Inside a vegetal frame is the scene of a right-facing lion against a mountainous backdrop. The denomination is rendered in exergue, above the date. This text reads 1 FLORIN 1921.

A ring of beading or denticles surrounds the design along the rim; these extend further into the field than the "Old Effigy" type.

Composition	Weight	Diameter	Alignment	Edge
.500 silver	11.6638 grams	30 mm	Medal	Reeded
Mintage	**Mint**		**Collecting Difficulty**	**References**
2	Ackroyd and Best (Morley, West Yorkshire)†		Virtually impossible	KM-17; Schön-19
	† Mintmark: A			

A fruit market in Zanzibar during its time as a British colony.

CZECHOSLOVAKIA 1937 GOLD 10 DUKATU

Artistry on a trade coin.

An earlier 10 dukatu depicting the design style of the 1937 coin.

Obverse. Offset to the left is the lesser coat of arms of the First Czechoslovak Republic: a left-facing, two-tailed Bohemian lion, wearing a three-pointed crown and carrying on its left arm the shield of Slovakia (a patriarchal cross surmounting the middle of three hills). A linden tree branch is to the right. Fourteen dots surround the shield and the number 10 is below the shield. Wrapping around the rim is the legend REPUBLIKA ČESKOSLOVENSKÁ. The date 1937 is separated from the legend by two crosses. Beaded denticles wrap around the rim.

Reverse. St. Wenceslas on a horse, facing right, holds a sword and branch aloft. His two fingers are extended in a Christian hand symbol. Wrapping around the rim is the inscription NEDEJ·ZAHYNOUTI·NÁM·I·BUDOUCÍM ("Do not let us and future ones perish"). The date is written as +929. Below are the designer's and engraver's initials, B-O-Š for Jaroslav Benda / Otakar Španiel.

Composition	Weight	Diameter	Alignment	Edge
.986 gold	34.909 grams	42 mm	Medal	Reeded
Mintage	Mint		Collecting Difficulty	References
<1,000	Kremnica Mint		Moderate	Fr-4; KM-14; Y-18

† Mintmark: A

Stained glass in St. Vitus Cathedral, Prague, depicting St. Wenceslas, patron saint of the Czech Republic.

The first Czechoslovak Republic was formed on October 28, 1918. The cutaway republic, formerly the industrial heart of the Habsburg monarchy, was one of nine new nations formed in the aftermath of World War I.

The Czechoslovakian 10 dukatu was a gold trade coin issued by the First Czechoslovak Republic between 1929 and 1938, and then again in 1951 when the country was under the yoke of communist rule.

The large size of the coin and its unique art style, a hybrid of ninth-century Ottonian art with more modern naturalist elements, combines to create an unforgettable look. The design was a collaboration between notable Czech artists Jaroslav Benda and Otakar Španiel. Of the two, Španiel was more known for his medal work, but the idiosyncrasies of Benda's design are apparent when one compares the 10-dukatu coin against Španiel's *Millennium of St. Wenceslaus* medal, also issued in 1929[1].

Jaroslav Benda (1882–1970) was a professional artist and professor at the Academy of Arts, Architecture, and Design in Prague, where he taught a number of influential twentieth-century Czech artists, including the great modernist illustrator Zdeněk Seydl. Benda was an immensely talented artist in his own right, notable not only for his painting and graphic work but also for his voluminous catalog of hundreds of original typefaces he designed and published throughout his lengthy career[2]. Numismatists should note that Benda was also the designer of the Czech 5-pět korun banknote of 1921, featuring the likeness of philosopher Jan Amos Komenský[3].

Otakar Španiel (1881–1955) was a leading sculptor and medalist. Inspired by his studies in Paris, Španiel's early work reflected the sentiments of the Art Nouveau movement. His later work, especially his portrait work, was imbued with angular masculinity. The jutting jawlines and jowls of Tomáš Garrigue Masaryk on the 20 koruna or Stalin on his 1949 100 koruna are two examples that illustrate this characteristic of his style. Španiel was honored in 1981, when the Czechoslovak Socialist Republic issued a commemorative 100 koruna silver coin featuring the artist's likeness.

Not legal tender in Czechoslovakia, the 10- and 5-dukatu coins were issued as trade coinage. Trade coins are generally bullion coins, struck in gold or silver, that do not have legal tender status within the borders of their issuing country but are used to facilitate international trade.

That the issue was struck in low numbers, typically 1,000 pieces or below, makes the 10 dukatu one of the most coveted twentieth-century gold types.

This design features the Czechoslovakian coat of arms on the obverse and a full-figured depiction of Wenceslas riding a horse. Wenceslas' figure is etched in crudely drawn lines, while his helmeted head and the horse are rendered in traditional relief. A smaller impression of this design was also used on the 5-dukatu trade coin, issued at the same time.

The coin's obverse features a modified portrait of the country's lesser coat of arms (the Bohemian lion holding the shield of Slovakia).

Struck to commemorate the 60th anniversary of the reign of Emperor Franz Joseph I, one of the longest serving monarchs in modern history (ruled 1848–1916), the Austrian 1908 100 corona is one of the most recognizable gold coins of the twentieth century.

The coin features the likeness of Franz Joseph, the penultimate emperor of the Austro-Hungarian Empire. Born on December 2, 1830, Franz Joseph was the eldest son of Archduke Franz Karl and Princess Sophie of Bavaria. His path to rule was indirect and made possible due to the revolutionary fervor that gripped much of the continent. His predecessor, Ferdinand I, was a kind ruler, though a man beset by a lifetime of physical ailments and considered ill-prepared to lead a modern state. In contrast, Franz Joseph was described by his contemporaries as a strong autocrat, one who took his duties as emperor seriously and who staffed his government with capable and competent people.

Still, Austria under Franz Joseph suffered numerous setbacks. Over the course of his 60-year reign, the balance of power in Europe continued to shift away from Austria-Hungary. Military adventurism under his rule put significant strains on his relationship with other monarchs and on the treasury. These decisions also exacerbated some of the rot that had begun to manifest itself within the European imperial system of the late nineteenth and early twentieth centuries. By the 60th year of his rule, Franz Joseph was still very much in control of Austrian politics but had grown out of step with the times. By the end of the first decade of the twentieth century, the course of European politics was being set by much younger monarchs and politicians. Yet still, even at the ripe old age of 78, Franz Joseph's most consequential decisions lay ahead, and with them came major repercussions for the House of Habsburg.

As a piece of numismatic art, the coin's design is perfection. Franz Joseph I cuts a distinct and noble profile in medalist Rudolph Ferdinand Marschall's rendition. It is at first an understated portrait, only revealing the full measure of its weight with close examination. The reverse, designed by medalist Rudolf Neuberger, is the coin's most famous side, featuring a beautiful female figure resting atop the clouds. It's a striking pose that projects the grand power of the state. Even simple details, like the two tips of the olive wreath connecting the dates 1848 and 1908, are imbued with deeper meaning, symbolizing the glory of the emperor's reign.

It is fortunate for collectors that this spectacular design was struck in sufficient numbers to remain relatively attainable even 100 years after its release. Not a major rarity in any true sense, non-impaired examples in grades AU to Choice Uncirculated sell for a gradually increasing numismatic premium. A PCGS-certified example in AU-58 with typical eye appeal for the grade brought US$5,040 at an August 2018 Stack's Bowers auction, while an example certified MS-61 by NGC brought $7,200 in April when offered by Heritage. Gem examples are extremely rare. In January 2017, Heritage sold an example graded Proof 65 Cameo by NGC, the single finest example recorded by either grading service, for $70,500.

AUSTRIA 1908 GOLD 100 CORONA

A striking depiction of a long-serving monarch.

Obverse. A right-facing bare bust of Emperor Franz Joseph I. The inscription wraps around the design and reads FRANC • IOS • I • D • G • IMP • AUST • REX BOH • GAL • ILL • ETC • ET AP • REX HUNG. ("Franz Joseph I by the Grace of God Emperor of Austria King of Bohemia, Galicia, Illyria, etc. and King of Hungary").

Reverse. Fame, facing left, reclines on a cloud and leans against a shield bearing Austria's imperial coat of arms. Sun rays are behind her on the left, and she is holding a wreath. The dual date 1848 1908 appears in the upper left. In the upper right, the denomination is written out 100 COR. The Latin inscription DVODECIM LVSTRIS GLORIOSE PERACTIS ("60 glorious years") is written in clouds at the bottom of the design.

Composition	Weight	Diameter	Alignment	Edge
.900 gold	33.8753 grams	37 mm	Medal	Lettered†
Mintage	**Mint**	**Collecting Difficulty**		**References**
16,026 (plus Proofs)	Mint of Kremnitz	Moderate		Fr-429; Herinek-317; J-400; KM-2812; Schl-646; Y-46

† VIRIBVS VNITIS ("United in Force")

An October 1908 illustration from the French magazine *Le Petit Journal* on the Bosnian Crisis of 1908. Bulgaria declares its independence and its prince Ferdinand is named czar. Austria-Hungary, depicted by Emperor Franz Joseph, annexes Bosnia and Herzegovina, while the Ottoman Sultan Abdul Hamid II looks on helplessly.

No. 75

SPAIN 1937 OLOT 15 CENTIMOS

The reality of a "romantic" civil war.

Obverse. A stylized design comprised of line segments and a protruding eagle's wing. This motif is enclosed in a semi-round box comprised of X-shaped hash marks. Encircling the design is the inscription A JUNTAMENT D'OLOT * ("Olot City Council"). The rim is raised and crudely rendered.

Reverse. A primitive depiction of a factory. On the left third of the coin are two billowing smokestacks. The date, rendered 24-IX-1937, wraps around the left of the design, text facing outward. The denomination wraps around the right and is partly obscured by smoke. It reads 15 CENTIM S.

Composition	Weight	Diameter	Alignment	Edge
Iron	5.51 grams	30.2 mm	Coin	Smooth
Mintage	Mint		Collecting Difficulty	References
100	Olot		Difficult	KM-2

Spanish Civil War soldiers at the Battle of Irún.

This crude 15-centimos coin was struck under the authority of the Olot City Council and was intended to be an emergency circulating coinage for the Catalonian city as the Spanish Civil War raged on. Seen through the literary modernist works of American volunteers for the republican cause (such as Ernest Hemingway and John Dos Passos), one might view the war as romantic adventurism. In truth, it was a brutal and vicious prelude to the great twentieth-century conflagration that was World War II. At least 150,000 civilians were killed and approximately 285,000 combatants were killed in action. It was a thoroughly modern conflict, fought between the supporters of liberal democracy and the proponents of fascism. But the roots of the war went deep, through the political instability of the nineteenth century all the way back to the death of the last Habsburg in Spain (Charles II) in 1700.

The coin's design is crude, yet distinctive. It has an artistic character that is neither necessary nor always present in the issuance of an emergency issue. The coin's obverse features a stylized and crude rendering of vertical lines with an extended eagle's wing. This motif is rendered in a much finer style on Olot's municipal paper money issues, which circulated at the same time.

Only 100 pieces of the 1937 Olot 15 centimos were struck, making this one of the rarest issues struck during the Spanish Civil War. The denomination was joined by a smaller 10-centimos coin. This coin features art that was even cruder, and in total 25,000 were reportedly struck. the 10 centimos is scarce in collectible grades, but the 15 centimos is rare and is, in many ways, an underrated coin. It carries a market value of US$15,000 to $20,000 in grades AU and above.

A Republican banner in Madrid reading, "They shall not pass! Fascism wants to conquer Madrid. Madrid shall be fascism's grave," during the siege of 1936–1939.

The Aramco gold sovereign and 4-pound "coins" are somewhat enigmatic, insofar as issues struck by the U.S. Mint go. Their existence was noted by the numismatic community as early as 1948, but the fog didn't begin to clear until Harry X Boosel wrote an in-depth recitation of his attempts to get to the bottom of why the Philadelphia Mint struck them.

Boosel's conclusion was that the issues were struck by the United States government on behalf of the Arabian American Oil Company (Aramco) as payment for a 60-year concession to explore and extract from Saudi oil fields[1]. While Saudi oil production in the 1940s was nowhere near as vital to the global fuel market as it is today, the newly formed gulf state did produce amounts sufficient enough to be strategically important as World War II unfolded—so much so that the Roosevelt administration provided the country with $12 million in foreign aid, paid mostly in the form of silver coin, as the war progressed.

Aramco was founded in 1933 by American oil giant Standard Oil of California. Originally called California-Arabian Standard Oil Co., it adopted the Aramco name in January 1944.

SAUDI ARABIA ARAMCO 1947 GOLD "SOVEREIGN" AND 1945 GOLD "4 POUNDS"

"Black gold" brings global trade to Saudi Arabia.

Common Obverse. The central motif is the seal of the United States of America: the heraldic eagle displayed with open wings. Its left talon holds an olive branch, and the right talon holds arrows. A shield (escutcheon) decorated like the U.S. flag covers its breast. The legend U.S. MINT wraps clockwise at the top, and PHILADELPHIA - U.S.A. wraps counterclockwise at the bottom. A thick rim area surrounds this. Note: an identical impression is used on the sovereign and 4-pound coins. The rim area is obviously larger on the larger format coin.
Sovereign Reverse. Three separate horizontal bars. The top bar's inscription is * CONTAINS *; the middle bar inscription is .2354 TROY OZS.; and the bottom bar inscription reads * FINE GOLD *. The rest of the field is empty.
4 Pounds Reverse. A similar motif as the sovereign, but slightly modified. The three horizontal bars are slightly inset. The top bar inscription reads GROSS WEIGHT - 493.1 GRAINS; the middle bar inscription is NET WEIGHT - 452.008333 GR.; and the bottom bar inscription reads FINENESS 916 ⅔.

Sovereign (1947 issue)				
Composition	**Weight**	**Diameter**	**Alignment**	**Edge**
.9167 gold, .0833 copper	7.9881 grams	21.7 mm	Medal	Reeded
Mintage	**Mint**		**Collecting Difficulty**	**References**
123,000 (most melted for bullion)	United States Mint (Philadelphia)		Moderate	Fr-19; KM-35; Schön-A20

4 Pounds (1945 issue)				
Composition	**Weight**	**Diameter**	**Alignment**	**Edge**
.9167 gold, .0833 copper (crown)	31.95 grams	39 mm	Medal	Reeded
Mintage	**Mint**		**Collecting Difficulty**	**References**
91,210	United States Mint (Philadelphia)		Moderate	Fr-190, KM-34, Schön-B20,

King Abdulaziz, Ibn Saud.

The company's relationship with its Saudi hosts was complicated. Drilling in the harsh environment proved difficult, and an entire infrastructure needed to be constructed in order to profitably refine and export crude oil. Development of a 750-mile pipeline began in 1947 and was finished in 1950. At the same time, the Saudi government put continuous pressure on Aramco in order to gain greater leverage and profits from extraction activities.

In light of these sensitive strategic developments, the Aramco gold discs can be seen as the complicated trade coinage that they were. Although gold coins no longer circulated in the United States, American businesses did have access to gold in the international market. Given the all-encompassing nature of the Second World War, gold could not be purchased in quantity without paying enormous premiums. And seeing that it was in America's strategic interests not to allow the Axis powers access to Arabian oil, the Treasury Department's willingness to produce gold bullion for use as payment to Saudi Arabia made sense.

As numismatic collectibles, the Aramco discs lack most of the hallmarks of a great coinage: the "coins" were never legal tender; they bear no date to signify when they were struck; the art, such as it is, is crudely rendered; and neither issue is known to be rare in the absolute sense. But few coins struck in the twentieth century carry the import of this two-issue series, not only in securing American interests abroad but also in their long-term impact on the daily lives of ordinary people.

The first to be struck was the larger 4-pound type. The U.S. Mint officially referred to the pieces as *gold discs*, not coins[2]. In total, 91,210 of this type were struck. The discs bore the seal of the United States Mint on the obverse and inscriptions detailing weight and fineness on the reverse. A second production run occurred in 1947, when the mint struck 121,364 pieces of the smaller type. The smaller type bears a similar design style but features slightly modified text on the reverse.

Until the private ownership of gold bullion was legalized in 1974, it was difficult—and possibly illegal—to acquire pieces like the Aramco gold bullion coins. Furthermore, the nature of the transaction from a U.S. company to the Saudi government meant a majority of the issue was likely melted down and converted into other forms. Anecdotal evidence exists that some number of these pieces passed from one hand to the next as a method of payment, and it is uncommon to find surviving examples in truly uncirculated states of preservation.

To date, NGC accounts for 284 grading events of the 4-pound issue, with two examples tied for finest at MS-63. PCGS reports 92 graded, with two at MS-63. The smaller type has proved to be the scarcer of the two. NGC reports 114 grading events, with a sole example at MS-65. PCGS accounts for 65 grading events, with three examples at MS-64. In April 2015, the finest known 4-pound coin, graded MS-63 by NGC, sold for US$5,170 at a Heritage auction.

King Abdulaziz Center for World Culture in Dammam, Saudi Arabia, developed by Saudi Aramco and inaugurated by King Salman bin Abdulaziz in December 2017. It is located where Saudi Arabia first discovered oil. The Center incorporates a museum, children's museum, library, cinema, theater, and exhibition halls.

Standard Oil tanks at Bakersfield, California, circa 1910.

The Mexican Revolution (1910–1920) of the early twentieth century was well underway when the Guerrero/Suriana 2 pesos was struck in 1915. A brutal, unpredictable, and confounding period for the people involved, the Mexican Revolution, when looked at through a numismatic prism, has proven to be one of the century's most fascinating periods for emergency coin production.

Of all the designs struck up by regional mints for local use, the Suriana/Guerrero 2 pesos may be the most fascinating. Struck at an impromptu mint built in the small town/mining camp of Suriana, located in the southern Mexican state of Guerrero, this crown-sized coin is made of a crudely blended alloy of gold and silver. The result is an "artisanal" coinage that was worth more in bullion than in face value. As a result, many of those struck were likely melted down, and few survivors remain.

To date, only one example has been certified by either NGC or PCGS. That coin, graded AU-58 by NGC, sold for US$27,600 when it was offered by Stack's Bowers and Ponterio in 2012. Three years later, the same piece brought $28,200 at a Heritage auction. Ira and Larry Goldberg Auctioneers sold the finest of two known of the plain edge variety for $35,000.

Similar pieces were struck in Guerrero in 1915 using slightly modified versions of the design. An example of a more common type sells for about $800 to $1,000 in About Uncirculated grades, with Mint State examples bringing more, based on eye appeal and other factors.

SURIANA 2 PESOS FOR THE REST OF US

While it is not possible for every collector to own a great numismatic rarity, the Mexican mint recognized the Suriana issue's importance to the country's numismatic community and in 2013 struck 8,000 silver and aluminum-bronze bimetallic coins, featuring the iconic sun and mountain reverse design. The piece was included in a six-coin set with other iconic Mexican coin designs. These sets trade online for about $200.

(Above) Mexican soldiers on a train during the Revolution.

(Right) Guerrero, Mexico.

MEXICO 1915 GUERRERO/ SURIANA GOLD WITH SILVER 2 PESOS

Making coins in the midst of upheaval.

Obverse. In the center, an eagle, clutching a rattlesnake in its beak and right talon, stands atop a cactus on a mound surrounded by water. The legend REPUBLICA MEXICANA. * DOS PESOS. GRO. 1915 * encircles the design. A border of small beads wraps around the design, just inside the rim.

Reverse. In the center, a heraldic sun with human facial features shines over mountains. The gold fineness ORO 0,595 is written above. The inscription REFORMA, LIBERTAD, JUSTICIA Y LEY * SURIANA … encircles the design. A border of small beads wraps around the design, just inside the rim.

Composition	Weight	Diameter	Alignment	Edge
Gold and silver alloy	22.93 grams	39 mm	Coin	Reeded

Mintage	Mint		Collecting Difficulty	References
Unknown	La Suriana		Extremely difficult	Eliz-MX-199; GB-223; KM-665

PANAMA 1931 SILVER BALBOA, PROOF

The quest to reach the Pacific.

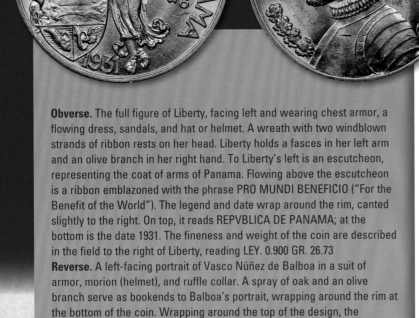

Obverse. The full figure of Liberty, facing left and wearing chest armor, a flowing dress, sandals, and hat or helmet. A wreath with two windblown strands of ribbon rests on her head. Liberty holds a fasces in her left arm and an olive branch in her right hand. To Liberty's left is an escutcheon, representing the coat of arms of Panama. Flowing above the escutcheon is a ribbon emblazoned with the phrase PRO MUNDI BENEFICIO ("For the Benefit of the World"). The legend and date wrap around the rim, canted slightly to the right. On top, it reads REPVBLICA DE PANAMA; at the bottom is the date 1931. The fineness and weight of the coin are described in the field to the right of Liberty, reading LEY. 0.900 GR. 26.73

Reverse. A left-facing portrait of Vasco Núñez de Balboa in a suit of armor, morion (helmet), and ruffle collar. A spray of oak and an olive branch serve as bookends to Balboa's portrait, wrapping around the rim at the bottom of the coin. Wrapping around the top of the design, the inscription: - V N - BALBOA -. A thin ring wraps around the corner next to the raised rim.

Composition	Weight	Diameter	Alignment	Edge
.900 silver	26.73 grams	38.10 mm	Coin	Reeded

Mintage	Mint		Collecting Difficulty	References
20	United States Mint (Philadelphia)		Extremely difficult	KM-13

While Panama's eventual independence from Colombia was all but inevitable in time, it was anything but assured after the Colombian Senate refused to ratify the Hay-Herrán Treaty in 1903. The treaty, had it been ratified, would have granted the United States a renewable lease for a six-mile-wide area running across the length of the Isthmus of Panama, allowing American engineers to finish a decades-long engineering debacle first undertaken by the French in the 1880s.

Considered the most complex engineering feat in history, the idea to cut a sea route through the Isthmus of Panama dates back to the earliest years of the European conquest of the New World. The Spanish, the English, and even the Americans contemplated the benefits of such a project, but it wasn't until the 1880s that the French made the first real effort. Coming off of the success of French engineers to construct the Suez Canal in Egypt, the Panama project proved to be far more difficult. Although the canal's length would be 40 percent shorter than Suez, the geography and climate proved overwhelming. Diseases like yellow fever and malaria ran rampant and killed thousands of workers. The rainy season caused flooding and mudslides and the project quickly overran its budget. In 1889, after five years of work, the French effort, led by Ferdinand de Lesseps, bowed out.

The Americans, under the administrations of President William McKinley and later President Theodore Roosevelt, saw the benefit of a canal to dramatically shorten the distance and cost of maritime commerce between the American coasts. Also, having acquired Guam, the Philippines, and Puerto Rico as spoils from the Spanish-American War, the United States was in an expansionist mood.

After the United States bought the rights to the canal, the project, already a boondoggle, was put under the purview of War Secretary William Howard Taft. Under the project's new administration, dramatic changes were undertaken to the canal's design and new modern equipment supplied by American companies proved to be more efficient in excavating through the tropical landscape. The American project better understood the threat of tropical diseases and developed a sophisticated sanitation system, which minimized disease. Still, construction of the canal was costly and dangerous. The canal opened in 1914 and changed the face of trade between the west and east coasts of North and South America.

Replacing the Colombian peso in 1904, the balboa—named in honor of Spanish conquistador Vasco Núñez de Balboa (1475–1519), the first European to travel to the Pacific Ocean—became the monetary unit of the Republic of Panama. The conquistador's portrait has appeared on the country's circulating coinage ever since (except for the centesimo, which features native chieftain Urracá (died 1531), a leader of the resistance against the Spanish).

However, a coin with the denomination of one balboa wasn't introduced until 1931. There were 200,000 circulation strikes reported to be struck that year, with a limited mintage of just 20 Proofs.

The reverse, designed by Panamanian artist and patriot Roberto Lewis (1874–1949), features a fluidly posed figure of Lady Liberty, hips swayed to her right to suggest movement towards the viewer. Liberty is facing left with her chin held up. Somewhat strangely, she is wearing armor that covers only her breasts. Her two-layered dress, rendered in a flowing, almost foamy manner, seems transparent in spots.

A wreath with two windblown strands of ribbon rests on Liberty's head. In her left arm, she cradles the fasces, a bundle of rods surrounding an axe and tied together with leather straps. Despite its adoption as an icon by fascist forces in the twentieth century, the ancient Roman fasces is a

Balboa claiming dominion over the South Seas on behalf of the king of Spain. Lithograph circa 1893.

traditional symbol of republican power in public art. In Liberty's right hand is a sprig of oak, a symbol of the country's independence and burgeoning strength.

To Liberty's left is a large escutcheon or shield, representing the coat of arms of Panama. The shield is divided into five scenes. In the sinister chief (upper left) is a depiction of a rifle and a sword, hung up, representing the laying down of arms after conflict. In the dexter chief (upper right) is a depiction of a shovel and rake, symbolizing the work to be done. In the fess point (center) is a depiction of the Isthmus of Panama. A sun crests the horizon on the left; a moon rises above the horizon on the right. In the sinister base (bottom left) is a depiction of a cornucopia, symbol of wealth and abundance. In the dexter base (bottom right) is a winged wheel, a symbol of progress. Flowing above the escutcheon is a ribbon emblazoned with the phrase PRO MVNDI BENEFICIO, which translates to "For the Benefit of the World." The legend REPVBLICA DE PANAMA and the date 1931 wrap around the rim, canted slightly to the right. Like bullion of a more recent vintage, the fineness and weight of the coin are described on the coin.

American sculptor William Clark Noble (1858–1938) designed the obverse, featuring a bust portrait of the conquistador. Noble also designed the 1925 Guatemalan quetzal.

Krause and NGC give a value of US$3,000 for the 1931 Proof, which—besides being the first year of the issue—was the only Proof issue for the type. Only two specimens have been certified by NGC; to date, PCGS has certified none. The PF-63 example was offered at a 2009 Ponterio sale with an estimate of US$15,000-$20,000, but the reserve was not met and the coin did not sell. The PF-65 coin, however, sold for $25,850 (including a buyer's premium) at an April 2015 Heritage Auctions sale.

Panama Canal construction, circa 1913.

Three men standing on lock gates of Panama Canal, circa 1913.

JAPAN 1943–1944 EAST INDIES OCCUPATION COINAGE

Puppet coins for a puppet government.

The Dutch East India Company took control of much of the Indonesian archipelago at the start of the seventeenth century, establishing for itself the newly built capital city of Batavia (on the location of present-day Jakarta) and assuming a monopoly of trade in the region.

Over the next few hundred years, the Dutch maintained and expanded their Southeast Asian colonial possessions. During the nineteenth century, however, the nations of Asia began to adapt to the new industrial age in a process often called "modernization", and perhaps none were more successful in this endeavor than Japan. By the beginning of the twentieth century, Japan's military and industrial might was even capable of defeating an imperial European country (the Russo-Japanese War). Suddenly, an ambitious new world power was on the rise.

Imperial Japan's long-term goal of establishing a pan-Asian empire—which it promoted as the Greater East Asia Co-Prosperity Sphere (大東亞共榮圏, *Dai Tōa Kyōeiken*)—developed, ironically enough, from a pacifist philosopher who envisioned an Asia comprised of countries that cooperated with each other, free from European influence. The Japanese government's

The surrender of Japan, Tokyo Bay, September 2, 1945.

true intent, however, was more self-serving. It saw its weaker neighbors not as potential allies in a reshuffling of the world order but as subordinate states, run by puppet governments for the benefit of the Japanese Empire.

To this end, the Japanese army was ruthless, rivalling the carnage unleashed by their World War II allies, Nazi Germany. By some estimates, the Greater East Asia Co-Prosperity Sphere resulted in the deaths of between six and ten million people before Japan's surrender in August 1945.

Japanese occupation of the East Indies formally began on March 8, 1942, when the Dutch colonial government capitulated to Japan's demands. With the war against the Nazis raging in Europe, the Dutch and their allies could ill afford to defend the large archipelago against invasion.

Initially, many Indonesians saw Japan's occupation in a favorable light, as they hoped that their country's "big brother" would end the racial hierarchy imposed upon them by their Dutch masters. While some Indonesians saw their lots improve due to the ouster of the Dutch from positions of power, the occupation ultimately proved more heinous for others who experienced war crimes such as torture, sex slavery, forced labor and execution.

Portrait of President Sukarno, circa 1949.

Sen				
Composition	Weight	Diameter	Alignment	Edge
Aluminum	0.55 grams	16 mm	Medal	Smooth
Mintage	**Mint**		**Collecting Difficulty**	**References**
233,190,000 (1943); 66,810,000 (1944)	Japan Mint (Osaka)		Easy	Y-A66

5 Sen				
Composition	Weight	Diameter	Alignment	Edge
Aluminum	0.85 grams	19 mm	Medal	Reeded
Mintage	**Mint**		**Collecting Difficulty**	**References**
Unknown	Japan Mint (Osaka)		Easy	Y-B66

10 Sen				
Composition	Weight	Diameter	Alignment	Edge
Tin alloy	3.5 grams	22 mm	Medal	Reeded
Mintage	**Mint**		**Collecting Difficulty**	**References**
69,490,000 (1943); 110,510,000 (1944)	Japan Mint (Osaka)		Easy	Y-66

After the end of the war and the removal of Japanese forces, nationalist leaders Mohammad Hatta and the mononymous Sukarno declared independence for Indonesia on August 17, 1945. The Dutch fought to regain their colony, but after four years of guerilla warfare, the Netherlands ceded control of most of the country in 1949.

Struck by the Osaka Mint, Japan began production of three denominations of East Indian occupation coinage in 1943, a year after they had successfully taken the island archipelago from the Dutch coalition forces. The denominations were the sen, 5 sen, and 10 sen (one-hundredth, one-twentieth and one-tenth of the yen). Production lasted for two years and was envisioned as a replacement for the Dutch colonial issues based on the gulden.

Of the three denominations, the 5 sen is by far the rarest. It was struck in unknown quantities and is seldom seen in the market, while the sen and the 10 sen, both minted in high numbers, are likewise seldom seen but are sufficient in numbers to command prices between US$1,000 to $2,500 for Mint State examples[1].

The designs are highly unusual, yet striking. They depict an important piece of Indonesian cultural heritage—the wayang kulit shadow puppets of the island of Java—and may have succeeded as an attempt to win locals over to this new monetary system had the coins actually been issued. With war in the Pacific interrupting the shipment of coins from Japan to the archipelago, most surviving examples were eventually melted.

The sen, struck in aluminum, was produced for two years and bears the close-up likeness of a puppet, its distinctive profile rendered in exacting detail with exaggerated facial features and hair that resembles an octopus tentacle.

Wayang kulit puppet.

The existence of off-metal trial pieces was confirmed by American pioneer of Asian numismatics Dr. Norman Jacobs, whose collection included a set of NE2603 (1943) silver trial strikings, one of each denomination. At a 2011 Heritage auction, the sen, certified by NGC in the grade of MS-62, brought US$10,350; the 5 sen, certified MS-61 by NGC, brought $29,910; and the 10 sen (NGC MS-62) brought $12,650.

POLAND 1942–1943 LODZ GHETTO COINAGE

A circulating coinage for the Living Hell.

When the Russian Army liberated the Polish city of Łódź from fleeing German forces on January 19, 1945, only 877 of the 230,000 Jews who once called the city home remained. Those left alive were spared simply because their overseers had run out of time.

On the streets of the ghetto, they were murdered by gunfire, hanging, starvation, exposure, and disease. They were murdered on the whims of soldiers of the German army, who fired upon them with impunity. They were even murdered on the orders of the Nazi's handpicked overseer, 65-year-old Jewish elder Mordecai Chaim Rumkowski, a controversial figure in Holocaust studies whose security detail included two members of the German SS[1].

Rumkowski was an autocrat who willingly conformed his administration to the desires of the Nazi regime. He thought he could render the Jews at Łódź useful to the German war effort and that this might ensure his and (one assumes) his community's survival.

Rumkowski is most remembered for a speech he gave in September 1942, when he asked the women and men of Łódź to hand over their children to the Germans for "relocation." The psychological terror of such a question is unimaginable, yet under pain of death most of the parents of Łódź acquiesced. Forbidden from leaving their homes, all they could do was watch from their windows as their sons and daughters piled into the backs of military wagons. Many dressed in their best clothes; little girls wore ribbons in their hair and boys wore suits. The children shrieked and cried out for their parents as the trucks drove away.

Within hours, they were all dead.

Such was the deal Rumkowski struck with his captors. Today, historians debate whether Rumkowski was a Nazi collaborator or merely a victim trying his best to give as many Jews as possible a chance to survive. There was no debate, however, on August 8, 1944, when he was bludgeoned to death at Auschwitz concentration camp by his fellow prisoners.

This is the historical backdrop in which the token coinage of Łódź must be considered.

The only coinage struck at a Jewish ghetto during the Holocaust, the ghetto coinage of Łódź consists of four denominations of eight major types. Three versions of a 10-pfennig denomination were struck in 1942, while 1943 saw production of two versions of a 5-mark coin. Two versions of a 10-mark coin were produced, as was a 20-mark coin.

Except the first two 10-pfennig design types, all of the coins were designed by ghetto resident Pinkus Szwarc and struck in a makeshift Jewish mint. Szwarc also designed the Łódź paper banknotes, called "Rumkies," that circulated before the introduction of the coins. The first 10-pfennig design type is widely credited to a resident artist named Tiefenbach. The designer of the second 10-pfennig design type is unknown.

While survivors are few, the first 10-pfennig design type was rejected by Hans Biebow, the chief Nazi administrator of the Łódź ghetto, because the design was deemed to be too similar to German types. The coins circulated for nearly three months (January-March 1942)[1]. The second design type, also criticized, entered production in August of that year[1].

Rumkowski had convinced Biebow to allow the ghetto to create its own money—really a receipt system—but it's clear, based on the surviving correspondence between the two men, that Biebow had little patience or consideration for any attempt on the part of the Jews to issue designs that were overtly prideful.

As a result, the approved coins are devoid of flourish but stand as a powerful testament of the Nazis' grotesque attempt at cultural erasure.

Holocaust survivor and author Primo Levi wrote of the coins in his novel *The Drowned and the Saved*, writing of the piece as a memento—a memory of the people and *lager* life. In that instance, the coin represented a truth that he, as a survivor, could never fully escape from.

As a numismatic artifact of one of the biggest crimes of the twentieth century, the importance of the Łódź Ghetto coinage should not be understated. Each surviving piece carries the burden of history and informs us that money remains vital and necessary even as humanity itself unravels.

Two design variants exist of the 1942 10-pfennig coin; the later variant was struck in aluminum-magnesium and bronze. The mintage of the first design type was largely destroyed as it was deemed too similar to the design of German coinage.

Jews in Łódź Ghetto. The Jojne Pilcer Market, at the intersection of Łagiewnicka and Berliński streets.

Chaim Rumkowski and Hans Biebow in the Łódź Ghetto.

10-Pfennig Obverse (first type). In the center, the Star of David, intertwined with sheaths of wheat. Wrapping around the rim in Gothic-style lettering: Litzmannstadt – Getto. Between two dots at the bottom: 1942.

10-Pfennig Reverse (first type). A large Gothic-style numeral 10. Wrapping around the rim, the inscription Der Aelteste der Juden. At the bottom, the Star of David is surrounded by two sprigs of oak leaves.

10-Pfennig Obverse (second type). In the center, a silhouette of the Star of David with the date 1942 inside. A circle frames the star. Wrapping around the rim, the inscription DER ALETESTE DER JUDEN IN LITZMANNSTADT.

10-Pfennig Reverse (second type). In the center, the large numeral 10. Wrapping around the rim, the inscription QUITTUNG UBER * PFENNIG *.

5-Mark, 10-Mark, and 20-Mark Obverse. A silhouette of the Star of David is large and offset to the upper left. At the bottom right corner of the star is the word GETTO, and below is the date 1943. Around the design is a semi-circle made of two lines intersected by six small Stars of David, which in this context resembles barbed wire.

5-Mark, 10-Mark, and 20-Mark Reverse. Wrapping around the rim is the inscription DER AELTESTE DER JUDEN IN LITZMANNSTADT ("The Jewish Elders of Litzmannstadt")—Litzmannstadt was the name the German occupiers gave to Łódź in honor of World War I general Karl Litzmann, who died trying to take Łódź during World War I. In the center is the denomination. A waving banner bisects the numeral and reads QUITTUNG UBER ("Receipt For").

10 Pfennig				
Composition	**Weight**	**Diameter**	**Alignment**	**Edge**
Magnesium	0.95 grams (Type 1); 0.76 grams (Type 2)	21.2 mm (Type 1); 19.1 mm (Type 2)	Medal	Smooth
Mintage	**Mint**		**Collecting Difficulty**	**References**
100,000 (Type 1); 1,000,000 (Type 2)	Łódź		Easy	KM-Tn5, Par-13

5 Mark				
Composition	**Weight**	**Diameter**	**Alignment**	**Edge**
Magnesium (Type 1); aluminum (Type 2)	1.03 grams (Type 1); 1.57 grams (Type 2)	22.7 mm (Type 1), 22.5 mm (Type 2)	Medal	
Mintage	**Mint**		**Collecting Difficulty**	**References**
800,000 (Type 1); unknown (Type 2)	Łódź		Easy	KM-Tn2

10 Mark				
Composition	**Weight**	**Diameter**	**Alignment**	**Edge**
Magnesium (Type 1); aluminum (Type 2)	1.75 grams (Type 1); between 2.6 and 3.4 grams (thin and thick planchet) (Type 2)	28.4 mm (Type 1); 28.3 mm (Type 2)	Medal	Smooth
Mintage	**Mint**		**Collecting Difficulty**	**References**
100,000 (Type 1); unknown (Type 2)	Łódź		Easy	KM-Tn3

20 Mark				
Composition	**Weight**	**Diameter**	**Alignment**	**Edge**
Aluminum	6.98 grams	33.5 mm	Medal	Smooth
Mintage	**Mint**		**Collecting Difficulty**	**References**
Approximately 600	Łódź		Easy	KM-Tn4

COLLECTOR'S WARNING: *Due to the simplicity of the design and the importance of this issue, Łódź Ghetto coinage is often counterfeited. Many of these counterfeits are deceptive. Third-party verification is highly recommended.*

NO. 81

ETHIOPIA EE1916–1917 (1924–1925) BIRR AND 6 BIRR PATTERNS

The pattern coinage of Ethiopia's Christian empress.

Obverse. A left-facing portrait of Empress Zewditu, wearing a crown and a veil. On the front of her blouse hangs a Christian cross necklace. The date is ፲፱፻፲፮. Wrapping around the rim is the inscription ዘውዲቱ፡ ንግሥ፡ ነገሥት፡ ዘኢትዮጵያ ("Zewditu: Empress of Ethiopia") and an ornamental border. Below the second- and third-to-last character of the inscription appears the word ESSAI. The engraver's name, M. DAMMON, appears to the left of the portrait.

Reverse. With its body facing left and head facing toward the viewer, a crowned lion holds a staff, the symbol of the Ethiopian Empire. Wrapping around the top of the design is the inscription ሞዓ፡አንበሳ፡ዘእምነገደ፡ይሁዳ፡፡ ("Conquering Lion of the Tribe of Judah"). A thin cutaway of ground creates the border for the exergue, in which the denomination አንድ፡ብር ("one birr") is written. Behind the lion's hind leg, following the curvature of the ornamental border, is the name J.C. CHAPLAIN.

Birr				
Composition	**Weight**	**Diameter**	**Alignment**	**Edge**
Silver	28.1 grams		Coin	Lettered†
Mintage	**Mint**		**Collecting Difficulty**	**References**
2 (known)	Paris Mint, Monnaie de Paris		Virtually impossible	Gill-Z5
† ሞዓ፡አንበሳ፡ዘእምነገደ፡ይሁዳ ("Conquering Lion of the Tribe of Judah")				

6 Birr				
Composition	**Weight**	**Diameter**	**Alignment**	**Edge**
Gold	18.21 grams		Coin	Lettered†
Mintage	**Mint**		**Collecting Difficulty**	**References**
2 (known)	Paris Mint, Monnaie de Paris		Virtually impossible	Gill-Y22
† ሞዓ፡አንበሳ፡ዘእምነገደ፡ይሁዳ ("Conquering Lion of the Tribe of Judah")				

The Ethiopian Empire adopted the birr (which literally means "silver") as its standard national monetary unit on February 9, 1893, during the reign of Emperor Menelik II (1844–1913).

Menelik, a politically astute ruler, spent years consolidating power in order to create a strong central government, and he saw the modernization of Ethiopia's monetary system as part of an overall package of reform and infrastructure development necessary for his empire to remain independent and out of the clutches of expansionist European colonial powers.

Complicating the situation was the fact that before his enthronement as emperor, Menelik had already entered into a treaty with Italy that had given the European state access to the port of Assab and surrounding lands, allowing for the establishment of the colony of Italian Eritrea. For Menelik, then king of Shewa, the move was a reprisal against his political rivals and an assurance of military support for his rise to power. There is no doubt that he viewed the rapid pace of Italian development in the region and its encroachment on the interior as a direct threat to his rule. Even as tensions with the Italians began to build, Menelik's Ethiopia introduced its own regime of modernization projects and governmental reforms.

One of Ethiopia's most pressing problems came from its reliance on foreign coin (primarily Maria Theresa thalers from Austria—see number 82) and a primitive money made from ingots of twine-bound salt called *amole tchew*.

Menelik sought to remedy Ethiopia's lack of national currency by establishing the birr, which literally translates to the word "silver." Ethiopians already called the circulating thalers "birrs," so this name had an established and historic meaning.

Menelik commissioned the Paris Mint to strike the first birr coins in EE1887 (1895). The first emission consisted of 20,000 pieces, which bore the likeness of the emperor on one side and an elegant representation of the Lion of Judah, an important Christian symbol of the Ethiopian Empire, on the other.

Empress Zewditu and a priest.

**A page from the French newspaper *Le Petit Journal*
depicting Menelik II at the battle of Adwa, August 1898.**

Merena, which realized US$15,400 (for an AU example), and a December 2008 Numismatica Genevensis SA auction, where an XF example brought $56,850. The difference in quality between a coin described as XF and AU is so slight that it is very possible these two listings were for the same coin!

Only two discrete examples are known of the EE1917 birr pattern, both have sold within the past decade by Heritage Auctions. A toned example certified MS-62 by NGC brought US$49,937.50 in January 2014, while a second piece, toned and ungraded but described as being in Mint State, brought $43,125 in a January 2011 Heritage auction.

The silver pattern coins were so elusive that Ethiopian coin expert Dennis Gill was unaware of their existence when he began work on his authoritative 1991 reference *The Coinage of Ethiopia, Eritrea, and Italian Somalia.*

Nevertheless, these elusive patterns do exist and are coveted treasures from one of history's longest running empires.

The royal palace in Addis Ababa, circa 1934.

The new coin saw some success in circulation, but certainly not enough to do away with the use of foreign coin, or salt money for that matter. Still, coins bearing the effigy of Menelik II would continue to see production and circulate for the remainder of his rule and in subsequent years after his death, while his successor Lij Iyasu served as the emperor-designate.

Iyasu's reign was enigmatic and ultimately cut short due to intrigue and fears that he had betrayed the royal mandate by converting to Islam. His regency was not marked by much in the way of strategic or diplomatic success. Succeeding Iyasu was Empress Zewditu, his aunt and the eldest daughter of Menelik II. Passed over initially due to her gender, Zewditu was the last empress in world history and served in that capacity until 1930, when she was succeeded by one of the twentieth century's most consequential African rulers, Emperor Haile Selassie (reigned 1930–1974).

While no coinage was struck to mark the reign of Iyasu, a pattern coinage was struck featuring the likeness of Zewditu. This coinage featured Jules-Clément Chaplain's elegant lion reverse (brought back from the second type of Menelik issues) and Paul Marcel Dammann's beautiful left-facing portrait of the empress. Both engravers were accomplished medalists, trained at the École nationale supérieure des Beaux-Arts.

The Zewditu coin design is elegant and ornate. It improves upon the Menelik design by adding a keyed border, embellished with a configuration of alternating dots and crosses. Dammann's portrait of the empress is regal and highly detailed, depicting her as a woman of great strength and piety.

As a collectible, only the EE1917 half birr was struck in significant enough numbers to be considered a regular issue. Pattern issues of EE1916 and EE1917 in denominations of 6 birr (in gold) and 1 birr (in silver) make up this Greatest Modern World Coins entry.

In his entertaining volume of *Unusual World Coins*, George Cuhaj reports a mintage of two for the gold 6 birr struck in EE1916 and reports two public sales for the issue: a March 1988 offering by Bowers and

Empress Zewditu's chair at the National Museum of Ethiopia, Addis Ababa.

AUSTRIA 1780 MARIA THERESA THALER

In far-off places, the Gray Lady.

Obverse. A right-facing profile of Empress Maria Theresa wearing a widow's veil and a regal gown, embellished by an ermine shawl and a small diadem pinned atop of her right shoulder. Below her bust truncation are the initials S.F., standing for Josef Faby and Tobias Johann Schöbel, officials of the Günzburg Mint. Wrapping around the edge of the coin is the inscription M·THERESIA·D·G·R·IMP·HU·BO·REG· ("Maria-Theresia, by the Grace of God, Roman Empress, Queen of Hungary and Bohemia"). Beaded denticles wrap around the edge.

Reverse. The imperial two-headed eagle of the Habsburg royal family is surmounted by a crown, centered between the heads. In front of the eagle is a shield bearing four quadrants, representing Hungary, Bohemia, Burgundy, and Burgau (wherein lies the Mint of Günzburg). The inscription reads ARCHID·AVST·DUX·BURG·CO·TYR·1780·X (*Archidux Austriae, Dux Burgundiae, Comes Tyrolis* ["Archduke of Austria, Duke of Burgundy, Count of Tyrol"]). Beaded denticles wrap around the edge.

Composition	Weight	Diameter	Alignment	Edge
.833 silver, .166 copper; Italian issues struck in .835 silver	26.067–28.07 grams	39-42 mm	Medal	Lettered†

Mintage	Mint	Collecting Difficulty	References
390,000,000+	Various inside and outside Austria, including the Royal Mints at Birmingham, Bombay, Brussels, and London; Paris; Rome; and Utrecht. Contemporary restrikes produced by the Austrian Mint (Vienna).	Easy	K-T1

† IUSTITIA ET CLEMENTIA ("Justice and Clemency")

At first glance, our inclusion of the Maria Theresa thaler, a coin that traces its origins back to the late eighteenth century, in a list of greatest modern world coins might seem to be a shocking lapse in judgement.

While a majority of world coin collectors active today are well aware that the majority of examples on the market of this commonly-traded coin bearing the 1780-dated design are restrikes (it is a fact the Austrian Mint to this day produces official restrikes; these are easily discerned by the crispness of their design features and their Proof finish), it seems fewer are aware of just how uniquely successful the coin was as a circulating medium. The Maria Theresa thaler traveled well beyond Austria's landlocked borders and circulated as money well into the twentieth century.

The Maria Theresa thaler we know is actually the culmination of a life celebrated on her nation's coins. Born in 1717, Empress Maria Theresa's first likeness appeared on a coin shortly after she assumed office in 1741. As a reformer, Maria Theresa directed coin production at her mints and paid attention to details such as weights and measures and the extent to which certain denominations would be struck. It was a July 1741 edict that set the weight and fineness of her trademark thaler to 28.82 grams and .875 silver.

After two wars ruined her country's finances, she debased the thaler, setting its weight to the 28.067 grams and .833 fineness that it still holds today.

The coins we know as Maria Theresa thalers today carry the date 1780 and were struck in the final year of the empress's life. The coins were struck at mints throughout the Habsburg's vast empire, including in the

Maria Theresa of Austria in her last state portrait, 1772.

cities of Kremnitz, Prague, Karlsburg, Vienna, and Günzburg. Josef Faby and Tobias Johann Schöbel, whose initials mark the Maria Theresa's bust truncation, were in charge of the Mint at Günzburg.

Almost immediately, the Maria Theresa thaler struck in Günzburg saw export, and the coins travelled throughout Europe, the Levant, East Asia, and Africa. This popularity of the coins abroad was a boon to the empire's finances, but it was foreign traders' reluctance to accept Austrian coins bearing the likeness of Maria Theresa' successor, Emperor Joseph II, that cast the die for the famous trade coin carrying on long after its intended production period.

Researcher John S. Davenport estimates the mintage of the "original" Günzburg thalers to exceed 15 million, a tiny fraction of the reported total mintage of 390 million (including myriad restrikes of various forms).

When used as a circulating coin in far-off lands, it was not uncommon for the Maria Theresa thaler to be counterstamped. HIJJAZ and NEJD appear on many that circulated in the Arabic world. The Mutawakkilite Kingdom of Yemen, which struck coin number 93 on our list, used the Maria Theresa thaler as planchets for its own silver coinage. Around the Horn of Africa, the Maria Theresa thaler circulated well into the twentieth century. In 1935, fascist Italy acquired the rights from Austria to mint the coin for 25 years as part of its colonial conquest in Ethiopia.

Today, it is still possible to see the Maria Theresa thaler, though well worn, circulating in isolated regions in Africa or worn as jewelry by tribal women.

The lettered edge features Maria's Latin motto, IUSTITIA ET CLEMENTIA ("Justice and Clemency").

As a collectible, the Maria Theresa thaler will likely never garner the respect it deserves from collectors looking to acquire scarce and valuable coins. This is an understandable limitation that separates coin collecting as it is commonly practiced from numismatics.

But with so many of the coins in our Greatest list being beautiful failures, oddballs, or important firsts, it's wonderfully refreshing to celebrate a coin for exceeding all expectations and being for centuries what a coin is meant to be—real circulating money. Maria Theresa, in life, may not have traveled the four corners of Europe, Africa, and Asia, but the silver thaler bearing her likeness did. If that doesn't equal greatness, we don't know what would.

A portrait of Joseph II, Holy Roman Emperor, created 1823 (posthumous).

Dowager Empress Maria Theresa with her family, circa 1776.

1860 map of the Austrian Empire, Italian States, Turkey, and Greece.

PHILIPPINES 1906-S SILVER PESO

Key date in the popular Philippines peso series.

Obverse. A full-figured woman, facing left in a flowing dress, strikes an anvil with a hammer in her right hand. In her left hand, she holds an olive branch. In the background to the right is a volcano with smoke billowing out of its top. The flat space between the ground the woman is standing on and the volcano gives the illusion of water separating two islands. Encircling the design is the inscription ONE PESO FILIPINAS and beading around the rim.

Reverse. In the center of the design is a federal shield surmounted by a bald eagle. The eagle holds in its talons an olive branch and three arrows. The legend UNITED STATES OF AMERICA encircles the design clockwise from the lower left to the lower right. Two dots separate the legend from the date, which is located below the shield. San Francisco's mintmark is located below the left dot. The rim is beaded.

Composition	Weight	Diameter	Alignment	Edge
.900 silver, .100 copper	26.95 grams	38 mm	Coin	Reeded

Mintage	Mint	Collecting Difficulty	References
201,000	United States Mint (San Francisco)†	Moderate	KM-168

† Mintmark: S

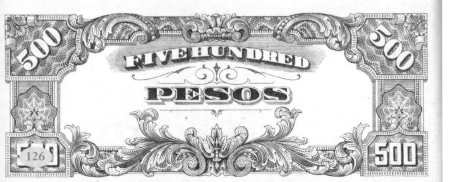

Beyond the 1907 Philippines peso in Proof (coin number 27 on our countdown), the Philippines peso series of 1903–1912 presents collectors a degree of difficulty that climbs rather steeply once one seeks examples of its more elusive issues in Mint State. Of the series' great condition rarities, none is as unforgiving as the 1906-S.

Struck at the San Francisco Mint and bearing the S mintmark, the 1906-S was the only 1906-dated Philippines peso struck for circulation. The Philadelphia Mint did strike up 500 Proof issues in 1906. PCGS and NGC have certified approximately 20 percent of that mintage and a nice, unimpaired Gem can be acquired for $3,000 in today's market.

The reported mintage of the 1906-S peso is 201,000, but most estimates have the number of surviving examples in all grades at below 200 examples. That number drops dramatically in Mint State. To date, PCGS reports 40 grading events of this rare issue, with just six pieces in Mint State and a sole example at the top of their condition census at MS-63. NGC reports 20 grading events, with just three in Mint State. It's not entirely clear whether these two reports include regrades or crossovers. A search online confirms that at least four of the nine in Mint State are unique pieces.

Gem examples of the 1906-S do not exist and the infrequent appearance at auction of a Mint State example in any degree of preservation should be considered a noteworthy event.

Stack's offered an example, the finest known at the time, in the Golden Horn Collection sale of January 12, 2009. That coin boasted gallimaufry toning in russet and eggplant. It is one of two examples certified by PCGS in MS-62. The other example in that grade is mostly brilliant but littered with bag marks, as one might expect for the grade. The aforementioned MS-63 is clearly in a league of its own. Were it not for one or two scratches (which are hidden underneath a layer of sandy rose-colored toning), the coin might warrant consideration for an upgrade. We've seen far less attractive coins in higher grades. High-resolution TrueView images are available to download on PCGS CoinFacts for readers interested in undertaking a more in-depth study of these census coins.

Three examples in MS-61 close out the entirety of the PCGS reported population of Mint State 1906-S pesos. One of the three was offered by Stack's at the January 2015 New York International Numismatic Convention.

It's noteworthy to point out that neither example sold for failure to meet the seller's reserve price. The MS-62 was offered as part of a four-coin grouping with an estimated price of US$80,000-$100,000[1]. The MS-61 example was offered at a reserve of $45,000-$55,000[2].

The current market value of an AU example is approximately $7,500.

The obverse of the 1906-S silver peso was designed by Filipino artist Melecio Figueroa (1842–1903). Educated in Spain, Figueroa returned to his homeland and taught the art of engraving. He also worked as an engraver for the Spanish colonial mint (Casa Moneda) in Manila. Figueroa was able to see his design first appear on this coin series in 1903, just prior to his death in July of that year.

The Imperial Japanese government issued paper currency denominated in pesos for local use during its occupation of the Philippines.

The South African city of Pretoria was founded in 1855 by Dutch settler Marthinus Pretorius, first president of the South African Republic, who named it to honor his father, Andries. At first, the city served as an economic and cultural center for area farmers. By 1870, the city had a population of about 1,500.

The discovery of nearby mineral wealth in the 1880s—gold in the Transvaal and silver in the greater Pretoria region—transformed the city. With mineral wealth came the opportunity for fortunes to be made, but it also brought about fierce competition between the Dutch and British Empires, which fought for decades to claim outright control of the region. Such was life in Africa during the Age of New Imperialism that spanned more than 40 years from 1870 until the start of World War I.

In 1910, under British rule, the South African republics and annexed Boer republics were merged into the Union of South Africa. The Union had four capital cities: Cape Town was home to the legislature; the former Orange Free State city of Bloemfontein was the capital of the judiciary; Pietermaritzburg housed the national archives; and Pretoria was the administrative capital.

As one would expect, the outbreak of World War I, which was essentially a supernova of the European imperial system, directed much of Britain's attention and resources away from colonial development. After the war, however, the government renewed its focus

Mine workers follow the compressed air drill, developing a drift in the Crown Mine, Johannesburg, circa 1935.

Marthinus Pretorius.

SOUTH AFRICA 1923-SA GOLD SOVEREIGN

Royal Mint expands to Britain's colonies.

Obverse. A portrait of George V, facing left. The initials B.M. are in the truncation. The inscriptions read GEORGIUS V D. G. BRITT: OMN: REX F. D. IND: IMP: (abbreviated Latin for *GEORGIUS V DEI GRATIA BRITANNIARUM OMNIUM REX FIDEI DEFENSOR INDIAE IMPERATOR* ["George V, by the Grace of God, King of all the Britons, Defender of the Faith, Emperor of India"]). Beaded denticles surround the rim.

Reverse. Pistrucci's *St. George and the Dragon* motif. St. George, scantily-clad in a Roman cape, helmet, and boots, rides a trampling horse. His gladius is in his right hand and a broken spear extends from the dragon's side. The mintmark SA is in the ground. Beneath is the date 1923, with the initials B.P. above and to the right.

Composition	Weight	Diameter	Alignment	Edge
.9167 gold	7.99 grams	22 mm	Medal	Reeded
Mintage	**Mint**		**Collecting Difficulty**	**References**
64	Royal Mint (Pretoria)†		Extremely difficult	Hern-S338; KM-21; Marsh-287; Spink-4004

† Mintmark: SA

on modernization and economic efficiencies in its most important territories, including India and South Africa.

The development of Royal Mint branch mints in Bombay and Pretoria was one such effort.

Struck at the Pretoria Mint in its first year of operations as a branch of the Royal Mint, the 1923-SA sovereign is known mostly to collectors in its Proof version, of which 655 were struck according to South African coin expert Brian Hern. Only 64 circulation strikes are believed to have been struck, making the coin one of the key collectible dates of the entire sovereign series.

The coin bears the effigy of King George V, a monarch who should by now appear very familiar to readers of this book as his likeness appears on 13 of our 100 Greatest, including five in the Top 10.

The reverse features Italian medalist Benedetto Pistrucci's *St. George and the Dragon* design that first appeared in 1817 on the British gold sovereign and some pattern crowns.

With just 64 struck, and not all accounted for, certified populations of the issue are understandably low. PCGS has six grading events, with a top population piece at MS-66. NGC reports 12 grading events with just four in Mint State, the highest also being at MS-66. The top pop coins at NGC and PCGS are confirmed to be different coins, but it is not clear whether each of the other grading events reported represent unique specimens.

The largest known cache of coins from the issue came to light in 1993, when the family of Raoul Robellaz Kahan, former assistant assayer at the Royal Mint in Perth and superintendent of the gold refinery Transvaal Chamber of Mines in Johannesburg, brought forward four pieces, all in Mint State, with two pieces being exceptional Gems.

The finest of the Gems was purchased in 1994 by collector Dr. Jacob Y. Terner and for nearly a decade was kept in his exemplary collection of English coins—one of the finest ever assembled.

Terner's coin surfaced at public auction in 2004 when Goldberg Auctions offered it, then conservatively graded MS-65 by PCGS (lot 414). The coin wildly beat pre-sale estimates, hammering at US$6,900[1]. The piece then entered into another world-class international coin collection, the Millennia Collection.

Five years later, the Terner-Millennia coin brought a record price of $27,600 (against a presale estimate of just $10,000 to $12,000). This time, it was offered in an NGC MS-66 holder.

That number was shattered in January 2013, when Heritage Auctions realized a US$49,937.50 hammer for the finest example yet certified in a PCGS holder. This example was described as prooflike by PCGS but was, according to cataloger Bruce Lorich, more accurately described as "satiny in texture with bright luster."[2]

One interesting observation about the market when it comes to coins struck at the Royal Mint branch mint in Pretoria: for many years, these coins were cataloged as Great Britain issues bearing the SA (South Africa) mintmark. In more recent years, however, catalogers have begun to list the coins as South African national releases. Precision and accuracy aside, it is clear the market has favored the latter approach.

Field Marshal Jan Smuts, prime minister of the Union of South Africa from 1919 to 1924 and 1939 to 1948.

Issued in silver from 1922 to 1928, the crown-sized Swiss 5-franc coin bearing engraver Paul Burkhard's effigy of William Tell was struck in two types.

The initial type was struck for two years only (1922 and 1923) and was strengthened in subsequent years to show more detail and strike up more fully. In addition, the coin's reverse lettering was changed so the denomination 5 Fr, reads 5FR.

Burkhard's design was chosen after it was entered into a 1919 design competition. His portrait of Tell is loosely based on sculptor Richard Kissling's Tell monument in Altdorf. While some may be thrown off by the lack of a beard in Burkhard's depiction, the hair detail is almost identical.

All issues of this series are highly collectible in Mint State. Especially scarce are Specimen strikings, which can be distinguished from circulation strike counterparts by their prooflike surfaces. These can bring several times more at auction than Mint State examples, and careful examination on the part of the collector is a must in order to avoid pieces of inferior quality. Prices of your typical silver 5 francs in this series are US$500 to $2,000 for Mint State examples, and $2,000 to $5,000 for Specimens.

For the 1928 issue, the collecting landscape changes dramatically. The mintage of the year is widely accepted to be 24,000 pieces, the lowest mintage of the entire series by a wide margin. But this mintage belies the true rarity of the issue. According to the estimates of experts in the field of Swiss coins, it is believed that fewer than 100 examples survive; some estimate that number could be as low as 50. The likely cause of this attrition? A massive melt of most of the mintage.

In certified grades, only two discrete examples have turned up, both in NGC holders.

The top pop specimen in the NGC census was offered for sale in 2016 at a Heritage Auctions ANA sale, where it brought $11,162.50. The coin had a muted golden hue, with dapple gray toning wrapping around the rim on the obverse and surrounding the devices on the reverse[1].

Specimen strikes are believed to be even rarer and bring even higher prices when offered for sale at auction.

In 2016, a PCGS-certified specimen graded SP-64 brought $19,975 at a Heritage auction; three years earlier, the finest-certified example at that service brought a record $25,853.53[2]. These coins account for half of the total certified by PCGS. NGC has yet to certify any Specimen examples.

No. 85

SWITZERLAND 1928-B SILVER 5 FRANCS

A low-mintage classic made rare by a great melt.

Obverse. A right-facing portrait of muscular William Tell in homespun clothes and a hood. The legend CONFOEDERATIO HELVETICA ("Helvetic Confederation" or "Confederation of Switzerland") encircles Tell in the upper portion of the field. The signature P BURKHARD is on the bust at the lower left. Beaded denticles wrap around inside of the rim.

Reverse. Sprigs of flowers (edelweiss on left, gentiana on right) surround the Swiss coat of arms (gules, a couped cross in argent). The denomination 5FR. ("Five Francs") in large text surmounts the coat of arms. Below is the date 1928, With a small B mintmark centered below the date. Beaded denticles wrap around inside of the rim.

Composition	Weight	Diameter	Alignment	Edge
.900 silver	25 grams	37 mm	Coin	Lettered†
Mintage	**Mint**		**Collecting Difficulty**	**References**
24,000	Swiss Mint (Bern)‡		Difficult	Dav-394; Divo-380; HMZ-2-1199g; KM-38

† DOMINUS *** | PROVIDEBIT | ********** ("The Lord Will Provide") ‡ Mintmark: B

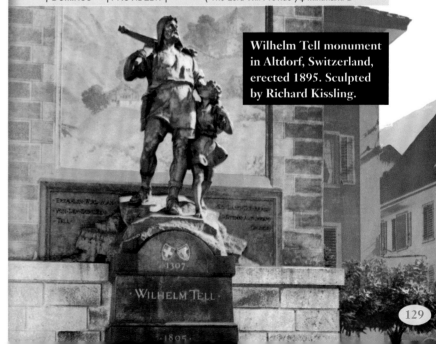

Wilhelm Tell monument in Altdorf, Switzerland, erected 1895. Sculpted by Richard Kissling.

WILLIAM TELL

The legend of William Tell plays an important role in the formulation of Swiss national identity.

The Tell story, which was adapted from a Proto-Germanic legend of the archer Egil and the evil King Nidung, sees the heroic Swiss herdsman forced to shoot an apple off the head of his beloved son as retaliation for his refusal to bow before the hat of the cruel Habsburg bailiff, Albrecht Gessler.

Tell, as the legend goes, splits the apple and saves the life of his son. But a second bolt from his crossbow felled Gessler and set into motion a peasant rebellion said to have led to the formation of the Old Swiss Confederacy. The date attached to the legendary standoff is 1307, and a bronze statue by artist Richard Kissling in Altdorf marks the supposed spot.

Today, the Tell story speaks to the Swiss people about the importance of the citizen soldier as a defense against tyranny and invasion. The leading gun advocacy organization in the country, ProTell, is named after the legendary marksmen.

Numismatically, the rifle and bow remain important symbols found on myriad Swiss medals and coins struck to honor annual shooting festivals. These pieces typically display beautiful artwork and are widely collected in and out of Switzerland.

No. 86
WEST GERMANY 1954-G MARK
The German miracle.

Obverse. In the center, the German federal eagle ("Bundesadler") is displayed (spread out) and langued (tongue protruding), facing left. Clockwise from the bottom, the inscription: BUNDESREPUBLIK DEUTSCHLAND ("People's Republic of Germany"). The mintmark is at the bottom of the design, bordered by one dot on either side. Beaded denticles surround the design. The rim is raised.

Reverse. Two sprigs of oak leaves fan inward toward a large number 1. The 1 is centered on the X-axis and its bottom tip touches the center of the Y-axis. Underneath, the remainder of the denomination DEUTSCHE MARK ("German Mark") is inscribed, and the date 1954 is in smaller text below. Beaded denticles surround the design. The rim is raised.

Composition	Weight	Diameter	Alignment	Edge
Copper-nickel	5.5 grams	23.5 mm	Medal	Ornamented and lettered†

Mintage	Mint	Collecting Difficulty	References
181,000	Karlsruhe Mint‡	Moderate	J-385; KM-110; Schön-108

† ~*~ ~·~ ~*~ ~·~ ~*~ ~·~ ‡ Mintmark: G

The Brandenburg gate in Berlin.

Twisted metal, burned and bombed-out buildings, shattered glass, broken spirits, and an indelible shame carried for generations were the spoiled fruits bestowed upon approximately 65 million Germans when the Allied bombs stopped falling on May 8, 1945. Hitler's thousand-year reich didn't make it to its second decade. Nazi Germany's vast military was crushed to pieces and the Austrian-born Führer, whose fiery demagoguery both captivated and terrorized the German people, lay dead of a self-inflicted gunshot wound in an underground bunker, feet below what was left of Berlin.

As bad as Germany felt aggrieved by the terms of peace negotiated in the Treaty of Versailles, the price it would pay culturally and economically for starting the Second World War would prove to be much worse. The Allied powers rejected the notion that fault for the war and the atrocities committed by the Nazi regime were solely the responsibility of the country's political leadership. Instead, they worked upon the assumption that the lawless conspiracy was carried out by the whole nation. Given these findings, Allied control over every facet of German life and the shaping of German national identity was comprehensive. Its effects, in many ways, continue to this day.

But out of the ashes, something incredible began to take shape. Three years after the end of the war, the German territories under the control of the Western Allies gained independence and formed the People's Republic of Germany (Bundesrepublik Deutschland, the "BRD," or simply West Germany). The Eastern territory, still under Soviet control, was fashioned into the German Democratic Republic (Deutsche Demokratische Republik, the "DDR," or East Germany). For the next 50 years, the rebuilt German territories existed as a real-world laboratory for the comparison of the capitalist and communist socioeconomic models. It was a comparison that did not favor the east.

The devastation that met the German people after the fall of Berlin cannot be understated; it was absolute. Life amid the ruin and rubble was difficult. Hunger was a major concern. So, too, was a cityscape and countryside littered with dangerous unexploded munitions. It is estimated that more than 1.4 million tons of bombs were dropped on Germany throughout the war's duration. Cleaning up and rebuilding was fraught with peril.

Eventually, better days did come. Good governance and the return of industry powered the West German economy. A currency reform in 1948 and the international community's forgiveness of half of the country's foreign debt set the stage for the infusion of capital at levels sufficient to build modern cities and infrastructure. International trade picked up and German products began to trade the world over. The rebirth of the West German economy and the prolonged period of economic growth and stability that followed was known as the *Wirtschaftswunder* (the "economic miracle").

The coin that helped lead this charge was the West German deutsche mark, a small base metal coin that circulated from 1950 until 2002. In the creation of the design, engraver J. Bernhardt was charged with the awesome responsibility of resetting the iconography of the German state in the post-Nazi world. His design, though modern, recalled the iconography of the Weimar Republic. The eagle depicted on the obverse is deceptively complex in its rendering, while the legend BUNDESREPUBLIK DEUTSCHLAND, which encircles it, is given equal weight. Gone is the threatening vulgarity of the iconography employed by the Nazi state. It was a welcome move.

As a collectible coin, the 1954-G has long been considered the key to this important series. Scarce in Mint State, the coin has also seen a dramatic decline in value from the peak prices it realized a decade or more ago, when the series was one of the darlings of the modern world coin collecting scene.

This decline is illustrated quite clearly when one compares auction prices realized to pre-sale estimates and the coin's value as described in Krause's *Standard Catalog*. In 2010, Stack's Bowers sold a near-Gem in PCGS MS-64 for US$548.70 against a $700 to $1,000 estimate. In 2018, against a much lower estimate of $200 to $300, Stack's Bowers sold another PCGS MS-64 for $192. This is hardly the direction one would hope to see for such a key issue of an important series.

Downward trend or no, the fundamentals remain unchanged. The West German mark is the most significant German issue of the second half of the twentieth century. It is no longer produced, it no longer circulates, and Gem Mint State examples are not likely to appear in number. Therefore, it is inconceivable that premium quality, Uncirculated German marks of this issue and around this period will be so easily overlooked by tomorrow's collector.

The Volkswagen Beetle was a symbol of West Germany's "economic miracle" after World War II.

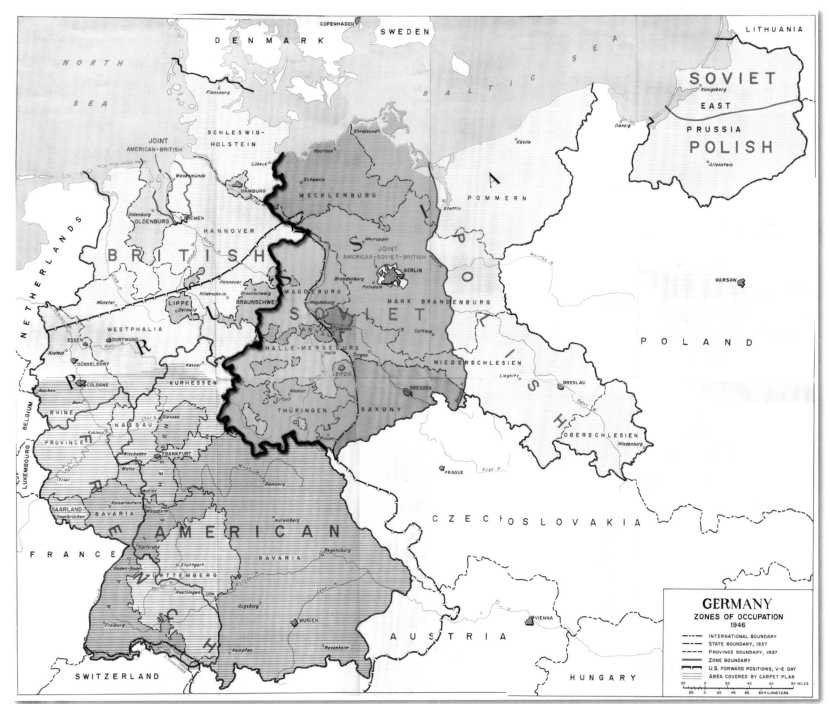

Map of the occupation zones of Germany in 1945, modified to show the inner German border and the zone from which Allied forces withdrew in July 1945.

MEXICO 1921 GOLD 50 PESOS

A contraband "American" hard money.

Obverse. In the center, an eagle, clutching a rattlesnake in its beak and right talon, stands atop a cactus on a mound of earth surrounded by water. The legend ESTADOS UNIDOS MEXICANOS ("United States of Mexico") wraps clockwise around the rim at the top. The denomination UN PESO ("One Peso") bookends the left and right sides of the cactus at its base. A wreath wraps around the rim at the bottom. A border of Mayan scrollwork encircles the design at the rim.

Reverse. Against a mountainous backdrop (showing the volcanos Iztaccihuatl on the left and Popocatépetl on the right), winged Liberty stands on a pedestal in the center of the coin, loosely wrapped in cloth, her breasts exposed. She holds her right arm aloft with a laurel crown in her hand. Her left arm reaches out to her side, a broken shackle around her wrist. To the left of the figure is the denomination 50 PESOS. To her right is an inscription denoting weight and purity: 37.5 Gr. ORO PURO (37.5 grams pure gold). Wrapping around the bottom of the rim and bookending the central figure is the dual date 1821 (left) and 1921 (right). A border of Mayan scrollwork encircles the design at the rim above the mountain scene.

Composition	Weight	Diameter	Alignment	Edge
.900 gold	41.666 grams	37 mm	Coin	Lettered†
Mintage	**Mint**		**Collecting Difficulty**	**References**
181,000	Mexican Mint, Banco de Mexico (Mexico City)		Moderate	BW-656; KM-481
† INDEPENDENCIA Y LIBERTAD ("Independence and Liberty")				

Struck as a bullion coin, the Mexican 50-peso "Centenario" gold coin was first issued in 1921 to mark the centennial of Mexican independence.

The coin had an initial run of 11 years and returned in 1944, when international demand for gold bullion prompted the Mexican Mint to resume production.

Production continued at an elevated level through 1947, and then the mint struck 1947-dated coins on a sporadic basis from 1949 to 2013.

The 1921 issue remains the most popular in the series, both because of its status as a first-year issue and because of its relative scarcity, especially for quality Uncirculated examples.

Before the South African Krugerrand became America's *de facto* gold bullion coin, the Mexican 50-peso gold coin served that purpose, albeit illicitly, as private ownership of gold bullion in the United States was prohibited by law from 1933 to 1974.

At .900 fine and weighing 41.666 grams (1.2056 actual gold weight), the 50 pesos had the same fineness as American circulating gold coins struck before 1933 but was appreciably larger in size than the $20 double eagle, our country's highest-denomination circulating coin.

While possession of bullion could lead to prosecution and seizure, some American speculators were able to circumvent the ban by using a special consideration in the law that allowed for ownership of small amounts of coin for collecting purposes. The 15-date set of 50-peso coins allowed one to possess 18 ounces of gold without being in violation of the law. Others bypassed the law altogether, utilizing the porous border to smuggle in some quantity of the gold coin.

Those not near the U.S.-Mexico border found it a bureaucratic nightmare to deal with the Federal Office of Gold and Silver Operations to import any quantity of gold coin. That office used the opinion of the curator of the National Numismatic Collection to determine whether coins had sufficient numismatic value to allow for import!

Designed by Emilio del Moral and perhaps inspired by Pillet's Caballito peso, the 50 pesos is a perennial favorite for world coin collectors and is one of the most popular types in the modern Mexican series. The coin's reverse features Winged Liberty, based on Antonio Rivas Mercado's Independence Monument, which was erected in Mexico City's Paseo de la Reforma in 1910.

When American Numismatic Rarities (ANR, Q. David Bowers's firm) offered the world coin section of the famous Louis B. Eliasberg Sr. Collection, it included a complete set of Mexican 50-peso coins, although many of his coins had significant issues that would make them less than desirable in today's market. In the catalog, Eliasberg's 1921 specimen was described as grading AU Details by NCS (Numismatic Conservation Services). Eliasberg's collection is just one of many that have found room for individual examples or the complete run of 50-peso gold coins.

The series offers collectors a chance to put together a complete date set for a modest premium over the cost of gold. Of the 15 dates, only three have reported mintages over one million coins (1945, 1946, and 1947, including restrikes). The 1921 and the 1931 have the lowest mintages (180,000 and 137,000, respectively), and of those two the 1921 carries the highest premium due to the fact that it's a first-year issue.

The Mexican golden eagle is depicted on the country's coat of arms and coinage.

The 20 srang is a curious Tibetan gold coin struck from 1918 to 1921, with the 1921 issue being the rarest. Numismatist Eduard Kann, whose catalog helped popularize the collecting of Chinese coins in the West, saw little point for the 28.3 mm gold coin, given the fact that Tibet in the post-Qing period had very little export industry to speak of.

Nevertheless, a gold coin it issued, and that coin was given a value of 20 times that of the srang, a 35 mm silver coin that typically weighed between 18 and 18.3 grams. The gold coin's design is intricate and exotic, using nearly every bit of the coin's surface to convey culturally and religiously important symbols. A galloping lion is surrounding by Buddhist symbols on the obverse. On the reverse is a flower surrounded by the Tibetan script.

The design retains the rustic charm of a coin that might have been struck hundreds of years earlier. Given Tibet's seclusion from the rest of the world, this is not surprising.

Mintage information for any Tibetan 20-srang coins of any date are not wholly reliable. Clearly these were not mass-produced coins, but examples from the dates 1918 to 1920 do appear every so often at auction. These issues come in two major varieties: with or without a dot on the reverse, in the center of the design. In Mint State, these bring between US$3,000 to $10,000. The 1921, which was struck without a dot, on the other hand, appears to be genuinely rare and collector enthusiasm for the elusive date shows quite clearly in the five-figure hammer price.

When an NGC-certified example in MS-63 from the Damkoehler Collection was offered at a Heritage Auctions sale in December 2015, it brought $50,190. Another example has yet to be offered in the United States at auction since. Those in the market for this truly great twentieth-century rarity may have a while to wait.

TIBET 1921 SER-KHANG GOLD 20 SRANG

"Tibet unquestionably never was in need of gold coins..." -Eduard Kann[1]

Obverse. In the center, inside an inner ring, is a running lion. Also inscribed is the date according to the Tibetan calendar. Enclosed within an outer ring, the eight auspicious symbols of Buddhism. Beads border the rim, encircling the design.

Reverse. In the center, inside an inner ring, is a stylized flower shape with eight points. A dot is in the center. The legend and denomination in Tibetan script encircle the design, enclosed within an outer ring. Beads border the rim.

Composition	Weight	Diameter	Alignment	Edge
Gold	11.19 grams	28.3 mm	Coin	Reeded
Mintage	**Mint**		**Collecting Difficulty**	**References**
2 (known)	Ser-Khang Mint		Virtually impossible	Fr-1, Y-22

THE EIGHT AUSPICIOUS SYMBOLS OF BUDDHISM

The Ashtamangala, also known as the Eight Auspicious Symbols in Buddhism, are frequently encountered in Tibet. Each symbol depicts a gift that the gods bestowed upon Gautama Buddha as well as representing qualities of spiritual enlightenment according to the Buddhist tradition.

- **Conch Shell:** A musical instrument that represents the omnipresent sound of the dharma, or cosmic law.
- **Endless Knot:** A knot pattern that represents the unity of all things.
- **Two Golden Fish:** A symbol of enlightened happiness and Fearlessness.
- **Lotus:** A flower that represents purity and transcendence.
- **Parasol:** An umbrella-like object that represents protection against negative forces. It also represents the sky and the vastness of the universe, and therefore the vastness of the dharma.
- **Vase:** An urn or vase that represents the Buddha's wisdom and the prosperity of enlightenment, as well as health and longevity.
- **Wheel of Law:** A spoked wheel that represents the Buddha himself and his teachings.
- **Victory Banner:** A banner or flag that represents the Buddha's overcoming of pride, desire, emotions, and the fear of death.

Carved wooden door in Nepal showing six of the eight auspicious symbols.

HONDURAS 1908/888/897 OVERDATE GOLD 20 PESOS

Why settle for one overdate, when you can have two?

Obverse. In the center, inside a circle, a pyramid is guarded by two castle towers. Inside the pyramid is a pileus cap atop a pole, with a glory of sun rays behind it. In exergue is a body of water representing the ocean. Inside a larger circle surrounding this motif is the legend REPUBLICA DE HONDURAS. A square dot is at the bottom center. Two cornucopias border the circle on either side. Wrapping around their base is a ribbon that reads PAZ PROGRESO I LIBERTAD ("Peace, Progress, and Liberty"). In a ribbon above the device is the inscription UNION. Above it are five stars, each with an incuse initial of one of the five states of the United Provinces of Central America (Guatemala, El Salvador, Honduras, Nicaragua, and Costa Rica). Wrapping around the bottom of the design is the date 1908 (with remnants of 888 and 897 under the date), VIENTE PESOS (20 Pesos), and 0.900 (for .900 fine). Thin reeded denticles encircle the design.
Reverse. In the center, a left-facing bust of Liberty wearing a pileus cap and a laurel wreath. The designer's name, FRENER, is engraved in incuse at the bottom of the bust truncation. Wrapping around the top of the design is the inscription 15 DE SETIEMBRE DE 1821. Wrapping around the bottom is CENTRO-AMERICA. A crossed caduceus and trident divide the two inscriptions. Superimposed on the left one is the letter P. The letter A superimposes the cross on the right. Thin reeded denticles encircle the design

Composition	Weight	Diameter	Alignment	Edge
.900 gold	32.258 grams	33 mm	Coin	Reeded
Mintage	**Mint**		**Collecting Difficulty**	**References**
Unknown	Tegucigalpa Mint		Moderately difficult	KM-57

The gold coins of Honduras were struck intermittently in denominations of 1, 5, 10, and 20 pesos beginning in 1871 and ending in 1925.

In the absolute sense, all Honduran gold issues are scarce to rare. This is evidenced by paltry certified population totals (NGC has certified fewer than 100 gold coins of all types) and the infrequency with which any emissions of the series are offered at auction.

Of course, scarcity and challenge only add to the appeal of the series, with only the most advanced collectors afforded the opportunity of assembling a complete date set by denomination and major variety.

But of all the rarities of the series, it is the rare 1908/897/888 20-peso gold coin that is not only one of the most challenging to acquire, but also the most interesting for numismatists.

An overdate, the 1908 is struck from a die that featured two underdates—one from 1888 and, on top of that, another from 1897. While visible to the naked eye, a strong magnifying glass will reveal the fine details of this blundered feature.

The coin's attractive design is the work of Swiss-born artist Johann Baptist Frener (1821–1892), who immigrated to Central America in 1854 to serve as the engraver of the mint in Guatemala[1].

Frener's design is rendered in the style of European neoclassicism. Characteristic of Frener, the sculpt is workmanlike, emulating elegance yet not wholly refined.

On the coin's reverse, a portrait of Liberty is surmounted by the date September 15, 1821, the day when Honduras and its Central American neighbors began their struggle to shed the yoke of Spanish colonialism by declaring their independence. Honduras was joined in the effort by Guatemala, El Salvador, and Costa Rica.

The obverse features an ornate representation of the national coat of arms, the blundered date, and the coin's gold purity, which is described as .900 fine.

In preparing this book, it was not possible to get a firm grasp on the number of known examples of this issue. World coin expert Lance Tchor can point to only two or three discrete examples but admits that he has handled none of them personally.

One well-known example was once owned by collector Mortimer Hammel of New York, who over the course of his collecting career assembled a spectacular and nearly complete type set of nineteenth- and twentieth-century gold coins. Stack's offered his collection for sale on September 15 and 16, 1982, wherein his example (lot 854) was described as rather weakly struck and extremely rare[2].

Current population totals by PCGS and NGC provide further illustration of the coin's status as a true twentieth-century rarity, with just one example certified by NGC (MS-61) and none by PCGS.

(Above) Close-up view of the spectacular overdate on this coin.

(Left) Honduras street scene in Tegucigalpa, circa 1911.

The introduction into circulation of the Irish 20-pence coin on October 30, 1986, marked the return of Percy Metcalfe's iconic horse design; a design that once served as the reverse on the Irish Republic's highest denomination coin, the half crown, but had for 15 years been held out of circulation after the denomination was deprecated in favor of a new system of decimalized coinage.

The half crown, which endures to this day as a collector favorite, was struck from 1928 through to 1967, with a lengthy gap in production taking place at the height of the Second World War and lasting until 1951. Pre-war issues were struck in .750 silver, while the post-war issues were struck in a slightly heavier copper-nickel alloy.

The 20 pence, by contrast, was a much smaller coin. It measured 27.11 mm to the half crown's 32.3 mm and weighed 8.47 grams. No longer emblematic of Ireland's highest-denomination circulating coin, Metcalfe's horse now represented a fifth of the Irish pound (punt) and primarily served as a change-making coin, used in quantity to pay for tolls, items in vending machines, or to make calls in pay telephones.

So it was because of this need to prepare tens of thousands of the country's pay telephones that in 1985, the year before the 20 pence was set to officially launch, the Central Bank of Ireland issued a limited number—according to some reports, as many as 500 pattern pieces—of the new coin for calibration purposes. By statutory requirement, these pieces carried the date of their current year of issue, and because of this a major modern rarity was born.

It's not clear how many 1985 20-pence coins survive. Those that are known in the market, and they number ten or so, all have provenance tying them to Irish telephone company Telecom Éireann. Some estimate that the survival rate could be upwards of 50 pieces, but given the high profile of the coin and the high prices examples have brought at auction, the existence of this many pieces is unlikely.

The Central Bank of Ireland's headquarters on North Wall Quay, Dublin.

An Irish Sport Horse in a cross-country competition at the Badminton Horse Trials.

IRELAND 1985 20 PENCE

A horse of a different color.

Obverse. In the center of the coin is a harp. To the left of the harp, wrapping around the rim, in lowercase is the legend éire ("Ireland"). To the harp's right is the date 1985.

Reverse. A left-facing Irish sport horse (also known as the Irish hunter) atop a thin line representing the ground. The exergue is beneath. Above the horse's back is the coin's denomination, written as 20P.

Composition	Weight	Diameter	Alignment	Edge
Nordic gold (.790 copper, .200 zinc, .010 nickel)	8.47 grams	27.1 mm	Medal	Security edged†

Mintage	Mint	Collecting Difficulty	References
500	British Royal Mint	Difficult	KM-25; Spink-6703

† Alternates plain to reeded, with three bands of six reeds

The Cliffs of Moher are one of the most famous tourist destinations in Ireland.

Irish coin expert and auctioneer Ian Whyte accounts for ten known pieces in private hands[1]. American dealer Del Parker specializes in Irish coins and accounts for slightly fewer. He has followed this issue closely and handled three examples, including two that he had at the January 2017 Florida United Numismatists convention in Ft. Lauderdale, Florida. One of these was an uncertified example in XF-AU condition, while the other was one of two that make up the totality of NGC's census (both graded MS-62[2]). These examples were part of a cache of three pieces belonging to the estate of a former Telecom engineer. Parker sold a third example a few years ago for $16,000.

Beyond these three pieces, Parker's tally does not quite add up to 10 known pieces.

He accounts for a Gem example sold in Dublin in 2005 by dealer Michael Kelly. This example, which might be the finest known, realized a record price of over US$20,000 at the prevailing exchange rate. A year later, another Choice to Gem Uncirculated example turned up and sold privately.

According to Parker, Whyte sold three pieces; two of these he believes would have graded MS-62 (perhaps one is the second NGC example). One of these three pieces sold at auction in 2015 for €8,970[3].

Dealer Dave Palin also had a circulated example at the Dublin Coin Fair in 1998, although Parker was not sure at the time whether the coin was authentic.

HISTORY REPEATS ITSELF

The chain of events that made the 20 pence of 1985 an important Irish rarity played out again in 1992, when the Irish Central Bank moved to reintroduce the 10-pence denomination, which had been out of production since 1986, in a new smaller size. Again, a smaller amount of pattern 1992 coins were made and distributed to engineers for testing and calibration. The exact number of 1992 10-pence coins issued is not known to the numismatic community, nor are the number of coins in private hands a settled matter.

To date, two are confirmed, but it is the belief of leading dealers that many more were retained by parties who held onto the coins, aware of the high prices that collectors were willing to pay for the 1985 20 pence. Because of this, it is difficult to establish a fair price for this second great modern Irish rarity.

The Irish 20 pence circulated from 1986 to the end of 2001. On New Year's Day 2002, Ireland and 11 other Eurozone members abandoned their national coinage in favor of the supranational coinage of the euro system. We discuss euro coinage in detail in our description of Greatest Modern World Coins entry number 100.

Note: Buyers of the 1985 20-pence coin should be advised that many counterfeits exist. Consult an expert in the field of Irish coins before making a purchase.

Before the outbreak of World War I, France produced three circulating gold coins in denominations of 20, 50, and 100 francs. After the war, only the 100-franc denomination saw continued production in gold, though its weight was sharply reduced to just under one-fifth of an ounce of gold—roughly the same weight and size of the Napoleonic era 20-franc coin. Such were the ravages of inflation.

Engraver Lucien Georges Bazor's facelift to the French 100 francs came about after a fierce open competition that included ten of the country's leading artists. Bazor's winning design was steeped in the Art Deco movement, which developed as a new style at the turn of the century but saw its peak in the late 1920s and early 1930s. Bazor, who trained in the classical style under his father and then later at the École nationale supérieure des Beaux-Arts, embraced the style and would return to it many times as chief engraver of the Paris Mint.

Although first struck in 1929, the French 100-francs type featuring Bazor's left-facing Art Deco female visage of Marianne saw only two years of production at levels sufficient to make it a practical circulating gold coin. In fact, the last French 100 francs only saw two years of substantial production, when the Paris Mint struck 6,102,000 and 7,689,000 coins in 1935 and 1936, respectively.

It's likely that most French at the time never had the opportunity to spend one of these coins.

The inflated mintage numbers of 1935 and 1936 are a far cry from the mintages of the type's earlier issues, whose reported mintages are scant and certified examples are nearly unheard of. By our count, only NGC has certified any examples of the Bazor 100-franc type in the rarer dates.

A paltry 50 circulation strikes are reported for 1929 and known survivors are few, which accounts for the fact that the issue is seldom encountered at auction unless it's an essai striking, of which variants in gold and aluminum-bronze were produced.

The gold version is scarce and often brings between US$4,500 and $5,000. NGC has certified three circulation strikes (PCGS none), with the finest being in MS-65. One would expect the circulation strike to bring a spirited price at auction.

Other issues are seldom encountered, either. The 1932 and 1934 issues are both reported in standard references as being "rare." Only one example, a 1932 in NGC MS-64, has ever been certified by either service. In 2017, that coin was listed for sale by its owner for a price in excess of $70,000.

Slightly more accessible is the 1933, with its estimated mintage of 300 pieces. These examples bring in excess of $3,000.

An Art Deco bas relief of *The Meditation of Apollo and the Nine Muses*, at the Théâtre des Champs Elysées in Paris.

A fire screen made in the Art Deco style from 1930.

FRANCE 1929 GOLD 100 FRANCS

Key date from France's final circulating gold coinage type.

Obverse. The left-facing winged head of Marianne, wearing a Phrygian cap and cockade. The legend wraps around the rim, reading REPUBLIQUE (left of the head) and FRANÇAISE (to the right of the head). Ornamental rectangular beading borders the rim. The designer's name, L. BAZOR, is under the neck truncation. Denticles of alternating raised beads wrap around the rim.

Reverse. Centered at the bottom is a head of wheat, an oak branch with four acorns to the right, and a laurel branch with three buds to the left. In the background is a sun with six visible rays. Above the wheat is the denomination 100 Francs. The first and last two numerals of the date bookend the wheat stalk. There are privy marks of a cornucopia (to the left) and a torch (to the right). Denticles of alternating raised beads wrap around the rim.

Composition	Weight	Diameter	Alignment	Edge
.900 gold	6.55 grams	21 mm	Coin	Lettered†
Mintage	**Mint**		**Collecting Difficulty**	**References**
15	Paris Mint, Monnaie de Paris		Difficult	KM-880

† *LIBERTE * ÉGALITÉ *FRATERNITÉ ("Liberty, Equality, Fraternity")

EAST GERMANY 1949-A 50 PFENNIGS

After war, Soviet-controlled Germany rebuilds.

The regular-issue 50 pfennigs of 1950, showing the design of 1949.

Obverse. In the background are the billowing smokestacks of a factory. In the foreground is a plow. The rim is raised.

Reverse. A large 50 is in the center of the design, below PFENNIG and the date 1949. The A mintmark of the Berlin Mint is centered in smaller text below the date. Wrapping around the top of the design is the legend DEUTSCHLAND. The rim is raised.

Composition	Weight	Diameter	Alignment	Edge
Aluminum-bronze	3.38 grams	20 mm	Medal	Smooth with incuse leaf design

Mintage	Mint	Collecting Difficulty	References
Unknown	Berlin Mint†	Virtually impossible	KM-4; Schön-4

† Mintmark: A

East Germany didn't officially come into being until October 7, 1949, but its origins trace back to April 20, 1945, when soldiers from the 1st Belorussian Front began shelling Berlin. It was Hitler's 56th birthday. He would be dead in ten days. For the advancing Russian army, paying Germany back for the horrors it inflicted upon the Russian people was deeply personal. For Stalin, who had seen Britain and France rebuff the Soviet Union's offer to send a million troops to the German border before the start of war, those horrors put him in a vengeful mood. If the Soviet army was to take Berlin, he had no plans to give it back.

Within hours of the shelling, Hitler's control over the situation was crumbling. In a last-ditch effort, the city's defense fell to General Helmuth Weidling and a ragtag force made from scraps of the German army and augmented by Hitler Youth boys, many of whom were as young as 12 years old but forced to the front lines nonetheless. It was a desperate situation.

With munitions running out and Soviet troops penetrating the city's borders, the Nazi regime collapsed. Weidling bore the responsibility of surrendering and did so on May 2. It was the last day he would live as a free man.

The Yalta Conference, held in February, set in motion a plan to split Germany into three zones: an American zone, a British zone, and a Russian one. Later, France would become a party in the international occupation of Germany, when the American and British zones were split. This split impacted the country as a whole and the city of Berlin. Austria and Vienna experienced a similar circumstance.

(Above) A memorial of Checkpoint Charlie from when Berlin was divided by the Berlin Wall.

(Left) British prime minister Winston Churchill, U.S. president Franklin Roosevelt, and Soviet leader Joseph Stalin met at Yalta in February 1945 to discuss their joint occupation of Germany and plans for post-war Europe.

Under Soviet influence, East Germany developed a character all its own. From Trabbis to Rotkäppchen wine to Zeha shoes, Germans who found themselves behind the Iron Curtain found ways to maintain their cultural identity, despite the obvious limitations imposed upon them. One way this cultural identity was celebrated was through the collecting of commemorative coins. From 1966 to 1989, the Berlin Mint struck these commemoratives in silver in the denominations of 10 and 20 marks.

The Berlin State Mint's visitor's center has a display of the complete catalog of East German commemorative issues. Viewed together as a complete collection, it is no wonder why these issues have a strong following. The designs are well executed, the themes are generally apolitical, and with few exceptions, the coins are affordable to most collectors.

In the western zones, rebuilding and reconstruction began with some delay. The Western powers were leery of postwar Germany becoming too powerful and spent a considerable time prosecuting Nazi officials and military figures for war crimes. They also felt that the communist system posed a major threat to liberal democracy. In the Soviet-occupied zones, German socialist groups, favored by the Kremlin, came into power. In 1949, the establishment of West Germany and East Germany formally solidified the splitting of Germany and set into motion one of the most concrete symbols of distrust between the Soviet Union and the Western allies.

Coinage operations in the newly formed East German state began in 1948. The Berlin Mint, one of five German state mints, was located in the eastern part of Berlin and was held under communist control. Its monetary unit was the same as the one used by the western part of the country but held considerably less value.

Production of the 1-, 5-, and 10-pfennig coin denominations began in 1948. The East German mark would not see production as a circulating coin until 1956.

In 1949, the Berlin Mint experimented with the production of a 50-pfennig coin. Large scale production would not take place until 1950, when the Berlin Mint struck 67,703,405 pieces of the aluminum-bronze coin, which featured designer Franz Krischker's industrial-themed design.

After this release, the denomination went into hiatus for eight years before it was reintroduced as a smaller aluminum coin with a different design. That, too, was a one-year design. In 1968, the denomination was again introduced and a third design was used. This iteration of the East German 50 pfennigs stayed in use until the fall of the Berlin Wall in 1989.

Not much information is really known about the 50-pfennig specimens struck bearing the 1949 date. Thought to be a pattern issue, the coin is rare and seldom offered at auction. We found no evidence of one selling in an American auction in the last decade. Krause puts a catalog value for an Uncirculated example at $10,000. Given the rarity of this piece, we feel this number is extremely conservative.

The Soviet War Memorial was erected by the Soviet Union in Berlin in 1945 to commemorate the soldiers lost in the Battle of Berlin.

YEMEN AH1358 (1939) GOLD 2 RIYALS

Modern coin, medieval look.

Obverse. An inset circle with a crescent cutaway. Arabic script and the date [AH]1322 are inset. There is an outer circle of Arabic calligraphy and a quatrefoil at the bottom. Rustic denticles surround the design.

Reverse. The inner circle has four flags in a crossed pattern. The outer circle features ornate Arabic calligraphy that reads ضرب في دار الخلافة ("Struck at the Capital of the Mutawakkilite Caliphate in Sana'a"). The date ١٣٥٨ [AH]1358 is at the bottom. Rustic denticles surround the design.

Composition	Weight	Diameter	Alignment	Edge
Gold	69.83 grams	45 mm	Medal	Reeded
Mintage	**Mint**		**Collecting Difficulty**	**References**
4 (known)	Sana'a Mint (صنعاء)		Virtually impossible	KM–16.1, 16.2; Schön-19

Arabic coinage often gets short shrift from Western collectors, which is unfortunate since the genre is replete with types, varieties, compositions, and major rarities for the adventurous collector.

One coin that certainly belongs in the major rarity column is the large gold Yemen 2 riyals dated AH1358 (1939).

Only four examples are known of this ornately inscribed issue. One, graded MS-64 by NGC, brought US$21,500 at a January 2015 Heritage Auction (lot 31318). As one might expect, other instances where one of these elusive pieces has been offered are few and far between.

When holding the coin, one is struck by the coin's almost medieval appearance. Such was the Mutawakkilite Kingdom of Yemen under the rule of Imam Yahya Muhammad Hamid ed-Din (1869–1948) as was the mint of the city of Sana'a, which he employed for the purpose of striking coins.

With few exceptions, Yemeni coins of this period were struck in the city of Sana'a at a hopelessly antiquated mint using medieval coining technology. The circulating coins were based on the Turkish system and struck in a quality that can charitably be referred to as artisanal.

Of Yahya Muhammad Hamid ed-Din, much can be said. He was a revolutionary and nationalist leader who became the imam of Yemen after the passing of his father, Imam Muhammad bin Yahya Hamid ad-Din in 1904. His rule marked the continuation of his father's efforts to resist and expel the occupying forces of Ottoman Turkey in order to establish an independent Yemeni state.

At the time of Yahya Muhammad Hamid ed-Din's rule, the geopolitical boundaries of Yemen were more aspirational than codified by international law. Yemen's proximity to the Suez Canal and its export coffee trade invited foreign interference in the country's domestic affairs; the Ottomans, British, and the Kingdom of Hejaz and Nejd to the north (present-day Saudi Arabia) all had designs on Yemeni territory. Ethnic and tribal rivalries among the people made governing even more difficult.

Yahya's 44-year reign came to an end on February 17, 1948, when he was assassinated. His son, Ahmad bin Yahya Hamidaddin, ruled ruthlessly and ultimately plunged the country into turmoil. A number of scarce-to-rare silver and gold coins were struck during his reign. When the Republic of Yemen emerged in 1962, it signaled the end of the modern-medieval period of Yemeni numismatics.

Further Reading: Hedges, Ken. "The Arabic Republic of Yemen." *Calcoin News*, Volume 18, no 4. 118-119.

A medieval copper-alloy coin made under Ottoman/Turkish rule.

City of Sana'a.

South Vietnam was an active participant in the FAO (Food and Agriculture Organization) program, working with the United Nations agency to improve its agricultural industry. It was also an active participant in the World Money Programme, with three coin issues included in FAO collector sets. The 1975 50 đồng was slated to be the country's fourth coin in the FAO series. All South Vietnam FAO coins were issued during the administration of President Nguyễn Văn Thiệu.

The first three—1 đồng, 10 đồng, and 20 đồng—were struck from 1968 through 1974 by an assortment of vendors, including the German State Mint at Hamburg, including the German State Mint, a private German mint, and the U.K. Royal Mint[1]. Today, these three coins are relatively common in Mint State even though they did circulate. Accounting for the large number of survivors in the Western coin market were various collector coin packages offered directly by the FAO and by third-party distributors such as Littleton Coin Company and Deutsche Münze.

In a contract with the Royal Mint, South Vietnam ordered the production of 50 million pieces of the 50 đồng. The nickel-clad steel coin went into production and a reported 1,010,000 coins were struck before a surprise Spring Offensive by North Vietnamese forces overran the South's defensive positions in 1975, leading to the fall of Saigon and the South Vietnamese government.

Realizing the coins would never be issued, the Royal Mint abandoned further production and disposed of those that had been struck. Save for approximately two dozen examples, the entire mintage was melted.

According to South Asian coin expert Howard Daniel, the survivors were likely smuggled out by workers during the melt. Curiously, despite never circulating officially, the condition of the surviving coins is typically poor—with most examples being unattractive and in Almost Uncirculated condition. It is hard to imagine that a Gem or even Choice example exists.

Estimated Value: $1,250 and up, more for an Uncirculated example.

THE FAO WORLD MONEY PROGRAMME

For a period of about 40 years, the Rome office of the Food and Agriculture Organization of the United Nations was engaged in a multi-faceted, multi-country numismatic endeavor known as the World Money Programme. Launched in 1968, the groundbreaking program centered around raising money for and awareness of food insecurity in the developing world.

It was a feel-good mission that mixed propaganda and collectibles to create one of the most comprehensive commemorative coin programs in history—one that consists of *more than 1,500 coins* if all varieties, finishes, and individual issues are tabulated, not to mention roughly 500 medals issued in gold, silver, bronze, gilded bronze, and aluminum. The F.A.O. was an aggressive marketer in Not-Intended-For-Circulation (NIFC) numismatic material.

Impressive, when you consider that the program had very limited engagement with the major developed countries.

The United States Mint at San Francisco struck FAO coins for the Philippines but none for itself. The Royal Mint was contracted to strike coins for various client governments, but no FAO commemorative from the UK was ever struck. Ditto for the Soviet Union, Japan, Canada, Australia, Mexico, Germany, or China.

Instead, collectors were offered a wide complement of coins from Algeria, Bangladesh, Bhutan, Cambodia, Egypt, Gambia, Ghana, India, Indonesia, Iran, Madagascar, Malta, North and South Korea, San Marino, Somalia, Thailand, Tonga, and Turkey, among others. In many cases, these coins actively circulated in their respective countries.

The theme of "Food for all" or "Fiat Panis" tied these issues together, as did a well-considered marketing effort on the part of the FAO office. Coins were available individually and in the secondary market as well as in subscription albums and boards, made by Dansco for the FAO.

SOUTH VIETNAM 1975 50 ĐỒNG

Saved from the dustbin of history.

Obverse. In the center, justified, the denomination is written with a large 50 above and ĐỒNG below. Wrapping around the rim is the legend and inscription VIỆT NAM CỘNG-HÒA ("Republic of Vietnam," above) NGÂN-HÀNG QUỐC-GIA VIỆT-NAM ("National Bank of Vietnam," below).
Reverse. Inside the circle is a scene of two Vietnamese farmers harvesting rice. An inscription wraps around the rim, reading TĂNG-GIA SẢN-SUẤT NÔNG-PHẨM ("Increase Food Production"). The date 1975 is centered at the bottom of the design. The rim is raised.

Composition	Weight	Diameter	Alignment	Edge
Nickel-clad steel	5 grams	26 mm	Medal	Reeded

Mintage	Mint	Collecting Difficulty	References
1,010,000	Various	Moderate	KM-14; Schön-48

Two Vietnamese women work in a rice field in summer.

No. 95

---◆---

PERU 1958 GOLD 100 SOLES

Underrated South American rarity.

Obverse. The center is Peru's coat of arms, a tripartite escutcheon with a left-facing vicuña at the upper left, a quinine tree at the upper right, and a cornucopia overflowing with coins at the bottom. A wreath of palm and laurel, tied together by a ribbon, surrounds the coat of arms. Surmounting the shield is an oak crown. The inscription wrapping around the rim reads PESOS : GRS. 46.8071 - REPUBLICA PERUANA - NUEVEDECIMOSFINO (Peruvian Republic - .900 fine). LIMA is in exergue.

Reverse. A seated Patria wears a flowing dress and ornamental chestplate featuring the sun. Held upright in Patria's left hand are a pole and Phrygian cap. Leaning against the base of her stool and propped up by her right hand is a sun-emblazoned shield. To her right is a column, and scrollwork with the word LIBERTAD wraps around the base. An upright oak crown wreath surmounts the column. The inscription CIEN SOLES ORO (left), GRS.42.1264DE ORO FINO (right) wraps around the rim. The date is below the exergue. The designer's initials A.P. (Antonio Pereja) are located to the left of the shield. Ornamental denticles wrap around the rim.

Composition	Weight	Diameter	Alignment	Edge
.900 gold	46.8071 grams	37 mm	Coin	Reeded
Mintage	**Mint**		**Collecting Difficulty**	**References**
101	Lima Mint		Difficult	KM-231

The motif carries forward the military symbolism of the revolution. Liberty, underneath her flowing dress, is dressed in military garb. The pole and shield are implements of war. The oak wreath atop the pedestal of Liberty is a symbol of newly won freedoms that must be defended in order to be preserved.

With just 101 coins issued, the 1958 stands as the key date for the 21-year run of the series. Scarce in any grade, the issue, which typically comes with a prooflike or semi-prooflike finish, is rare in Gem. Of the eight certified examples that NGC has reported, three are in the top-population grade of MS-65, three examples grade MS-64, and MS-62 and MS-61 are represented by one specimen each.

The certified market for world coins is not as fully developed as is the case with U.S. issues, so it may take some time get a true measure of the coin's survival rate. What is clear is this connoisseur coin continues to grow in stature around the world as collectors turn their attention to the fantastic modern coinage of South America.

Over the past ten years, the 1958 100 soles has experienced significant price increases at auction. An NGC-graded MS-64 example brought US$6,900 at a 2006 Goldberg's sale. Ten years later, that same piece brought $12,925 at a Heritage Auctions Platinum Night offering at the American Numismatic Association's World's Fair of Money. Demonstrating the demand for this coin beyond the Western Hemisphere, in February 2017, German auctioneer Künker offered an uncertified Uncirculated example. It brought €8,500 (US$10,024).

A recent sale of an NGC-graded MS-64 example of the 1958 100 soles brought $19,975 (Heritage Auctions, April 2015, lot 30345). Lance Tchor, a notable world coin expert and co-president of WINGS Coins, suggests that an example in Gem would find a buyer at a price of $45,000.

Besides 1958, the Peru 100 soles gold series offers collectors tremendous buying opportunities, as there are a number of issues with low mintages. The 1952 issue, for instance, has a mintage of just 126 pieces, while the Lima Mint struck fewer than 500 pieces in both 1953 and 1970.

ANOTHER PERUVIAN BEAUTY

While not as rare as the 1958 100 soles, the Peru 50 soles gold coin series, produced 1930–1931 and again 1967–1969, is one of South America's most beautiful coins of the twentieth century. It features the likeness of Inca governor Manco Capac and is popular on both sides of the equator.

Frist issued in 1950, 20 years after Peru left the gold standard, the 100 soles is a crown-sized gold coin that weighs 46.8071 grams, with 42.164 of that being *Oro Fino* ("fine gold"). That makes the 100 soles one of the largest gold coins struck for circulation in the twentieth century.

Featuring an attractive design, the 100 soles carries forth the classic Peruvian Seated Patria motif that traces its origins back to the mid-nineteenth century, when the newly independent country abandoned the Spanish monetary system in favor of a national coinage that used the *sol* (Spanish for "sun") as the primary unit of denomination. In truth, the 100 soles design is a re-rendering—an inferior one—of British Royal Mint engraver Leonard Charles Wyon's design, first featured on the Peruvian pattern coinage of 1886[1].

PERU 100 SOLES YEAR-BY-YEAR MINTAGE CHART

1950: 1,176	1957: 550	1964: 11,000
1951: 8,241	1958: 101	1965: 23,000
1952: 126	1959: 4,710	1966: 3,409
1953: 498	1960: 2,207	1967: 6,431
1954: 1,808	1961: 6,982	1968: 540
1955: 901	1962: 9,678	1969: 540
1956: 1,159	1963: 7,342	1970: 425

1958 is, by classical definition, the "key date." However, many other dates should garner serious collector interest, as low mintage numbers were the rule and not the exception for nearly half of the series' 21-year run.

The 1931 100 mils from the British Mandate of Palestine is the second entry in our rundown of greatest modern world coins from the short-lived Palestine Mandate series—a series comprised of 59 coins (not counting Proof versions).

In terms of complexity and scarcity, assembling a complete set of circulation-strike Palestinian Mandate coins is a challenge, but it is within the means of most collectors. The degree of difficulty increases dramatically as soon as one tries to assemble a collection with only Choice or Gem Mint State examples.

One of the stoppers for most collectors is the 1931 100 mils.

Over the years, collectors have debated which 100 mils coin is the key to the series. Was it the 1931, with its 250,000 mintage? Or the 1934, which has a mintage of just 200,000 pieces? Both are known to be scarce in all grades and are seldom seen in Mint State.

It's only now, after 30 years of third-party coin certification and population tracking, that we have a clearer picture of the Mint State survival rate of the two coins. In Mint State, the 1931 is the rarer of the two, a fact that has not gone unnoticed by collectors of the series.

When Heritage Auctions offered a PCGS-graded MS-62 specimen at their 2014 Chicago International Coin Fair Signature Auction, they reported the coin was but one of three that the company had graded in Mint State. The PCGS MS-62 coin brought US$28,200[1]. PCGS estimates that the one example graded finer (MS-63) has a value of $35,000.

Studying the NGC populations, the coin is equally elusive in Mint State. Like PCGS, NGC reports three grading events of a Mint State example, the finest grading MS-62. The possibility exists that cross-pollination has taken place and PCGS coins may be in NGC holders and vice-versa.

Leaving that aside, for a modern coin with a mintage of 250,000 to remain so elusive in Mint State speaks to the fact, too often ignored, that mintages sometimes only tell part of the story.

PALESTINE 1931 SILVER 100 MILS

Key date of important Middle East crown type.

Obverse. The legend is written in Hebrew, English, and Arabic: פלשתינה(וא) (aleph and yod letters in parenthesis are acronyms for "*Eretz Yisra'el*" [land of Israel]) • PALESTINE • فلسطين. In the center is an olive tree with seven branches and six berries growing out of a wavy ground, which forms the exergue. The date, written in Western and Eastern Arabic numerals, bookends the trunk of the tree. Beaded denticles surround the rim.

Reverse. Inside the circle, in the center, written in large font: 100, below ١٠٠. Outside the circle, wrapping around and separated by dots, the denomination is written in English on top (ONE HUNDRED MILS), Hebrew on the bottom left (מאה מיל), and Arabic on the bottom right (مائة ملم). Beaded denticles surround the rim.

Composition	Weight	Diameter	Alignment	Edge
.720 silver	11.6638 grams	29 mm	Medal	Reeded

Mintage	Mint	Collecting Difficulty	References
250,000	British Royal Mint (London)	Condition rarity; Uncirculated examples, difficult	KM-7; Schön-7

Arab protestors with clubs charged by British police in Jaffa, Palestine, Oct. 29, 1933. In Jaffa Square, mounted officers follow.

Palestine currency, 1929.

SAXE-MEININGEN 1914-D DUKE GEORG II GOLD 20 MARKS, PROOF

By Georg! A great beard and a major rarity in the German gold series.

Obverse. A left-facing portrait of Duke Georg II. Somewhat canted to the left and wrapping around the rim, slightly inside the denticles, is the inscription GEORG II HERZOG VON SACHSEN-MEININGEN. Below the bust truncation is the D mintmark of the German State Mint in Munich.
Reverse. The imperial German eagle. Wrapping around the rim, slightly inside the denticles, is the legend DEUTSCHES REICH 1914 (top) and the denomination 20 Mark (bottom). Separating the legend and denomination are two canted five-pointed stars.

Composition	Weight	Diameter	Alignment	Edge
.900 gold	7.965 grams	23 mm	Medal	Lettered†

Mintage	Mint	Collecting Difficulty	References
Unknown	Bavarian Central Mint (Munich)‡	Difficult	J-281; KM-205

† GOTT MIT UNS ("God with Us") ‡ Mintmark: D

Duke Georg II (1826–1914) was a significant and colorful figure during an important time in German history.

The penultimate duke of Saxe-Meiningen, Georg was highly educated, deeply cultured, and a lifelong artist and patron of the arts. He restored credit to his house after his father's abdication by exhibiting loyalty to the Prussians at a time of German unification. Georg found success at war, earning the position of lieutenant general of the Prussian Army, where he built a lifelong friendship with Wilhelm I (1797–1888), the first emperor of the German Second Reich.

Thrice married, Georg was popular amongst his people and seemed to genuinely care. After his first two wives died of disease, he married actress Ellen Franz. Together, they founded the Meiningen Theater, a progressive and innovative troupe known across Europe for its accurate representations of period and manner in its productions. He also established the Meiningen Court Orchestra, which served as a proving-ground for composers Johannes Brahms and a then-unknown 20-year-old named Richard Strauss.

The duke's later years were marked by declining health and the onset of deafness. Having retired from public life, he had little direct involvement in the onset of hostilities between Germany and its neighbors. He died on June 25, 1914, little more than a month before the start of World War I.

His passing was the end of an era. His eldest son Bernhard III became duke of Saxe-Meiningen. Bernhard's reign was short-lived, as animosity from being passed over for a military command, coupled with Germany's defeat in World War I, caused the duke to abdicate his position. The Duchy would remain without a head until its dissolution in 1920.

Georg II's effigy appears on coins in various denominations from 2 marks to the 20-mark coin you see here. The 1914-D 20-mark gold coin is the second issue of the type and was produced in the year of Georg II's death. It is one of the most impressive and sought-after German coins of the imperial period. The total mintage of the issue is believed to be either 1,000 or 1,001 pieces, with an unknown but very small mintage of Proofs included in that number.

One example, believed to be possibly the finest extant at NGC PF-67 Ultra Cameo, sold for $29,375 at Heritage Auctions' August 2015 World and Ancient Coins Platinum Night sale at the American Numismatic Association's World's Fair of Money.

SAXE-MEININGEN

Saxe-Meiningen was located in the center of Germany, immediately north of Bavaria and bordering Saxony to the east. Meiningen served as its capital city and in 1830, it was a base camp for the Russian Grand Duke Alexander during his campaign against Napoleon. Upon the dissolution of the duchy in 1920, the area was absorbed into the new state of Thuringia. Thuringia is now a federal state of Germany. Its economy is largely based on agriculture, tourism, automobile production, and mining.

Georg II, duke of Saxe-Meiningen (1826-1914), and his third wife, actress and pianist Ellen Franz (1839-1923).

Nicaragua, the largest country in Central America, is situated to the north of Costa Rica and to the south of Honduras. Its eastern shores open up to the Caribbean Sea, while its western coastline touches the Pacific Ocean.

In pre-Columbian times, the Nicaraguan region was populated by multiple indigenous tribes, most of which were heavily influenced by Mayans and Aztecs from the north and the Muisca from the south.

In 1912, a major effort was undertaken to reform Nicaragua's monetary system. In part aided by investment capital from the United States, the Central American republic introduced into circulation a new series of paper currency and six circulating coin denominations based on the new unit of one córdoba.

The córdoba was named after Spanish conquistador Francisco Hernández de Córdoba, whose likeness is depicted on the obverse of many of the new coins. The notes carry effigies of the heroes of the Revolution.

The new coin denominations were: ½ centavo, centavo, 5 centavos, 10 centavos, 25 centavos, 50 centavos, and the córdoba. All six were struck at the private Heaton Mint in Birmingham, England.

For the córdoba, the 1912 emission would mark its only year of production. When the córdoba coin returned in 1972, the coin would be smaller, made of copper-nickel, and have considerably less value.

As a collector coin, the 1912-H córdoba has three things going for it: it is the only crown-sized silver coin struck for circulation for Nicaragua; its low mintage and low survival rate in Mint State make it a challenge to collect (yet not unobtainable at today's levels); and the coin's design is one of the most striking in the Latin American series.

Gem-quality circulation strikes for the 1912 córdoba are seldom encountered; so, too, are Gem-quality Proof strikings. To date, PCGS has certified just seven examples of the issue in Mint State, with the top of the condition census being an attractively toned MS-66 from the Heaton Mint Archives/Luis H. Flores Collection, which brought US$11,750 in a 2013 Stack's Bowers Auction (lot 1607).

NGC has certified a mere 16 examples in Mint State and only one reached Gem status. That coin was also graded MS-66.

In Choice Uncirculated grades, this scarce and popular one-year type can be acquired for less than $2,500. In circulated grades up to AU-50, the 1912-H córdoba is affordable at $300 or less.

It's also worth mentioning that uniface trial strikes of the obverse and reverse of this coin survive in very limited numbers. In 2005, Heritage Auctions sold a pair in aluminum at auction for $5,462.50.

THE HEATON MINT

The Heaton Mint was a private mint founded in 1850. Before that, it was a multi-generational family business headquartered in Birmingham, England, which produced various metallic objects, including chandeliers and brass fixtures.

As a coin-producing business, the Heaton Mint struck coins for the Royal Mint and for a number of foreign countries that did not have the facilities necessary to strike their own coins. The Heaton Mint also, on occasion, assisted its foreign customers in the process of establishing their own mints. In Central America, the Heaton Mint struck coins for Colombia, Costa Rica, and Guatemala.

The diagnostic of a coin struck at the Heaton Mint was either the inscription HEATON, HEATON MINT, or the mintmark H. On the Nicaraguan córdoba, the mark appears as a tiny H located underneath the date, between the 9 and the 1.

NICARAGUA 1912-H SILVER CÓRDOBA

Struck for only one year.

Obverse. In the center circle is a portrait of Francisco Hernández de Córdoba. Wrapping around the outside of the circle, at the top, is the legend REPÚBLICA DE NICARAGUA. Two five-pointed stars separate the legend from the date, which is centered at the bottom.

Reverse. In the center circle is a portrait of five mountain tops. An anthropomorphized sun peeks out behind the far-left mountain, and sun rays fill the sky. Wrapping around the outside of the circle, at the top, is the inscription EN DIOS CONFIAMOS ("In God We Trust"). At the bottom, separated from the inscription by two stars, is the denomination UN CÓRDOBA.

Composition	Weight	Diameter	Alignment	Edge
.900 silver	25 grams	38 mm	Medal	Reeded
Mintage	**Mint**		**Collecting Difficulty**	**References**
35,000	Heaton Mint†		Easy‡	KM-16

† Mintmark: H ‡ Examples in high Mint State grades can sell for $10,000 or more.

National Palace, Managua, Nicaragua, circa 1910s.

GERMAN EAST AFRICA 1916-T GOLD 15 RUPIEN

End of the empire.

Obverse. A German crowned imperial eagle is in the center. Wrapping around the rim above is the legend DEUTSCH OSTAFRICKA; below is the denomination 15 RUPIEN.

Reverse. An elephant, facing right, raises its head in a roar, with a mountain range in the background. The ground forms the exergue, below which the date 1916 is written between two dots. Below the date is a T, for Tabora.

Composition	Weight	Diameter	Alignment	Edge
.750 gold	7.168 grams	22 mm	Medal	Smooth
Mintage	**Mint**		**Collecting Difficulty**	**References**
9,035 (KM-16.1); 6,395 (KM-16.2)	Tabora Mint (German East Africa, now Tanzania)†		Moderately difficult	KM–16.1, 16.2; Schön-19
† Mintmark: T				

African soldiers with cannons and European officers during the East African Campaign during World War I.

German East Africa was a German colony established in 1891, six years after adventurer Carl Peters set out to establish a protectorate of the mineral- and resource-rich territory located in the Great Lakes region of the African East Coast. As the largest and most populous of four German colonies on the continent, German East Africa supplied Germany with fine woods, clay, coconuts, coffee, rubber, copper, iron, and, to a limited degree, gold. German investment in the territory saw the improvement of roads and infrastructure as it suited the extraction of these materials. The largest and most vital of these improvements was the creation of a rail line that bisected the territory, connecting Lake Tanganyika at Kigomo to the coast at Dar es Salaam.

German interest in the region coincided with a period of European expansion defined by historians as the Age of New Imperialism. Germany's ambitions were facilitated by the opening of the Suez Canal, which significantly lowered the cost and time it took to conduct trade with and exert control over the region.

And Germany wasn't alone. German East Africa was surrounded by the colonies of its European rivals. It bordered British East Africa to the north, Belgian Congo to the west, and Portuguese East Africa to the south. The porosity of its border would play an important part in the colony's undoing once hostilities with its neighbors broke out at the onset of World War I.

German control of the colony was quite often tenuous and fraught with conflict. The territory of German East Africa was also claimed by the sultan of Zanzibar, ruler of the chain of islands located immediately to the east. The sultan's claim ended after Otto von Bismarck sent German warships to the region.

On the mainland, German authorities were met with resistance and violence. The most famous and consequential of these conflicts played out over many years as the Hehe tribe, led by the warrior chief Mkwavinyika Munyigumba Mwamuyinga (usually referred to in the West simply as

East African official for Germany, formerly a sultan, in Tanganyika, circa 1902.

Chief Mkwawa, "conqueror of many lands"), led a spirited resistance. Unfortunately, Mkwawa's resistance was no match for German military dominance and in the end, when faced with capture, the chief took his own life. Germany celebrated its victory by shipping his head back to Europe and putting it on public display.

By the end of the conflict, Germany had lost administrative control over the area, but it was the signing of the Treaty of Versailles on June 28, 1919, that officially marked an end to German East Africa and the rest of Germany's colonial holdings.

European control over the region continued for another 25 years and lasted through the outbreak of World War II. Like the Great War that preceded it, World War II brought incredible violence to the African continent as Germany and Italy sought to re-establish their claims.

Ultimately, colonialism in Africa came to an end when the European powers, faced with years of rebuilding and total economic collapse, realized that foreign adventurism was no longer worth the price.

Sadly, the leadership vacuum created a post-colonial order filled with revolution, social turmoil, and economic upheaval from which it took decades to recover. To make matters worse, in many cases the European political division of the continent created boundaries that proved unnatural to the African people, leading to even more war and suffering.

Today, the territory of former German East Africa is contained in the independent nations of Burundi, Kenya, Mozambique, Rwanda, Tanzania, and Uganda.

The coinage of German East Africa, as initially conceived, was based on the Indian rupee, with one German East African *rupie* having the equivalent value of one Indian *rupee* and the German East African denomination of the *pesa* (64 to a rupie) being the equivalent of the Indian *paisa*. In 1904, Germany decimalized the colonial monetary system, with the unit of one *heller* taking over for the pesa with a value set at a hundredth of a rupie. The decimalized rupie had a value of 1⅓ times the value of a German mark.

Before the outbreak of World War I, production of German East African coinage was produced by the German mints in Hamburg and Berlin. Typically, this coinage bore the J mintmark of Hamburg or the A mintmark of Berlin, but this was not always the case. Occasionally, German East African coins bear no mark to indicate where they were struck.

World War I caused considerable strain to Germany's ability to defend and service the colony. A British naval blockade shut off trade routes by sea, while Belgian and British ground forces encroached upon the territory by the north and west. At the end of 1915, facing a siege at Dar es Salaam, German East Africa's government moved inland to the railway city of Tabora.

With circulating money drying up, the colonial administration attempted to relieve the situation with an emission of paper notes. These were rejected by the local population, and so, facing a total economic breakdown, the colonial governor instructed Kironda mine engineer Dr. Friedrich Schumacher to strike emergency coinage at an improvised mint established at a railway warehouse at Tabora[1]. Coins struck at the Tabora emergency mint bore the T mintmark.

Schumacher had no first-hand knowledge of the coin production process and the machinery available to him was crude, with replacement parts difficult to come by. Dies had to be cut by hand and coining metal for the 5- and 20-heller coins came to the mint in the form of military scraps. Gold for the 15-rupien coins, which were used to pay soldiers, had to be transported in secret by porters over 200 miles through the African brush, from the Senkeke gold mine to Tabora.

Given these circumstances, it's hard to believe the plant produced more than two million coins. The 5- and 20-heller coins were as crudely designed as one might expect. The gold 15-rupien coins, which were struck on different equipment and feature a now-classic design, were of better quality.

Usambara railway tracks.

Drawn by railway cashier R. Voght, the design depicts a roaring African elephant in a natural scene with mountains in the background. The design was executed by an African engraver from Zanzibar. The coin's reverse carries forward the German imperial eagle design with new inscriptions.

The 15 rupien was made of an unusual gold alloy consisting of 75 percent gold, 20 percent silver and 5 percent copper. Because of this debasement, the value of the 15 rupien was essentially on par with that of the German mark.

Production of the coin began in April and continued through July, when equipment failure ended production. An estimated total of 6,400 15-rupien coins were struck. A steam press used to extract oil from nuts was located in the nearby town of Lulanguru, where an additional 3,400 pieces were struck before Belgian forces launched an offensive to seize the city, bringing an end to the 1916-T emergency coinage of German East Africa. The total mintage of the issue is widely reported as being 9,803; however, German sources claim a larger mintage, with 6,395 examples struck at Tabora with a small Arabesque on the first A in OSTAFRICA, and 9,803 examples struck at Lulanguru with a large Arabesque on the A in OSTAFRICA[2].

While issues surrounding colonialism and the striking of these emergency issues are complex and seldom fully explored by collectors, the 1916-T 15-rupien gold coin's rustic yet iconic design is a standout in a century of great designs.

A typical uncirculated example of the issue costs between US$7,500 and $10,000 in today's market.

EUROZONE 1999 EURO COIN SETS

Toward the creation of a continental currency.

W hereas the early half of the European twentieth century was fraught with the decline of empires, political intrigue amongst rival nations, and two utterly devastating world wars (not to mention many local and regional wars), the latter half of the century was noteworthy for its relative sense of peace, brought about by the realignment of the world order after the emergence of the United States and the Soviet Union as the nuclear age's two global superpowers. Given the stakes, this

National Obverses:

Belgium: All designs: the inner circle features a portrait of King Albert II. Wrapping around the design are 12 stars symbolizing Europe. The king's monogram, a capital A underneath a crown, is located on the right. The date is located at the lower right. The designer is Jan Alfons Keustermans.

Finland: The minor coinage has Finland's heraldic lion encircled by 12 stars. The date appears on the left, below the lion's outstretched left paw. An M (for mintmaster Raimo Makkonen) is below the bottom sword. The designer is Heikki Aulis Häiväoja.

The euro features two left-facing swans flying over a hilly lake scene. Twelve stars encircle the design. The date appears in incuse over the landscape in the middle right portion of the coin. The designer is Pertti Kalervo Mäkinen. An M (for mintmaster Raimo Makkonen) is located on the left, bordering the outer ring.

The 2-euro coin has two cloudberry flowers. Twelve stars encircle the design. An M (for mintmaster Raimo Makkonen) is below the right flower. The designer is Raimo Isma Heino.

France: The 1-, 2-, and 5-cent coins feature a two-thirds portrait of Marianne, facing forward from a slightly rightward perspective. A stylized RF is located to the right of her face. Twelve stars encircle the design. The date is rendered at the lower right, inset slightly from the stars. A bee privy mark is located to the upper right of the date and a cornucopia privy mark is to the upper left. The designer's name F. COURTIADE (Fabienne Courtiade) wraps around the inside of the rim at the lower right.

The 10- to 50-cent coins include the French flag with a modernist interpretation of Oscar Roty's "Sower" design inset within it. The design represents France staying true to itself, while integrating into the European Union. The date appears on the left and RF appears to the right, below the sower's outstretched right hand. The designers' names are represented on the right, oriented vertically, as L. JORIO (for Laurent Jorio) and d'ap. (adapted from) O. ROTY.

The 1- and 2-euro coins feature a tree, symbolizing life, continuity, and growth. The tree is contained in a hexagon and encircled by the motto LIBERTÉ, ÉGALITÉ, FRATERNITÉ ("Liberty, Equality, Brotherhood"). Edge for 2 euro: 2 **2 ** 2 * 2 ** 2 ** 2 **.

Netherlands: The minor coinage features a stylized portrait of Queen Beatrix, facing left. The queen's effigy is surrounded by small dots and the 12 stars of Europe. Encircling the design is the effigy BEATRIX KONINGIN DER NEDERLANDEN ("Beatrix, Queen of the Netherlands"). The date is at the bottom, surrounded by privy marks. The designer is Bruno Ninaber van Eyben.

The 1- and 2-euro coins have a bisected, stylized portrait of Queen Beatrix, facing left. Twelve stars wrap around the left side of the design in the outer ring. Starting in the center and continuing toward the right are vertical lines, in which is the inscription BEATRIX KONNINGIN DER NEDERLANDEN ("Beatrix, Queen of the Netherlands"). Privy marks are at the bottom right of the design. The designer is Bruno Ninaber van Eyben.

Spain: The 1-, 2-, and 5-cent coins feature the cathedral Santiago de Compostela, encircled by 12 stars. ESPAÑA is written to the left and the mark of the Spanish Mint is to the right. The date is above the cathedral. The designer is Garcilaso Rollán.

The 10-, 20-, and 50-cent coins show a portrait of author Miguel de Cervantes. Cervantes' name and a quill appear to the left of the portrait, and ESPAÑA is on the upper left. Twelve stars encircle the design. The mark of the Spanish Mint is to the left, and the date is below the bust.

The 1- and 2-euro coins feature a two-thirds portrait of King Juan Carlos I, encircled by 12 stars. ESPAÑA is written to the left, and the date is below. The mark of the Spanish Mint is to the left.

1 Cent

Composition	Weight	Diameter	Alignment	Edge
Copper-plated Steel	2.3 grams	16.25 mm	Medal	Plain

Mintage	Mint	Collecting Difficulty	References
See chart on right	Various	Easy	Various

2 Cent

Composition	Weight	Diameter	Alignment	Edge
Copper-plated Steel	3.06 grams	18.75 mm	Medal	Grooved

Mintage	Mint	Collecting Difficulty	References
See chart on right	Various	Easy	Various

5 Cent

Composition	Weight	Diameter	Alignment	Edge
Copper-plated Steel	3.92 grams	21.25 mm	Medal	Plain

Mintage	Mint	Collecting Difficulty	References
See chart on right	Various	Easy	Various

10 Cent

Composition	Weight	Diameter	Alignment	Edge
Nordic gold	4.1 grams	19.75 mm	Medal	Indented

Mintage	Mint	Collecting Difficulty	References
See chart on right	Various	Easy	Various

20 Cent

Composition	Weight	Diameter	Alignment	Edge
Nordic gold	5.74 grams	22.25 mm	Medal	Smooth Edge with Indentations

Mintage	Mint	Collecting Difficulty	References
See chart on right	Various	Easy	Various

50 Cent

Composition	Weight	Diameter	Alignment	Edge
Nordic gold	7.8 grams	24.25 mm	Medal	Indented

Mintage	Mint	Collecting Difficulty	References
See chart on right	Various	Easy	Various

1 Euro

Composition	Weight	Diameter	Alignment	Edge
Bimetallic Copper-Nickel Clad, Nickel Center in Nickel-Brass Outer Ring	7.5 grams	23.25 mm	Medal	Segmented Reeds

Mintage	Mint	Collecting Difficulty	References
See chart on right	Various	Easy	Various

2 Euro

Composition	Weight	Diameter	Alignment	Edge
Bimetallic Nickel-Brass Clad, Nickel Center in Copper-nickel Outer Ring	8.5 grams	25.75 mm	Medal	Various †

Mintage	Mint	Collecting Difficulty	References
See chart on right	Various	Easy	Various

† Fine ribs with alternating sequence of stars and the number 2 (Belgium), fine ribs with incuse lettering SUOMI FINLAND and three lion's heads (Finland), 2 ** in sequence of six (France), GOD*ZIJ*MET*ONS ("God Be With Us") (Netherlands). 2 ** in a sequence of six (Spain).

Mintage

Belgium: 40,000 sets only (10,388 Proofs)						
Finland: 75,000 sets (15,000 Proofs). For circulation: 1 cent: 8,175,000						
2 Cents	5 Cents	10 Cents	20 Cents	50 Cents	1 Euro	2 Euros
1,860,000	63,380,000	133,520,000	42,350,000	20,696,000	16,210,000	16,090,000
France: 35,000 sets (15,000 Proofs). For circulation: 1 cent: 794,016,000						
2 Cents	5 Cents	10 Cents	20 Cents	50 Cents	1 Euro	2 Euros
702,104,013	616,192,000	447,249,600	454,291,200	105,753,613	301,050,000	56,695,000
Netherlands: 65,000 sets (16,500 Proofs). For circulation: 1 cent: 47,800,000						
2 Cents	5 Cents	10 Cents	20 Cents	50 Cents	1 Euro	2 Euros
109,065,000	213,065,000	149,700,000	86,500,000	99,600,000	63,500,000	9,900,000
Spain: 49,030 sets. For circulation: 1 cent: 721,049,030						
2 Cents	5 Cents	10 Cents	20 Cents	50 Cents	1 Euro	2 Euros
291,651,000	483,500,000	588,100,000	762,300,000	370,100,000	100,150,970	60,500,000

Postcard depicting Oscar Roty's *The Sower*,
which is featured on some of France's Euro coinage.

distrust of the West increased, this sphere of influence hardened into an Iron Curtain. Coerced cooperation and foreign-controlled governments took shape. Only the potential of mutual destruction kept these two worlds from direct conflict.

As the second half of the twentieth century unfolded, a political movement toward a unified Europe emerged. British Prime Minister Winston Churchill was an early proponent, calling for a United States of Europe in a 1946 speech at the University of Zurich. Other political thinkers followed suit and gradually, over the course of many years through codification and cooperation in the business sector, a viable roadmap to a European "Union" was born. At first, the union took shape around the shared goal of making war among European nations impossible.

The founders sought to create a supranational organization that emboldened cross-border trade in areas of steel, energy, and agriculture production. This interlinking of economies eventually led to a reduction or removal of customs duties for cross-border trade on several products. The success of these programs led other nations to join and by the time the Maastricht Treaty, which put a plan for a common currency into place, was ratified in 1992, the EU had 12 member states.

Today, the EU has 28 members. In the near future, that number will likely change as the United Kingdom plans its exit and other members complete the accession process.

The "euro" was born in 1995, after Belgian teacher Germain Pirlot suggested the name to then-President of the European Commission Jacques Santer. Pirlot also put forth the name "ropas" to mean one hundredth of a euro. Instead, the term "cent" was adopted.

newfound sense of stability and cooperation was born out of necessity more so than a sense of shared values and community.

Under the umbrella of American influence and protection, the Western European powers rebuilt their cities and institutions, carrying out much-needed social and political reforms.

The nationalism that had laid waste to the continent had given way. In its place, sprigs from the tree of globalism grew. For Eastern Europe, a story in mirror image played out. A "buffer zone" of Eastern European states were given by the Western allies to the sphere of Soviet influence. As

The Roman Colosseum lit up in celebration of the 60th anniversary of the European Union, 2017.

On January 1, 1999, the euro came into existence, with 12 countries adopting the currency. Of those 12, Belgium, Finland, France, the Netherlands, and Spain struck and issued euro coin sets dated 1999, 2000, and 2001. Reservations for these sets were made available to collectors and the sets were issued once the euro coins entered official circulation in 2002. These five countries were joined by Austria, Germany, Greece, Ireland, Italy, Luxembourg, and Portugal as issuers of the coins in 2002.

The adoption and release of the euro into circulation signaled the dawn of a new epoch.

Consigned to history were some of numismatics' most notable currencies: the drachma, the escudo, the franc, the guilder, the lira, the mark, the markka, the peseta, and the schilling, among others. In their place was a new modern coin that crossed cultural and physical boundaries and tied the continent together in ways both symbolic and practical.

The new coins were uniform in their reverse design, composition, and denominations of issue (with some countries opting out of issuing the low-denomination coins), but the obverse of each coin allowed the issuing country to retain some national character on their issued coins.

The greatness of the euro lies within the daring and improbable nature of its existence. Even now, as the currency enters its second decade, its future as the circulating money of Europe is not certain.

As a collectible, the euro has been a true success story. The 1999 sets, coveted upon their release, continue to excite collectors. And while the value of these sets will never match the rarity or value of any of the other coins described in this book (an individual set might set you back $10-$12), the sets' value to the health of the modern numismatic marketplace, especially amongst European collectors, continues to grow.

The launch of the euro created a fresh start for a whole generation of collectors and allowed them to collect money anew. By supplanting the old monetary systems, the introduction of the euro has also hastened the culling of each issuing country's preceding issues, making the coin great for its destructive power and in the power of its creation. This is all the more reason why modern world coin collectors should love the euro.

View of the main nave of the church of the monastery of San Martiño Pinario, Santiago de Compostela, Galicia, Spain.

CREDITS AND ACKNOWLEDGEMENTS

This book is dedicated to Scott, Eve, Ha, Owen, Stella, Fiona, and Philip.

The authors would like to thank Howard Berlin, Q. David Bowers, Ivan Che, Michael Chou, Jeff Garrett, Ira Goldberg, Heritage Auctions, Joshua McMorrow-Hernandez, Christine Karstedt, Julian Leidman, Numismatic Guaranty Corporation, Del Parker, Professional Coin Grading Service, Scott Purvis, James Ricks, Bill Rosenblum, Allan Schein, Larry Stack, Harvey Stack, Stack's Bowers Galleries, Lance Tchor, and the staff of Whitman Publishing.

The publisher would like to thank the following: Donald Scarinci for writing the foreword to this book. Heritage Auctions for opening its voluminous archives and sharing coin images. Stack's Bowers Galleries, A.H. Baldwin & Sons, APMEX, Aureo & Calicó Subastas Numismaticas, Baldwin's, Bonham's, Colin Cooke Ltd., European Central Bank, PCGS, NGC, Numista, Roma Numismatics, Royal Mint Museum, St. James Auctions for sharing coin images. Jeff Starck of *Coin World* for assisting with image gathering.

ABOUT THE AUTHORS

Charles Morgan is an award-winning numismatic writer, industry analyst, and editor of one of the hobby's most visited online publications, *CoinWeek.com*. At *CoinWeek*, he has written about and covered the entire gamut of numismatic topics. As the host of the *CoinWeek Podcast*, Morgan has dug deeper into the history of numismatics with some of the hobby's leading personalities.

His main areas of collecting interest are numismatic literature and the coins and medals of the Food and Agriculture Organization (FAO) of the United Nations. He also collects U.S. coins, classic films, and comic books.

Morgan studied English at Susquehanna University and the University of Virginia and served in the U.S. Army as a Russian linguist. He lives in Virginia with his wife, two children, and a very temperamental Maine Coon cat.

Hubert Walker is the assistant editor of *CoinWeek.com* and along with Charles has written numerous award-winning articles and columns, both online and in print. He studied English at the University of Virginia, though he is also keen on history, music, and art. Hubert currently resides in Virginia; his cat does not.

IMAGE CREDITS

Images are credited by page number. Coin images are credited first. Where multiple auxiliary illustrations are found on a given page, they are credited by location, starting with number 1 at upper left and reading left to right, top to bottom. LOC = Library of Congress. NARA = National Archives and Records Administration. NGC = Numismatic Guaranty Corporation. NYPL = New York Public Library. PCGS = Professional Coin Grading Service.

The "Greatest Coins by Country" with additional "Great" coins from select countries.

Australia
1902-S 5 Pounds
1916 Mule Half Penny
1919–1921 Square Kookaburra Patterns (55)
1920 Sydney Gold Sovereign (4)
1923 Half Penny, Proof
1930 Melbourne Penny, Proof (7)
1934 Six-Coin Proof Set (16)
1945 Penny

Austria
(1780) Maria Theresa Thaler (82)
1908 Gold 100 Corona (74)

Brazil
1902 10,000 Reis
1922 Gold 10,000 Reis (45)
1935 20 Reis

British Honduras
1901 50 Cents, Proof

British North Borneo
1907-H Cent, Proof

British West Africa
1928 2 Shillings

Bulgaria
1912 Gold 100 Leva, Proof

Canada
1911 Silver Dollar Pattern (1)
1916-C Sovereign (43)
1921 50 Cents (17)
1936 Six-Coin Specimen Set (with "Dot" Issues) (8)
1979 Gold Maple Leaf (66)

Central African States (Cameroon, Central African Republic, Chad, Republic of Congo, Equatorial Guinea, and Gabon)
1956 Pattern Set

Ceylon
1904 Copper 5 Cents Pattern

China
1903 Silver Fengtien Tael Pattern (2)
1903 Silver Hu Poo Tael Pattern (13)
1906 Gold Kuping Tael Pattern (11)
1910 Yunnan Spring Silver Dollar (3)
1911 Long Whisker Silver Dollar Pattern (54)
1912 Republic of China Gold Dollar (41)
1914 Republic of China Gold Dollar (38)
Yuan ShiKai "Giorgi" Gold 10 Dollars Pattern (18)
1921 Republic of China Gold Dollar
1926 Shantung Dragon and Phoenix Gold 20 Dollars (23)
1927 Chang Tso-Lin Gold 50 Yuan, Specimen (20)
1928 Kweichow Silver Auto Dollar (59)
1929 Sun Yat-Sen Flag and Globe Silver Dollar Pattern (28)
1949 Kweichow 50 Cents (15)
1982 Panda Four-Piece Gold Set (65)

Colombia
1901 Leprosarium Coinage 50 Centavos
1902 2-1/2 Centavos

Costa Rica
1917 50 Centavos (without Counterstamp)

Crete
1901 5 Drachmai, Specimen

Croatia
1941 500 Kunas

Cuba
1915 Gold Proof Set
1916 Six-Coin Gold Proof Set (60)

Cyprus
1928 45 Piastres, Proof

Czechoslovakia
1937 Gold 10 Dukatu (73)

Danish West Indies
1904-H Gold 10 Dalers, Proof (42)

Danzig
1935 10 Gulden

Denmark
1924 HCN GJ Krone
1964 CS Gold 5 Kroner

Dominican Republic
1939 Peso, Proof

East Africa
1921 King George V Florin (72)

Ecuador
1975 5 Sucres

Egypt
AH1338 (1920-H) 20 Piastres

El Salvador
1914 Proof Set
1925 20 Colones

Eritrea
1918 Talero

Estonia
1926 10 Marka

Ethiopia
EE1916–1917 (1924–1925) Birr and 6 Birr Patterns (81)

Euro-Producing Countries
1999 Euro Sets (100)

Falkland Islands
1919 150 Pounds

Fiji
1934 Proof Set

Finland
1912-L Grand Duchy of Finland Gold 20 Markaa (64)

France
1929 Gold 100 Francs (91)
1950-B 50 Francs
1976 Platinum Piedfort 50 Francs

French Indochina
1931 Piastre Essai Set (62)

Gabon
1925 Elephant Token

German East Africa
1916-T Gold 15 Rupien (99)

Germany
1905 Mecklenburg-Strelitz 20 Marks
1905-D Saxe-Meiningen Georg II 20 Marks, Proof
1911-A Saxe-Coburg-Gotha 2 Marks, Proof
1913-E Saxony Albertine 3 Marks, Matte Proof (25)
1913-F Württemberg Gold 20 Marks, Proof (46)
1914-D Saxe-Meiningen Duke Georg II Gold 20 Marks, Proof (97)
1949-A East Germany 50 Pfennigs (92)
1954-G West Germany Marks (86)

Great Britain
1921-B Silver Trade Dollar (53)
1926 Peace Crown Pattern
1933 Penny (10)
1937 King Edward VIII Gold Sovereign (6)
1937 King Edward VIII Proof Set (26)
1952 King George VI Half Crown (35)
1953 Queen Elizabeth II Four-Coin Gold Proof Set (9)
1954 Penny (19)

Greece
1915 Silver 2 Drachmai Pattern (52)
1963 30 Drachmai

Guadeloupe
1903 Franc, Proof

Guatemala
1995 Gold 1 and 10 Quetzales Patterns

Guinea-Bissau
1933 10 Centavos

Guyana
1904 4 Pence, Proof

Honduras
1908/888/897 Overdate Gold 20 Pesos (89)

Hong Kong
1941 Cent

Hungary
1907-KB Gold 100 Korona Coronation 40th Anniversary

India
1939-B Rupee (31)

Iran
SH1342 (1963) Gold 5 Pahlavi (70)

Iraq
1932 Riyal, Proof

Ireland
1938 Penny Pattern (40)
1938 Silver Half Crown Pattern (36)
1943 Florin
1985 20 Pence (90)
1992 10 Pence

Israel
JE5723 (1962) (b) 50 and 100 Lirot without "mem"

Italian Somaliland
1921-R Rupia

Italy
1901-R Silver 5 Lire (71)
1902-R 20 Lire
1925-R 100 Lire
1926--R 100 Lire
1927R 100 Lire
1928-R Gold 20 Lire, Proof (14)
1939-R 100 Lire
1940-R Gold 100 Lire (32)

Japan
Meiji 1901 Silver Yen Pattern (44)
Meiji 1903 Gold 20 Yen (34)
Showa Year 5 (1930) 5 Yen
Showa Year 7 (1932) 20 Yen

Jordan
1949 Proof Set

Korea
1902 Chon, Russian Denomination (47)
1902 20 Won
1908 Gold 5 Won
1909 Yunghui Three-Coin Gold Set (5)
1909 Yunghui Copper-Nickel 5 Chon (61)

Kuwait
AH1380 (1961) 5 Dinars

Latvia
1923 2 Santimi
1929 5 Lati

Liberia
1906-H 50 Cents, Proof

Liechtenstein
1924 5 Franken

Lithuania
1938 Gold 10 Litu Pattern

Maldives Islands
1978 5 Rufiyaa and 25 Rufiyaa FAO Gold Set

Mexico
1909 Caballito Peso Pattern (69)
1915 Guerrero/Suriana Gold With Silver 2 Pesos (77)
1916 Oaxaca Gold 60 Pesos (58)
1921 Gold 50 Pesos (87)
1931/0 50 Pesos
1984 50 Pesos, Proof

Monaco
1904-A 100 Francs

Montenegro
1910 Gold 100 Perpera, Proof (51)

Morocco
AH1371 (1951) Gold Off-Metal Strike 50 Francs

Muscat and Oman
AH1367 (1947) 1/2 Dhofari Rial, Proof

Nepal
SE 1826 (1904) Prithvi Bir Bikram, Gold Mohar

Netherlands
1980 2-1/2 Gulden in Gold

Netherlands East Indies
1943–1944 Occupation Coinage (79)

New Hebrides
1979 Platinum 500 Francs Pattern

New Zealand
1949 Silver Crown Proof (49)

Nicaragua
1912-H Silver Córdoba (98)

Norway
1902 10 Kroner

Palestine Mandate
1927 Proof Set (67)
1931 Silver 100 Mils (96)

Panama
1931 Silver Balboa, Proof (78)

Peru
1958 Gold 100 Soles (95)

Philippines
1907-S Peso, Proof (Large Size and Small Size) (27)
1906-S Silver Peso (83)

Poland
1925 Gold 5 Zlotych (33)
1942–1943 Łódź Ghetto Coinage (80)

Portugal
1925 50 Centavos

Rhodesia
1975 Proof Set

Romania
1940 Six-Coin Gold Set (24)

Russia
1902 Gold 37 Rubles, 50 Kopeks (22)
1904 5 Kopeks (37)
1908 Gold 25 Rubles, Proof (12)
1912 Czar Alexander III Memorial Silver Ruble (50)
1914 Ruble
1921 Soviet Federative Socialist Republic Silver Ruble (56)
1991/1992 Government Bank Eight-Coin Set (63)

Saarland
1955 100 Franken Pattern

San Marino
1935-R 20 Lire

Saudi Arabia
Aramco 1947 Gold "Sovereign" and 1945 Gold "4 Pounds" (76)

Serbia
1904 5 Dinara

South Africa
1902 Veld Pond (39)
1923-SA Gold Sovereign (84)
1928-SA Bronze Sovereign Pattern (21)
1928 Sterling Silver Sixpence, Specimen (29)
1936 Proof Set
1939 Proof Set
1967 Gold Krugerrand (57)

Southern Rhodesia
1937 Proof Set

South Vietnam
1975 50 Đong (94)

Spain
1904 SM-V 20 Pesetas
1937 Olot 15 Centimos (75)
1949 Gold 5 Pesetas (52) (68)

Straits Settlements
1920 5 Cents

Sweden
1910 5 Öre

Switzerland
1910–1911 Gold 10 Francs, Essai (48)
1925-B Gold 100 Francs, Specimen (30)
1928-B Silver 5 Francs (85)

Thailand
RS127 (1908) Rama V Baht

Tibet
1921 Ser-Khang Gold 20 Srang (88)

Venezuela
1900 5 Bolivares

Yemen
AH1358 (1939) Gold 2 Riyals (93)

NO. 1: CANADA 1911 SILVER DOLLAR PATTERN

1. Haxby, James A. *Striking Impressions: The Royal Canadian Mint and Canadian Coinage.* Ottawa: The Royal Canadian Mint, 1983. 73.
2. *Ibid* 96.
3. "Notes and Queries: Rare Canadian Dollar Sold." *Numismatist*, Volume 90, Issue 1, January 1977. 79.
4. "The Emperor and the King Hold Court at PCGS," Ad. *Numismatist*, March 1990. 441.
5. The Sid and Alicia Belzberg Collection of Canadian Coinage. Public auction sale, January 13, 2003. Heritage Auctions. https://coins.ha.com/itm/canada/world-coins/1911-pattern-dollar-dc-6-specimen-65-pcgs-considered-the-greatest-and-most-storied-rarity-in-all-of-canadian-numismatics-/a/312-15545.s

NO. 8: CANADA 1936 SIX-COIN SPECIMEN SET (WITH "DOT" ISSUES)

1. The Sid & Alicia Belzberg Collection of Canadian Coinage. Public auction sale, January 13, 2003. Heritage Auctions. https://coins.ha.com/itm/canada/world-coins/1936-1-cent-dot-specimen-66-red-pcgs-onlythis-exceptional-rarity-was-lightly-lacquered-at-the-mint-to-preserve-the-origi/a/312-15608.s?ic4=ListView-ShortDescription-071515

NO. 10: GREAT BRITAIN 1933 PENNY

1. "1933 penny." The Royal Mint Museum. http://www.royalmintmuseum.org.uk/collection/collection-highlights/coins/1933-penny/
2–3. "O'Brien Rare Coin Review: Why is the 1933 British Penny so valuable?" The Old Currency Exchange, August 20, 2014. https://oldcurrencyexchange.com/2014/08/20/rare-coins-the-1933-british-penny/
4. "The 1933 Penny." *The Baldwin's Blog* (blog), April 9, 2016. http://www.baldwin.co.uk/news/the-1933-penny/

NO. 24: ROMANIA 1940 SIX-COIN GOLD SET

1. Iliescu, Octavian. *The History of Coins in Romania (cca. 1500 B.C. - 2000 AD).* Bucharest: EDITURA ENCICLOPEDICĂ, 2002.
2. ROMANIA. Galben Mare (12 Ducat), 1940. PCGS MS-63+ Secure Holder. Public auction sale, Aug. 12, 2016. Stack's Bowers Galleries. https://auctions.stacksbowers.com/lots/view/3-4QLOW
3. Romania Carol II gold 100 Lei 1940. Public auction sale, April 10-16, 2014. Heritage Auctions. https://coins.ha.com/itm/romania/romania-carol-ii-gold-100-lei-1940-/a/3032-25748.s?hdnJumpToLot=1x=0&y=0
4. Romania Carol II gold 20 Lei 1940. Public auction sale, April 10-16, 2014. Heritage Auctions. https://coins.ha.com/itm/romania/world-coins/romania-carol-ii-gold-20-lei-1940-/a/3032-25745.s?

NO. 32: ITALY 1940-R GOLD 100 LIRE

1. "To His Majesty Victor Emanuel III King of Italy." Farran Zerbe. *Numismatist*, December 15, 1908. 66.

NO. 34: JAPAN 1903 MEIJI GOLD 20 YEN

1. The Winter Collection of United States, Ancient, and Foreign Coins. Public auction sale, January 31, 1974. Stacks-Bowers Galleries, Santa Ana, California.

NO. 37: RUSSIA 1904 5 KOPEKS

1. Kosinski, Thomas Gregory & Tomasz Kosinski. *Coins of RUSSIA 1901-2014: Coins of Europe Catalog 1901-2014.* 2014. https://books.google.com/books?id=wkl7AwAAQBAJ&pg=PA54&dq=Coins+of+RUSSIA+1901-2014:+Coins+of+Europe+Catalog+1901-2014&source=gbs_selected_pages&cad=3#v=onepage&q=5%20kopeks&f=false>

NO. 44: JAPAN 1901 SILVER YEN PATTERN

1. Haxby, James A. *A Guide Book of Canadian Coins and Tokens.* Atlanta: Whitman Publishing, 2012.
2. Cross, W.K. *Canadian Coins, Volume One: Numismatic Issues.* Kitchener, Ontario: Charlton Press, 2014.

NO. 45: BRAZIL 1922 GOLD 10,000 REIS

1. Norweb Collection Brazilian, Bolivian, Columbian, and Chilean Coins. Public auction sale, March 3-4, 1997. Spink America. http://www.christies.com/LotFinder/print_sale.aspx?saleid=6237.
2. The RLM Collection of Brazilian Coins (Part III). Public auction sale, January 5-6, 2014. Heritage Auctions. https://coins.ha.com/itm/brazil/world-coins/brazil-republic-gold-10000-reis-1922-/a/3030-23157.s?ic4=ListView-ShortDescription-071515#

NO. 50: RUSSIA 1912 CZAR ALEXANDER III MEMORIAL SILVER RUBLE

1. Singer, Isidore and Cyrus Adler, editors. *The Jewish Encyclopedia: A Descriptive Record of the History, Religion, Literature, and Customs of the Jewish People from the Earliest Times to the Present Day. Volume 6.* New York: Funk & Wagnalls, 1906. 92.
2. Heritage World Coin Auctions Long Beach Signature Auction Catalog #378. Public auction sale, June 2–3, 2005. Heritage Auctions.
3. Russia: Nicholas II, Alexander III Commemorative Rouble 1912. Public auction sale, September 18-21, 2008. Heritage Auctions. https://coins.ha.com/itm/russia/russia-nicholas-ii-alexander-iii-commemorative-rouble-1912-/a/3002-22227.s?type=NGC3002

NO. 51: MONTENEGRO 1910 GOLD 100 PERPERA, PROOF

1. 1910 100 P Bare Head, DCAM (Proof). Public auction sale, August 15, 2019. Heritage Auctions. https://www.pcgs.com/pop/valueview.aspx?s=609461
2. Montenegro: Nicholas I gold "Bare Head" Proof 100 Perpera 1910 PR63 Ultra Cameo NGC. Public auction sale, August 3, 2017. Heritage Auctions. https://coins.ha.com/itm/montenegro/world-coins/montenegro-nicholas-i-gold-bare-head-proof-100-perpera-1910-pr63-ultra-cameo-ngc-andnbsp-/a/3056-30413.s?ic4=ListView-ShortDescription-071515

NO. 52: GREECE 1915 SILVER 2 DRACHMAI PATTERN

1. Greece: Constantine I silver Essai 2 Drachmai 1915. Public auction sale, April 25–May 1, 2012. Heritage Auctions.https://coins.ha.com/itm/greece/world-coins/greece-constantine-i-silver-essai-2-drachmai-1915-/a/3019-24849.s?ic4=ListView-ShortDescription-071515
2. Greece: Constantine I copper-nickel Proof Essai Drachma 1915 PR65 NGC. August 8, 2014. Heritage Auctions. https://coins.ha.com/itm/greece/world-coins/greece-constantine-i-copper-nickel-proof-essai-drachma-1915-pr65-ngc-/a/3033-23317.s?ic4=ListView-ShortDescription-071515
3. Greece: Constantine I copper-nickel Specimen Essai Drachma 1915 PR65 PCGS. January 8-9, 2017. Heritage Auctions. https://coins.ha.com/itm/greece/world-coins/greece-constantine-i-copper-nickel-specimen-essai-drachma-1915-sp65-pcgs-/a/3051-34280.s?ic4=OtherResults-SampleItem-071515&tab=ArchiveSearchResults-012417

NO. 55: AUSTRALIA 1919–1921 SQUARE KOOKABURRA PATTERNS

1. "Australia's Square Coinage 1919–1921." *CoinWorks.* https://coinworks.com.au/file/11056/10275
2. Australia: George V copper-nickel Pattern Penny 1919. Public auction sale, January 2–3, 2012. Heritage Auctions. https://coins.ha.com/itm/australia/world-coins/australia-george-v-copper-nickel-pattern-penny-1919-/a/3016-23336.s?ic4=ListView-ShortDescription-071515

NO. 56: RUSSIA 1921 SOVIET FEDERATIVE SOCIALIST REPUB. SILVER RUBLE

1. Harrison, Mark and Andrei Markevich. "Russia's National Income in War and Revolution, 1913 to 1928." VoxEU.org, May 11, 2012. http://voxeu.org/article/russia-s-national-income-war-and-revolution-1913-1928
2. Russia: R.S.F.S.R. Proof Rouble 1921 АГ. KM-84, Proof 67 NGC. Public auction sale, September 27–28, 2007. Heritage Auctions. https://coins.ha.com/itm/russia/world-coins/russia-rsfsr-proof-rouble-1921-a-/a/441-52269.s?ic4=ListView-ShortDescription-071515
3. The D. Moore Collection. Public auction sale, January 8–9, 2017. Heritage Auctions. https://coins.ha.com/itm/russia/world-coins/russia-rsfsr-silver-proof-rouble-1921-a-pr66-cameo-ngc-/a/3051-33112.s?ic4=ListView-ShortDescription-071515

NO. 58: MEXICO 1916 OAXACA GOLD 60 PESOS

1. Sorenson, M. "The Oaxaca Coinage of 1915." *The Numismatist*, Volume 33, Issue 4, April 1920. 142-144.
2. Bailey, Don and Lois. *Whitman Encyclopedia of Mexican Money, Volume I: An Illustrated History of Mexican Coins and Currency*. Atlanta: Whitman Publishing, 2014. 274-275.

NO. 67: PALESTINE 1927 SEVEN-COIN PROOF SET

1. Fox, Mark. "Palestine Gets Own Coinage in 1927." *World Coin News*. February 9, 2011.
2. Howard Berlin, email message to author, May 21, 2017.
3. Palestine: British Mandate Proof 50 Mils 1927 PR65 NGC. Public auction sale, September 17–22, 2015. Heritage Auctions. https://coins.ha.com/itm/palestine/world-coins/palestine-british-mandate-proof-50-mils-1927-pr65-ngc-/a/3042-30262.s?ic4=GalleryView-ShortDescription-071515

NO. 73: CZECHOSLOVAKIA 1937 GOLD 10 DUKATU

1. Millennium St. Vaclav 929–1929—Czechoslovak medal 1929." https://www.zlate-mince.cz/MedSVNK.htm
2. "Exhibition: Jaroslav Benda 1882–1970." The Briefcase Type Foundry (website), June 12, 2017. https://www.briefcasetype.com/blog/exhibition-jaroslav-benda-18821970
3. "Gallery Hnídková RIHA Journal 0011: Fig. 2." Journal of the International Association of Research Institutes in the History of Art (website), 2010. http://www.riha-journal.org/articles/2010/galleries-2010/gallery-hnidkova-riha-journal-0011/fig.-2/view

NO. 76: SAUDI ARABIA ARAMCO 1947 GOLD "SOVEREIGN" AND 1945 GOLD "4 POUNDS"

1. Boosel, Harry X. "Why: Those Saudi Arabian Gold Discs." *Numismatist*, July 1959. 805-809.
2. *Annual Report of the Director of the Mint for the Fiscal Year Ended June 30, 1946*. Washington: United States Government Printing Office, 1947. 3.

NO. 79: JAPAN 1943–1944 EAST INDIES OCCUPATION COINAGE

1. The Dr. Norman Jacobs Collection of Japanese and Korean Coins. Public auction sale, September 7-12, 2011. Heritage Auctions. https://coins.ha.com/itm/japan/netherlands-east-indies-japanese-occupation-tin-alloy-1-sen-ne2604-1944-/a/3015-24419.s?ic3=ViewItem-Auction-Archive-ThisAuction-120115

NO. 80: POLAND 1942–1943 LODZ GHETTO COINAGE

1. Grabowski, Hans-Ludwig. *Das Geld des Terrors: Geld und Geldersatz in deutschen Knozentrationslagern und Gettos 1933 bis 1945*. Regenstauf: Battenberg, 2008. 390.

NO. 83: PHILIPPINES 1906-S SILVER PESO

1. The Golden Horn Collection. Public auction sale, January 12, 2009. Stack's, New York. 181. https://www.archive.org/stream/2009_01Stck_IntGoldenHorn_LR#page/n181/mode/2up
2. Philippines. Peso, 1906-S. PCGS MS-61. Public auction sale, January 2015. Stack's Bowers Galleries, New York International Numismatic Convention. https://auctions.stacksbowers.com/lots/view/1-1KAQL

NO. 84: SOUTH AFRICA 1923-SA GOLD SOVEREIGN

1. Great Britain, Sovereign, 1923-SA. Public auction sale, 2004. Ira and Larry Goldberg Auctioneers, Los Angeles. http://images.goldbergauctions.com/php/lot_auc.php?site=1&sale=20&lot=414&lang=1
2. South Africa: George V gold Sovereign 1923-SA. Public auction sale, January 6–7, 2013. Heritage Auctions. https://coins.ha.com/itm/south-africa/south-africa-george-v-gold-sovereign-1923-sa-/a/3021-22688.s

NO. 85: SWITZERLAND 1928-B SILVER 5 FRANCS

1. The Redwood Collection. Public auction sale, August 11, 2016. Heritage Auctions. https://coins.ha.com/itm/switzerland/world-coins/switzerland-confederation-5-francs-1928-b-ms63-ngc-/a/3048-30098.s?ic4=OtherResults-SampleItem-071515&tab=ArchiveSearchResults-012417
2. Switzerland: Confederation 5 Francs 1928-B. Public auction sale, September 25–October 1, 2013. Heritage Auctions. https://coins.ha.com/itm/switzerland/switzerland-confederation-5-francs-1928-b-/a/3026-25920.s

NO. 88: TIBET 1921 SER-KHANG GOLD 20 SRANG

1. Kann, Eduard. *Illustrated Catalog of Chinese Coins: Gold, Silver, Nickel, and Aluminum*. Los Angeles: Self Published, 1953. 441.

NO. 89: HONDURAS 1908/888/897 OVERDATE GOLD 20 PESOS

1. "Communications: J.B. Frener. Chief-Engraver to the Mint of the Republic of Guatemala, 1854-1892." *Proceedings of the American Numismatic and Archaeological Society. Thirty-Ninth Annual Meeting. 1897*. American Numismatic and Archaeological Society. New York. 1897. 56.
2. The Mortimer Hammel Collection: 19th & 20th Century Foreign Gold Coins. Public auction sale, September 15–16, 1982. Stack's, New York. 169.

NO. 90: IRELAND 1985 20 PENCE

1. "O'Brien Rare Coin Review: Why is the 1985 Irish 20p coin so valuable?" *The Old Currency Exchange* (blog), August 21, 2014. https://oldcurrencyexchange.com/2014/08/21/rare-coins-the-1985-irish-20p/
2. "Ireland—Republic—1928 to Date 20P." NGC. Numismatic Guaranty Corporation. https://www.ngccoin.com/census/world/ireland-republic-1928-to-date/sc-170/20p/?c=760449
3. Murray, Niall. "Rare 20p coin fetches €9,000 at auction." *Irish Examiner*, October 20, 2015. http://www.irishexaminer.com/ireland/rare-20p-coin-fetches-9000-at-auction-360226.html

NO. 94: SOUTH VIETNAM 1975 50 ĐỒNG

1. Cheek, Ron, FCNRS. "The Coins of South Vietnam." *Supplement to the North York Coin Club Bulletin for August 2016*. 9.

NO. 95: PERU 1958 GOLD 100 SOLES

1. Christensen, William B. "Pattern Coinage of Peru." *The Coinage of El Peru: Coinage of the Americas Conference Proceedings No. 5*. American Numismatic Society, 1989. 186.

NO. 96: PALESTINE 1931 SILVER 100 MILS

1. 1931 100 Mil (Regular Strike). Public auction sale, April 10, 2014. Heritage Auctions, CICF World Coin Signature Auction, Chicago. http://www.pcgs.com/pop/valueview.aspx?s=398743

NO. 99: GERMAN EAST AFRICA 1916-T GOLD 15 RUPIEN

1. Williams, Ken. "The Tabora Mint." *Norwich Coin and Medal Society* (blog), September 7, 2016. http://www.norwichcoinandmedalsociety.co.uk/index.php/the-tabora-mint/
2. Price Guide. *MunzenRevue: International Coin Trend Journal*. February 2017.

In addition to the following reference works, auction catalogs from the following firms are useful sources of information: A.H. Baldwin and Sons, American Numismatic Rarities, Aurea Numismatika, Baldwin's of St. James, Bonham's, Champion Auctions, Dix Noonan Webb, Geoffrey Bell Auctions, Glendining's, Goldstein Auctions, Heritage Auctions, Ira and Larry Goldberg Auctioneers, London Coins Limited, Lyn Knight Auctions, Numismatica Genevensis, Paramount Rare Coins, Ponterio, Rare Coin Galleries, Roma Numismatics, Sincona, Sotheby's, Spink America, Spink Auctions, Spink of London, St. James Auctions, Stack's, Stack's Bowers Galleries, and Superior Stamp and Coin Company.

Bailey, Don & Lois. *Whitman Encyclopedia of Mexican Money, Volume I*. Atlanta: Whitman Publishing, 2014.

Berlin, Howard. *The Coins and Banknotes of Palestine Under the British Mandate, 1927–1947*. Jefferson: McFarland & Company, 2005.

Bitkin, Vladimir, *Composite Catalogue of Russian Coins, 1700–1917*. Kiev: IŪ nona-Moneta, 2000.

Cross, W.K. *Standard Catalogue of Canadian Coins*. Quebec: The Charlton Press.

Cuhaj, George S. & Thomas Michael. *Unusual World Coins: Companion Volume to the Standard Catalog of World Coins: 6th Edition*. Iola, Wisconsin: Krause Publications, 2011.

Davenport, John S. *European Crowns and Talers, Since 1800, 2nd Edition*. London: Spink & Son Ltd., 1964.

Divo, Jean-Paul. *Modern Greek Coins: 1828–1968*. Zürich and Amsterdam: Bank Leu, 1969.

Drake, M. *Charlton Coin Guide*. Quebec: The Charlton Press.

Elizondo, Carlos A. *Eight Reales and Pesos of the New World*. San Antonio: Roy's Coin Center, 1968.

Friedberg, Arthur & Ira. *Gold Coins of the World: From Ancient Times to the Present*. Clifton: The Coin & Currency Institute, Inc.

Gill, Dennis. *The Coinage of Ethiopia, Eritrea and Italian Somalia*. Dennis Gill, 1991.

Guthrie, Hugh S. *Mexican Revolutionary Coinage: 1913–1917: Based on the Bothamley Collection*. Beverly Hills: Superior Stamp & Coin Co., Inc., 1976.

Haxby, James A. *Striking Impressions: The Royal Canadian Mint and Canadian Coinage*. Ottawa: The Royal Canadian Mint, 1984.

Hede, Holger. *Danmarks og Norges Mønter 1541–1814–1977*. Copenhagen: Dansk Numismatisk Forening, 1978.

Hedges, Ken. "The Arabic Republic of Yemen." *Calcoin News*, Volume 18, no 4. 118-119. California State Numismatic Association, 1964.

Herinek, Ludwig. *Österreichische Münzprägungen von 1740–1969*. Wein, L. Herinek, 1970.

Hern, Brian. *Hern's Handbook of South African Coins and Patterns*. Potchefstroom: JD Numismatic Corporation, 2018.

Hodder, Michael & Q. David Bowers. *The Norweb Collection: An American Legacy*. Bowers and Merena Galleries, 1987.

Howard, Emma & Geoff Kitchen. *Coins of England and the United Kingdom: Pre-Decimal Issues*. London: Spink Books.

Jacobs, Norman & Cornelius Vermeule III. *Japanese Coinage: A Monetary History of Japan*. Ishi Press, 1953.

Jaeger, Kurt. *Die deutschen Münzen seit 1871: Bewertungen mit aktuellen Marktpreisen, Die Münzprägungen der deutschen Staaten vom Ausgang de alten Reiches*. Battenberg Verlag, 2007.

JNDA. *The Catalog of Japanese Coins and Bank Notes*. Tokyo: Japan Numismatic Dealers Association.

Kann, Eduard. *Illustrated Catalog of Chinese Coins: Gold, Silver, Nickel, and Aluminum*. Hong Kong: Ye Olde Printerie, Ltd., 1954.

Kosinski, Tomasz. *Coins of Europe*. Tomasz Kosinski, 2014.

Krause-Mishler. *Standard Catalog of World Coins*. Iola: Krause Publications, 2014.

Lin Gwo Ming & Ma Tak Wo. *Illustrated Catalog of Chinese Gold & Silver Coins*. Hong Kong: Ma Tak Wo Numismatic Company, 2012.

Marsh, Michael. *The Gold Sovereign*. Cambridge Coins, 1980.

McDonald, Greg. *Pocket Guide to Australian Coins and Banknotes*. Lavington: Greg McDonald Publishing.

Parchimowicz, Janusz. *Katalog Monet Polskich*. Wydawn Nefryt.

Pridmore, Fred. *Coins of the British Commonwealth of Nations*. London: Spink & Son Ltd., 1975/

Richter, Juerg, and Ruedi Kunzmann. *Der neue HMZ-Katalog, Band 2: Die Münzen der Schweiz und Liechtensteins 15//16. Jahrhundert bis Gegenwart*. Battenberg Gietl Verlag, 2011.

Russo, Arnaldo. *Catalogo de Moedas do Brasil*. Arnaldo Russo, 1978.

Schön, Günter. *Welt-Münzkatalog*. Regenstauf: Battenburg, 2004.

Schou, H.H. *Besrivelse af Danske og Norske Mønter, 1815–1923*. Copenhagen, Numismatisk Forening, 1926.

Severin, H.M. *Gold and Platinum Coinage of Imperial Russia*. New York: Crown and Taler Publishing Company, 1958.

Uzdenikov, V.V. *Russian Coins 1700–1917*. Moscow: IP Media, 2011.

Vogt, George & Colin Bruce. *Standard Catalog of Mexican Coins, Paper Money, Stocks, Bonds and Medals*. Krause Publications, 1981.

Wilkinson, Endymion. *Chinese History: A New Manual*. 5th Edition. Boston: Self-Published, 2018. 626.

Wood, Howland. *The Coinage of the Mexican Revolutionists 1913–1917*. New York: American Numismatic Society, 1928.

Wright, Richard N. J. *The Modern Coinage of China 1866–1949: The Evidence in Western Archives*. London: Spink, 2012.

Yeoman, R.S. *Catalog of Modern World Coins, 1850–1964*. Atlanta: Whitman Publishing.

A NOTE ABOUT TRANSCRIPTIONS OF ASIAN PROPER NOUNS AND NAMES

When referring to Chinese names and places in this book, we use Pinyin instead of the traditionally used Wade-Giles style for Chinese transliteration. This style change, much like BC and AD being BCE and CE in academic history circles for the past 40 years, is long overdue. Our decision to do this was to facilitate further research on the part of the reader. In addition, we use revised romanization for Korean. For Japanese, we use Hepburn romanization. This is an older system, but it is in common usage around the world and whatever flaws it may have in reproducing Japanese grammar they do not outweigh its familiarity to most readers. The over-reliance on Wade-Giles in the numismatic hobby is, at this late point, an unnecessary detriment to the future study and enjoyment of Chinese numismatics in the United States.

INDEX

INDEX